PRAISE FOR

TOGETHER AT SOBO

"Very few chefs are able to capture their surroundings the way Lisa does. In this beautiful cookbook, Lisa's brilliance and skill shine through in every single page."

CLAUDIO APRILE, JUDGE ON *MASTERCHEF CANADA*

"*Together at SoBo* captures the soul of Tofino and Chef Lisa's love for culinary adventure. She is a rock star of the culinary world, committed to her craft, and her Fried Chicken Dinner, Southern Style is absolutely delish! This beautiful book is filled with her delicious recipes and is a must-have for anyone who wants to explore the Tofino food culture and cuisine."

MARILYN DENIS, HOST OF *THE MARILYN DENIS SHOW*

"Not only have I always been jealous of the magical restaurant Lisa owns, but now I'm jealous of this perfect cookbook she's written. SoBo is the restaurant everyone wishes that they had on their corner and with this book we can all feel lucky to have it in our homes."

AMANDA COHEN, CHEF AND OWNER OF DIRT CANDY

"This cookbook is a perfect example of when love of food and craft is transported onto a plate. Chef Lisa's generous spirit shines brightly on every page."

NICOLE GOMES, WINNER OF *TOP CHEF CANADA: ALL-STARS* AND CO-FOUNDER OF CLUCK 'N' CLEAVER

TOGETHER AT

SoBo

TOGETHER AT

SoBo

MORE RECIPES AND STORIES FROM
TOFINO'S CHERISHED RESTAURANT

appetite
by RANDOM HOUSE

Appetite by Random House® and colophon are registered trademarks of Penguin Random House LLC.

Library and Archives of Canada Cataloguing in Publication is available upon request.

ISBN: 978-0-52-561063-2
eBook ISBN: 978-0-52-561064-9

Cover and book design by Andrew Roberts
Cover and book photography by Jeremy Koreski
Photo on page 95 by Steven Gomez-Harvey
Chalkboard image: Patty Chan/Shutterstock.com

Printed in China

Published in Canada by Appetite by Random House®,
a division of Penguin Random House Canada Limited

www.penguinrandomhouse.ca

10 9 8 7 6 5 4 3 2 1

I would like
to dedicate this
book to my family.
I am blessed
and grateful for
the support you've
all shown me on
this journey.

To my loving mother,
who supports
everything I do.

To my astute son,
Barkley. Truly an
old soul—a special,
empathetic old soul.

To my radiant
daughter, Ella.
You have always
brought so much
joy and laughter
to our family.

TABLE OF CONTENTS

Foreword by Lynn Crawford   1

Foreword by Ella Ahier   5

*Felled Parsnips and Waved Cucumbers
   by Susan Musgrave*   9

Introduction by Lisa Ahier   15

Key Ingredients   19

LIGHT STARTERS

Charcuterie with Grilled Peaches   27

Wild Salmon Tartare   29

Heirloom Tomato Quiche   31

Smoked Salmon, Farro and Sorrel Fritters   33

Grilled Pattypan Squash, Green Polenta
   and Garlic Aioli   35

Crab Louis   37

Seared Halibut Cheeks and Tomato Dashi   39

Halibut, Cucumber and Grapefruit Ceviche   40

Fried Green Tomatoes with Spiced Shrimp
   and Herbed Mayonnaise   43

SOUPS AND SANDWICHES

Classic Tomato Gazpacho   49

Watermelon Gazpacho   50

Melon and Coconut Milk Soup   53

Chilled Pea and Mint Soup   54

Chanterelle Mushroom and Corn Chowder   57

White Bean and Chicken Chili   58

Fall Harvest Vegetable Soup   61

Roasted Cauliflower and Garlic Soup   62

Silky Parsnip, Apple and Celeriac Soup   64

Cream of Mushroom Soup   67

Hot and Sour Chicken Noodle Soup   69

Falafel Pockets with Sumac Onions
   and Herbed Yogurt Dip   71

Shrimp, Avocado and Tomato Roti Wrap   75

Grilled Halloumi and Sun-Dried Tomato Tapenade
   on Focaccia   77

Tuna Melt   81

Crab Salad on French Baguette   83

Smoked Turkey, Bacon, Tomato and Arugula
   on Sourdough   85

SALADS

Kale, Farro and Grilled Halloumi Salad with Lemon
   Parsley Vinaigrette   90

Wedge Salad   93

Waldorf Salad   94

Green Goddess Salad   96

Curried Wheat Berry and Lentil Salad with
   Poached Eggs and Turmeric Cauliflower   99

Seaweed, Sea Asparagus and
   Brassica Shoots Salad   101

Warm Asparagus, Farro and King Oyster Mushroom Salad
   with Poached Eggs   104

Panzanella with Fresh Mozzarella   107

Roasted Brussels Sprouts and Sunchokes   109

Seared Scallop and Quinoa Salad   113

PIZZA

Pizza Dough, Tofino Style   119

Pizza Sauces   122

Classic Margherita Pizza   124

Roasted Acorn Squash and Kale Pizza   127

Mushroom, Caramelized Onion and Goat Cheese
   Pizza   128

Mystic Clam Pizza   131

Asparagus and Potato Pizza   134

Lamb Pizza   137

Mediterranean Pizza   138

ENTRÉES

Summer Ratatouille and Polenta   142

Lentil Vegiballs with Chimichurri and Fresh
Cheese   145

Buckwheat Crepes with Rhubarb, Fiddleheads,
Asparagus and Fennel   147

Spaghetti Squash Patties with Poached Eggs
and Salsa Verde   151

Seafood Saffron Risotto   155

Clam and Corn Vongole   158

Nettle, Clam and Shrimp Tagliatelle   160

Braised Chicken and Roasted Brussels Sprouts
Pappardelle   163

Orecchiette, Braised Lamb and Cauliflower
with Kalamata Olives   165

Halibut Cheeks with Morels, Fiddleheads
and Celeriac Cream   169

Shrimp and Polenta Grits   171

Chinook Salmon with Cauliflower Purée
and Parsnip Puffs   175

Seared Wild Salmon with New Potatoes, Broccolini
and Parsley Sauce   178

Seared Halibut, Black Beans, King Oyster Mushrooms
and Almond Cream   181

Pacific Halibut, Chanterelles and Corn Purée   183

Fried Chicken Dinner, Southern Style   187

Braised Beef Cheek Tacos with Black Bean Salsa   189

DESSERTS

Chocolate Mascarpone Cookies   196

Salted Caramel Cashew Cookies   199

Vegan Chocolate Almond Cookies   202

Fruit and Nut Cookies   203

Triple Chocolate Chip Cookies   204

Chocolate Mousse Tarts   206

Fresh Rhubarb Tarts   207

Grilled Peach and Raspberry Melba   211

Ice Cream Sandwiches   213

Root Beer Float   216

Toasted Hazelnut Brownies   217

Cherry Pie   219

Peach Pie   222

DRINKS

SoBo Caesar with Pickled Bull Kelp   226

SoBo Sunset   228

Mezcal Paloma   228

Lavender Lemonade Spritzer   230

Tijuana Go Surfing   230

Batched Vesper   232

Stubbs Island Mule   232

Cedar Negroni   234

Port of Tofino   234

Tofino 75   236

Red-Eye Medusa   236

Sangria for a Crowd   238

STAPLES

Sourdough Bread   245

Biscuits and Honey Butter   248

Vegan Butter   249

Egg Pasta Dough   250

Stocks   252

Simple Syrup   255

Chips   256

Onion Rings   257

Roasting   258

Chimichurri Sauce   260

Left Coast Kimchi   261

Pickling   262

Acknowledgements   **269**

Index   **272**

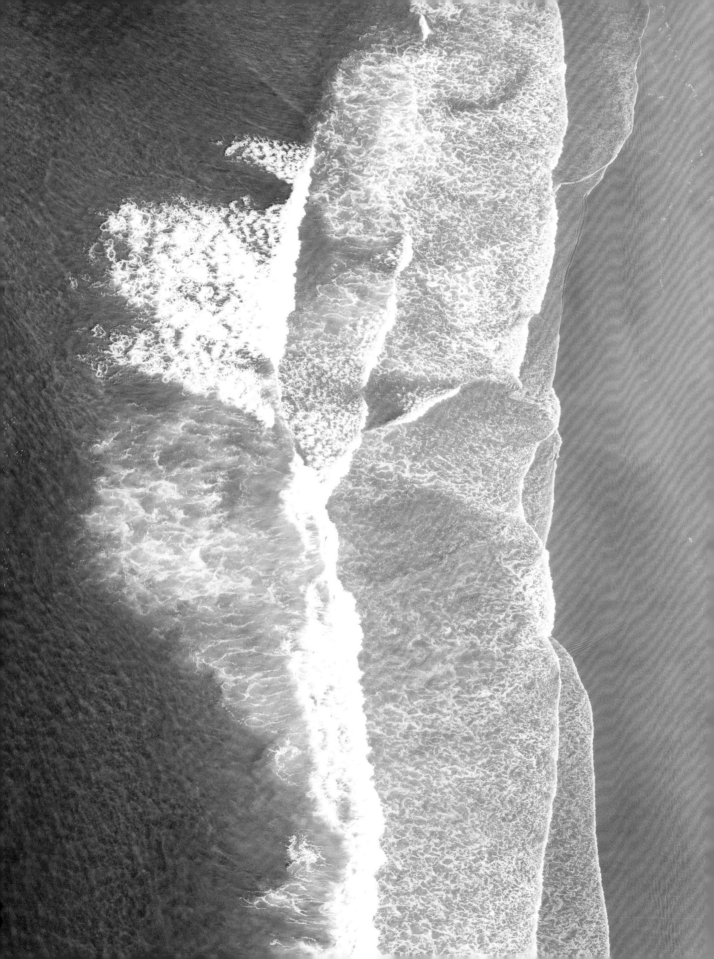

FOREWORD

BY LYNN CRAWFORD

Tofino is a magical place. On the extreme west coast of Vancouver Island, it's a beautiful gem at the end of the road, surrounded by ocean, rainforest and infinite wildlife. Hundreds of thousands of world travelers come to surf the majestic, icy cold waves and hike the Pacific Rim National Park Reserve's trails, and I know that I could walk the endless beaches lined by weathered driftwood and evergreen forests for days. At the core of the coastal town is Chef Lisa, who has inspired me like no other.

Going back to the early 2000s, before I ever visited Tofino, I read about Chef Lisa and SoBo in *Saveur* magazine: This iconic purple food truck, helmed by a trailblazing woman chef, served up "killer" fish tacos, crispy shrimp cakes, miso udon soup and tofu pockets. Just seeing her menu, I wanted to order everything from it. At that time, I was cooking at the Four Seasons in New York City, while Chef Lisa was cooking from a food truck parked outside the Tofino Botanical Gardens. Talk about two different worlds! I remember reading about life on Vancouver Island—to me, Chef Lisa had a chef's dream job, with all the amazing local ingredients at SoBo's fingertips every day . . . I knew that I would have to meet this chef one day and cook with her! After all, while many people understand that in order to become a better cook, you must know your food's journey on its way to your table, the next (equally important) step that many don't consider is getting to know the local chefs who are cooking with those ingredients far better than you are (for now!).

Fast forward to my first Tofino trip in 2011. I was hosting my television show *Pitchin' In*, on this ridiculously awesome adventure traveling the country in search of the most precious ingredients—this time, Dungeness crab off the shores of Tofino. It was then that I finally met Lisa. She opened her kitchen and her world up to us, and I finally got to know this talented chef I had read so much about.

I am always on a quest to find the rock stars of the culinary world. Lisa is certainly one of them. From the moment we met, I knew we would become true friends. To be honest, I was in awe of her then, and to be *perfectly* honest, I am more in awe of her today than ever before. Lisa is inspiring on so many levels . . . not only is she a dynamic and creative chef with a total commitment to her craft, she's also an incredible mother, friend, supporter, motivator, community leader and ambassador for real food. She embraces life to its fullest, takes on any challenge with strength and clarity, and shares her positive energy and humor with everyone around her.

Although the purple truck retired 16 years ago, she and SoBo have since firmly established their restaurant in downtown Tofino. Surrounding herself with a team as passionate as she is, Lisa has created a restaurant where people have fallen in love with her food for all the right reasons.

When Lisa cooks, she cooks with all her heart. Lisa is, and has always been, committed to providing fresh, delicious, innovative food and memorable times for all those who come to experience Vancouver Island's bounty at SoBo, whether from Tofino or faraway. It's about the taste of the organic ingredients and the incredible relationships she has fostered with the local farmers, growers, foragers, ranchers, food artisans, wineries, breweries, distilleries and fishers—those she has supported over the years and who, in turn, have supported her.

With *Together at SoBo*, Lisa has created one of the most stunning cookbooks about food culture and cuisine in Tofino and beyond, destined to become a classic. I know that as you dive in, you'll want to cook from it every day (SoBo fans will be thrilled to discover some of their favorite recipes in here).

When Lisa cooks, she cooks with all her heart.

Despite our different takes on the culinary world, I've wondered many times . . . if I had cooked with her sooner, where would I be now? Lisa's kitchen was my classroom when we first met, and she continues to open my eyes to her journey. The one thing I do know is that I am a far better chef now for having met Lisa. And now, together with Lisa, her 25 years of culinary experience and her passion for craft and community in your kitchen—get ready to cook.

SOBO

FOREWORD

BY ELLA AHIER

My favorite story from my childhood comes from back when SoBo was in the purple truck at the Tofino Botanical Gardens. I was only about seven months old, strapped to my mum's chest as she worked in the narrow kitchen. As she chopped ingredients I shot my hand out from my swaddle and grabbed a piece. Mum's knife just barely missed my fingers. After that incident, she kept me well away from the working area—and knives. When my brother and I were at the gardens over the years while my mom served out of the truck, our time was mostly spent looking at birds and sniffing flowers, not getting our fingers cut off. I swear.

When I was about three years old, SoBo moved to a brick-and-mortar space on Neill Street in downtown Tofino. Apart from when I was at school, I spent most of my time in or around the restaurant. In the summer, I would build forts out of cardboard boxes in the parking lot to hide from the sun or fall asleep in the cool basement of the building. In the winter, when we were closed for the off-season, I would run around the empty restaurant while my father painted the walls in preparation for the following year.

I have no idea what it's like to grow up in a city or even a town much larger than two thousand people. But in Tofino, my friends and I would ride our bikes to the local Saturday market to stuff our faces with cinnamon buns and tamales while getting colorful feathers clamped into our salty, surf-tousled hair. Winters were quiet, with all the tourists having gone back home, leaving us kids to run free. Even our school was unconventional: many classes were held outside, and I learned about the mushrooms, tree bark and microorganisms in our "backyard." (Thanks, Mel and Andy!)

And always, even at school, SoBo was there. My mum would even occasionally come teach cooking classes to the older kids, and she made lunchtime my favorite thing about school: nearly every day, she would walk down the trail behind SoBo to Wickaninnish Community School to deliver my brother and me hot, fresh food from the restaurant, ranging from warm polenta fries to, my favorite, fish tacos. It was rare that she wouldn't take the 10 minutes off the line to come see us, but if she was ever stuck, she would send Katrina Peters or Jen Scott to make the delivery (meet them on pages 68 and 221).

When my mum was wrapping up the first SoBo cookbook, about 10 years ago, we all stayed over at the Koreski family farm on the east side of Vancouver Island, and with the Lawson family out on Wickaninnish Island—Wick Island for short. While our parents worked tirelessly on the photography and other finishing touches, we kids got to swim in the rivers, ride the Koreskis' horses, play on rope swings and explore the forests. These are some of my most treasured memories from childhood, days filled with family, friends, fun and, most importantly, food.

To me, SoBo has always been a place where people come together. They laughed over food and margaritas while their children played out back in the purple wooden truck, modeled after SoBo's very own. Teachers would gather on the first day of spring or summer break. Nurses and dentists from the nearby hospital and dental office would pop in on their lunch breaks. First dates were had there (even mine!), graduation dinners, local theater actors eating dinner in between shows. Nearly everyone in Tofino and the surrounding coastal communities will have a story to tell you about SoBo, if you have time to sit with them over some chowder and cornbread.

Now, I'm not trying to get too overconfident here and claim that SoBo is the very heart of Tofino, but it *is* a vital organ that has contributed so much to the community over the years that it—and my mum —has been around. My mum is easily the hardest-working person I know; watching her build the SoBo name and business *and* write two books all while raising two kids will always be inspiring to me.

To me, SoBo has always been a place where people come together.

I may not have picked up her cooking abilities but I would like to believe I have picked up her creativity. Where she uses fresh ingredients to create dishes she's passionate about, I use words to tell stories that I believe are worth sharing. My mother and I both use our art forms to connect with our community, friends and family. Having my mum in my life is the greatest gift in the world, and with book number two, I'm glad you're able to have a little bit more of her in yours.

FELLED PARSNIPS AND WAVED CUCUMBERS
BY SUSAN MUSGRAVE

Back in the day when SoBo was the kickass purple food truck parked in Tofino Botanical Gardens, I would lug armfuls of parsnip puffs and crab cakes to the cabin my mother rented for our family every Thanksgiving. When *The SoBo Cookbook* was published, I bought a copy—I even *used* it. Still use it. The iconic key lime pie. The hippest Hippy Chicken. It's one cookbook that feels friendly, unintimidating and, best of all, lacking in pretension.

As a result of my own foray into the world of food writing with my cookbook *A Taste of Haida Gwaii*, I was invited to the Ballymaloe Literary Festival of Wine & Food, near Cork, in Ireland. I found myself at the "cool table" with a hastiness (yes, that is the collective noun) of highly respected chefs but quickly realized that my tablemates spoke a different language. While discussing overnight cold proofing of sourdough bread, one of my dining companions rolled her eyes when I told her I didn't think my fridge had a thermometer, or, if it did, I didn't know how it worked or where it was located. If the temperature fell below 40°F, she assured me, the flavor and profile of my loaf would be severely compromised.

Well, if you can't run with the big dogs, as they say in the South, stay under the porch. My sourdough bread tasted awesome. All my neighbors on Haida Gwaii think so. Then, two summers ago, I crawled out from under my porch to visit my friends Chris Taylor and Sharon Whalen in Tofino. "Lisa wants to meet you," they warned me. "She owns SoBo."

SoBo, by this time established as a restaurant downtown, was still my go-to when I was in Tofino. How would I be able to sneak in for my SoBo fix while avoiding this curious chef whom I feared would be the likes of the Ballymaloe hastiness? Lisa Ahier, I had gathered from eavesdropping, was a force to be reckoned with. But what Lisa Ahier turned out *not* to be—as I discovered after slipping in for a few discreet meals with Chris and Sharon—was one of those scary, highfalutin' purist chef type people. In fact, she'd be right at home under the porch with me, any day.

After preparing one after another of her masterful creations for us, Lisa sat down to chat. It was then that she asked if I would consider helping her finish her second book. "I can't write," she said humbly. *Of course* she could write, I assured her between mouthfuls of Thai chicken. Then, seizing the moment—which, I hoped, would mean the chance to sample more of her dishes in the future—I said, "Send me some recipes. Let's do this thing."

But soon after our initial meeting came the COVID pandemic, which, for Lisa, meant closing time. And although we spent the next year exchanging a few "Yes, we must get to work" emails, it wasn't until February 2021 that Lisa wrote saying her book was overdue at her publishers. After a year of the pandemic, of finding it hard to focus, hard to feel excited, hard to conceive of a future where writing any kind of book could brighten your day, I was ready.

Lisa sent me all the recipes she had collected for this book, including some recipe introductions she thought she "couldn't write." As I'd told her, with her experience and unique way of saying things, I had no doubt she *could* write. What she couldn't always do was spell. But it turns out that wasn't her fault: she was working with one eye that spring (awaiting a lockdown-postponed cataract surgery) on a computer that didn't have spell-check (that, or, like my fridge thermometer, she didn't know how to use it). She sent me one recipe calling for "1 carrot, washed; 1 cucumber, waved." I spent the better part of an afternoon researching "how to wave a cucumber," but after I sent Lisa my inspired writing, she called me right away.

"Waved?" she said, sounding perplexed. "It's supposed to be *washed*."

We set up regular phone calls to go over everything in detail. These conversations became a high point of my week—they offered connection, and the longer we worked together, the more comfortable we both became, even playing off one another's writing, channeling each other. Lisa eased into her writing voice, letting her natural humor spill onto the page. I added a smear of ranch dressing here, a glug of hot sauce there, delivered with a dash of twang, spurred on by Lisa's Southern influence. I never would have put it this way before channeling Lisa, but I haven't had so much fun since the hogs *et* (sic) my little brother. You'll even see our banter in the Biscuits and Honey Butter recipe (page 248).

By the time I reached a recipe that called for "12 medium parsnips, felled," I was hip to her slips. I made the change: "12 medium parsnips, peeled." Although I later found myself stumped by "I adore the rich *rage* of vegetables on top of the silky polenta."

"Ragu, of course," she said on another call, "it's ragu." My bad. Like I said: a unique way of saying things.

INTRODUCTION

When I set out to write this, my second cookbook, I knew I wanted it to be a bit of a step up from my first. *The SoBo Cookbook* is full of tried-and-true standards—in it, you'll find recipes for our famous tofu pockets and killer fish tacos—many going way back to when SoBo was a swinging little spot, serving out of an '80s-era purple food truck in Tofino's Live to Surf parking lot, where we set up in 2003.

Our truck later moved from that surf-shop parking lot to Tofino Botanical Gardens, then finally, in 2007, we settled into a spacious, floor-to-ceiling-windowed restaurant in downtown Tofino. And now, even though the purple truck has been let out to pasture, we keep a miniature homage to it in our fancy "new" digs. Throughout all this change, our essence has remained *un*changed. We haven't lost our grassroots essence —after all, "SoBo" is short for "Sophisticated Bohemian." In this brick-and-mortar spot that we can call our own, we still offer our signature globally influenced, gourmet-level selections that fuse Asian and Southwestern standbys with the freshest local products, with menus for all mealtimes. Here, we can serve a dinner crowd looking for a night out, making the most out of our bigger kitchen to prepare complex dishes such as Warm Asparagus, Farro and King Oyster Mushroom Salad with Poached Eggs (page 104).

I first thought this second book might be inspired by the daily specials that show up on the SoBo chalkboard, often with a focus on product availability on any given day—we're all about fresh food from here and there. And some of those certainly made it in (like the Chinook Salmon with Purée of Cauliflower and Parsnip Puffs, page 175), but as I began to write this book of recipes, something became overwhelmingly clear: as much as the product itself contributes to our great menu, it's also undeniably the people surrounding me who have led to our experimental cooking style that locals and visitors alike have taken a shine to.

To watch a young cook's eyes light up when asked to help create a daily special is truly wonderful. Together, like a couple learning how to dance, I work with them to set our intention, usually talking about the product, the flavor profile. I urge them to draw on their own memories of food, their culture, their passion that has brought them into the culinary arts. Then the cooking starts. All while tasting and thinking about how it might change from one moment to the next. When you involve those around you in the creations, they take ownership and really sink their teeth into the task.

Then there are the folks who have been with me since day one—whether that was day one of my moving to Tofino in 2000, or my day one on Earth.

Many of these recipes are from my childhood growing up in and around the South (for example, Fried Chicken, Southern Style on page 187, and Grilled Peach and Raspberry Melba on page 211), which I have come to know and love through my mom (you'll get to know her on page 95). The community of friends I've made in Tofino have all left their touch on SoBo, whether it's in the décor, the kitchen or the supplies and ingredients we use for these excellent recipes. Even Susan, my wondrous coauthor, was brought into my life by my circle of friends one night at SoBo.

The restaurant's appeal rests, in part, on the fact that we have created a culture that people want to immerse themselves in. SoBo is an extended family that people want to be a part of, whether they're in the dining room or behind the scenes. It's very much a product of its place: we have the cross-cultural, open-spirited air of the West Coast, and we foster a sense of belonging, for both regulars and visitors who are trying the restaurant for their first time. Therein lies one of the secrets of SoBo's success. The sense of connection is important to us. We've always wanted that openness and rapport. It puts everyone on the same level—SoBo was built on a platform of down-to-earth, natural food meant to nourish the soul and warm the heart.

SoBo's food is unsurpassed in flavor and adventurous in its selections. We have a strict commitment to quality, and to organic and regional sourcing. We pick and choose the best ingredients and the best growers and harvesters around. That's deceptively simple: all of it is built on long, long (did I say long?) hours of work and a truckload of passion.

So, with this second book, I want to give a shoutout to those before, after and currently involved in my culinary journey. I want to share not only *my* stories but also those of people who have helped shape SoBo over the years, to show how we have come together as a like-minded community.

LISA AHIER
TOFINO

SoBo was built on a platform
of down-to-earth, natural food
meant to nourish the soul
and warm the heart.

KEY INGREDIENTS

Throughout this book, you'll find some ingredients pop up over and over again. I've put together some key notes on these key ingredients that I feel particularly strongly about. But overall, my top advice is to always buy local ingredients when you can, which also means you'll be eating these foods in season. It's a beautiful way to get to know when produce in your part of the world is at its peak deliciousness. For us on the West Coast, that usually means acorn squash in the fall, heirloom tomatoes as early as mid-August and, if the weather holds out, corn into October. You can really, truly taste the difference—not to mention that you'll feel good supporting your community at the same time, and maybe even get to know the folks behind the food.

BUTTER

When baking, use unsalted butter in order to control the amount of salt (or omit the salt called for in the recipe and instead add it gradually, to taste). When cooking, why not use salted?

CANOLA OIL

With a high smoking point and relatively low saturated fat level (compared with peanut or sunflower oil, for instance), canola is a popular neutral oil. Give the label a close look—you want organic and non-GMO canola oil, to ensure it's untainted. Grapeseed oil is a great substitute.

CORIANDER

Coriander (the seeds of cilantro) can be purchased whole or ground. If you buy the seeds whole, you can grind them yourself. Try roasting them at 325°F for 5 minutes (watch them closely—they burn easily), then grinding in a spice grinder, to be added to curries or Southwestern dishes.

CUCUMBERS

When it comes to cucumbers, garden (tough-skinned), English (medium-skinned) or lemon (thin-skinned) work equally well in these recipes. To reduce the chance of a bitter taste or the cucumber causing indigestion, peel it before serving, removing both the skin and some of the flesh just under the skin.

EGGS

Free-range, organic and large. These are my preferred stats when it comes to eggs and will give the best results for these recipes.

FLOUR

If you take no other advice from this book, please at least take this: always use fresh flour! If you're not using it within a few weeks of purchase, store it in the freezer. For my recipes, all-purpose flour is unbleached, organic white flour; spelt flour is for bread; 00 flour is for pizza (Tipo 00 flour or

Caputo 00 are top-notch). I also call for buckwheat flour, in the crepes, which should be purchased especially fresh, as it just doesn't move quickly off store shelves, so the stock you're buying might even be past its best-before date already.

GARLIC

My recipes all call for fresh garlic. I always recommend buying local products whenever possible—especially garlic. There's a noticeable difference in the smell, taste and overall quality of local or even Californian garlic, compared with the bulk-packed overseas imported bulbs.

GINGER

It's always best to use fresh ginger for my recipes, buying it for straightaway use or for storing in the fridge or freezer. Check to make sure it's not greenish-blue inside (that means it's old) and that it's cleaned, without wrinkles or mold. I like to grate or freshly mince mine; typically, you'll want to at least peel its outer skin ahead of cooking.

MAPLE SYRUP

For cooking, I make sure to use pure maple syrup, either Grade A (which is lighter) or Grade B (darker). Avoid maple syrups that are blended, since they often contain corn syrup or cheaper sweeteners.

MILK

For milk, 2% milk is my go-to—unless the recipe says otherwise—although whole milk or even 1% or skim will also work well for my recipes. The heavy cream I call for is between 33% and 36%.

MUSHROOMS

Cremini, portobello, shiitake and white button mushrooms are readily available in most North American supermarkets. Foraging can make it easier to try different combinations, but always consult a mushroom expert, who can correctly identify anything you might pick. Personally, I adore morels, chanterelles, pine and porcini ("bolete"), but these can get costly in the grocery store and are highly seasonal.

OLIVE OIL

With a lower smoking point than canola oil, olive oil is great to cook with at lower heats. For cooking, I use pure olive oil; extra virgin is best for dressings, spreads and condiments. Basil Olive Oil's Golden Olive Eleni is the crème de la crème!

OLIVES

In this book, I call for either green or Kalamata olives. Avoid canned, pre-sliced olives (they're often artificially ripened and picked when underripe, making them blander yet overly salty). Agrinion and Sicilian are some spectacular green olives, and for Kalamata, there is only one company for me: Basil Olive Oil

ONIONS

Unless stated otherwise, onions in my recipes are medium yellow onions. Red onions will often be raw and thinly sliced; white are for Southwestern or Mexican dishes.

PARSLEY

Italian parsley (also called flat-leaf parsley) and curly parsley can be used interchangeably, but most chefs (including me) prefer flat-leaf, as it usually has the more robust taste and is ideal for flavoring. Curly parsley can be tough and is better suited to fine chopping. In the end, it's your preference. And, of course, dependent on what's available to you.

SALT

I cook with kosher salt—Diamond Crystal brand only! It's my preferred because there's only one ingredient: salt. That might sound obvious, but it can be difficult to find a kosher salt with no additives or anti-clumping agents.

TOMATOES

Throughout the recipes, you'll find me calling for heirloom tomatoes. Compared with mass-market tomatoes, which are hybridized for "ideal qualities" (you'll find a story all about them in my Heirloom Tomato Quiche recipe, page 31), heirloom tomatoes grow from seeds passed down generation to generation. They're rich in flavor and come in a spectrum of colors.

Light
Starters

FRESH CHEESE

Fresh cheese is a mild-flavored cheese in its youngest, purest form. It's made from fresh curds that have not been pressed or aged. Fluffy ricotta, tangy goat cheese, creamy mozzarella, crumbly feta, sweet mascarpone . . . these are but a few examples.

CHARCUTERIE WITH GRILLED PEACHES

What we have here is a wee bit more exciting than your average cheese and meat platter—the grilled peaches make it exceptional! Freestone peaches are best, still slightly firm so that they don't fall apart while grilling, and easily sliced. Overly ripe peaches will mush up, and the higher sugar levels will burn more easily. Always source locally when you can and when in season (see Cook's Note). When it comes to the bread, the sourdough on page 245 is there if you feel like going all the way! Or the simple French Baguette (page 83) is a bit less challenging and works very well with cheese and meat.

SERVES 4

2 peaches, halved and pitted

1 tsp olive oil

8–10 slices Sourdough Bread (page 245) or French Baguette (page 83)

¼ lb salami, thinly sliced

1 cup spreadable fresh cheese (see sidebar and Cook's Note)

½ lb grapes

Preheat the grill to medium.

Grill the peaches: Brush the cut sides of the peaches with some of the oil. Place them on the grill, cut side down, until the fruit develops grill marks and starts to soften, about 3 to 5 minutes.

Turn the peaches, brush the skin with the remaining oil and grill for another 2 to 3 minutes.

Alternatively, you can broil the peaches in your oven: Preheat the broiler to high heat (or an oven to 500°F or a toaster oven on the highest setting). Place the peaches skin side down in a broiler pan. Set the pan under the broiler and broil the peaches until they start to caramelize, 3 to 4 minutes. Remove and, once cool enough to handle, cut into thick slices.

To serve: Arrange the assortment of bread, meat, cheese and fruit on a platter or individual plates. There's lots of room for creativity here! Now, where to put the grilled peaches . . .

COOK'S NOTE: Concord, Coronation or Champagne (Corinth) are some of my favorite B.C. grapes. For fresh cheese, my go-to is Little Qualicum Cheeseworks' Fromage Frais (a West Coast twist on a traditional European quark). Oyama Sausage Co. from Vancouver carries my salami of choice; Picnic Charcuterie here in Tofino offers extra-special goodies like porcini salami (with wild harvested Pacific Northwest porcini mushrooms, Manchego cheese and sage).

WILD SALMON TARTARE
WITH SEED CRACKERS

This is a recipe where the freshness of the salmon is key. When I fillet my whole salmon to make individual portions for a meal of Seared Wild Salmon (page 178), there's usually a small portion of trim left over. Tartare is an efficient and creative (not to mention delicious) way to utilize it. This makes for a super sexy little starter course, or for an elegant canapé at your swanky cocktail party. The crackers are ridiculously addictive—their salty crispiness satisfies like a potato chip, while the hemp seeds are an excellent plant-based protein.

SERVES 4

Seed Crackers

¾ cup all-purpose flour

¾ cup whole-wheat flour

3 tsp salt, divided

6 Tbsp mixture of seeds (I use a combination of flax, sesame and hemp—but whatever you have on hand will do)

2 Tbsp butter, room temperature

Salmon Tartare

½ lb wild salmon, deboned, very finely diced

1 tsp salt

1 Tbsp freshly squeezed lemon juice

½ tsp capers, rinsed and minced

1 Tbsp minced shallot

1 Tbsp extra virgin olive oil

3–5 sprigs fresh herbs (I use radish sprouts and fennel pollen or bur chervil), for garnish (optional)

Chill a medium bowl in the freezer for 1 hour.

Prepare the crackers: Preheat the oven to 350°F. Line two 13- × 18-inch baking sheets with parchment paper.

In a large bowl, mix together the flours, 1 tsp of the salt and the seeds until well combined. Work the butter into the dry ingredients until incorporated. Add ½ cup water and mix using a wooden spoon until everything comes together in a sticky-ish ball in your bowl.

Divide the dough into two pieces. (If your pans are smaller than suggested, simply divide the dough into three, or more, to fit.) Sprinkle a pastry board with flour to keep the dough from sticking, then use a rolling pin to roll the dough out thin. Place the dough on the prepared baking sheets. Sprinkle with the remaining 2 tsp salt.

Bake until crisp and lightly browned, about 10 minutes. Rotate the sheets halfway through. Remove from the oven and let cool to room temperature, then break the crackers into your desired size.

Prepare the salmon tartare: Remove the chilled bowl from the freezer. Add the salmon, salt, lemon juice, capers, shallot, oil and herbs to the bowl and gently toss together. To serve, spoon some tartare onto a cracker and enjoy.

COOK'S NOTE: I usually make my tartare with the trim from a whole salmon, one that's being portioned for the restaurant, but I realize that most folks won't be doing that. The most important part of this recipe is getting hold of an ultra-fresh wild salmon. Health guidelines advise freezing salmon for a few hours before using.

PAR-BAKED PIE CRUST

The problem: As pie dough bakes, the fat melts, causing the crust to shrink down the sides of the dish. And as the fat melts, it creates steam. Steam is both good and bad: it creates scrumptious layers of flakiness, but it also causes the dough to puff up because there's no heavy filling weighing it down.

The solution: Prick holes in the unbaked pie crust to allow the steam to escape. Line the pie crust with parchment paper or aluminum foil and weigh it down with pie weights or dry beans (about 1½ lb) so that the bottom doesn't puff and the sides don't slouch.

Bake for 10 minutes. Once the crust is set—the edges will have turned golden—remove the weights and let the crust cook a few minutes longer. You want the bottom of the partially baked crust to look dry and flaky, but still pale.

HEIRLOOM TOMATO QUICHE

One summer, I was given a standard, mass-market-type tomato. I left it on my windowsill and promptly forgot about it. When I found it two months later, there wasn't a single spot, wrinkle or blemish on its glow-in-the-dark (well, almost) skin. It was so unnatural, I threw it out. Mass-market tomatoes just can't compete with my favorite member of the nightshade family: the heirloom tomato. I've never met an heirloom tomato I didn't want to devour. And if it has a few bumps or cracks on it, so much the better. This quiche spotlights heirlooms beautifully. If mozzarella isn't your cup of tea, there will be another cheese out there to suit your personality. But there's only one kind of tomato (for me).

SERVES 6

½ recipe Jen's Pie Crust (page 219) (1 single pie crust)

1 cup shredded mozzarella cheese

2 heirloom tomatoes, sliced ¼ inch thick

1 small leek, rinsed well and thinly sliced

5 eggs

1½ cups heavy cream

2 tsp salt

1 tsp hot sauce (I like Frank's RedHot or Louisiana)

Preheat the oven to 350°F.

Prick the bottom of the prepared pie crust with a fork. Par-bake for 10 minutes (see sidebar). Remove from the oven and sprinkle the mozzarella over the bottom of the pie crust. Layer the tomatoes on top, then the leeks.

In a blender, combine the eggs, cream, salt and hot sauce. Blend on medium-low speed for 1 minute or until frothy. Slowly pour half the blended mixture into the pie crust. Let the mixture settle into the tomatoes and cheese before pouring in the rest.

Place the quiche on a baking sheet to catch any overflow and put in the preheated oven. After 20 minutes, the quiche will start to rise. At this point, loosely cover it with a piece of aluminum foil to prevent excess browning.

Bake for 15 minutes or until the quiche is completely set.

Dan Law

When I think of Dan Law, I think: husband, father, friend, artist, handyman, good human. I also think: solver of acoustic problems, maker of funky eyeglass frames, carver of wooden raccoons and ravens.

After earning his nursing degree in Victoria in 2001, Dan and his wife, Mollie, settled in Tofino after a 10-day tour around the province in search of just enough wilderness. With the pull for a more creative life ever-present—Mollie and Dan met in art school, they directed community theater, taught art at the elementary school—Dan eventually returned to school for his Master of Fine Arts.

Today, you can spot Dan's art around Tofino, most notably his stunning fire-blackened cedar ravens at the Seashack at Chesterman Beach. Several of Dan's pieces have rotated through SoBo—including a raccoon carved out of old-growth cedar that perched at the end of the bar. We all loved that piece; it was one of Dan's favorites, too. "It did everything I wanted a piece to do," he says. "It had a special point of tension between fear and curiosity." It was so popular with our guests that Dan had to refinish the spot on its torso that had worn out from people petting it so often.

To see Dan's permanent SoBo installation, sit at the bar and look up. Solving our previously unsolvable problem of lousy acoustics in the restaurant's glass, slate and concrete structure, we turned to Dan, who designed a sinuous installation on the ceiling. The curves of its salvaged wood planks soften the din of echoes and clatters, setting the greatest eating atmosphere—all while looking beautiful.

There's actually one more permanent piece of Dan's at SoBo: every day, I wear a pair of wood-framed eyeglasses handmade by Dan. He worked out the design with a local optometrist, crafting them from salvaged ironwood, with antler used for the hinges. Along with my purple bandana, my glasses are my signature look. The time and care he takes with his art in general echoes what I do with the food I prepare.

SMOKED SALMON, FARRO AND SORREL FRITTERS

This is a creation of one of my all-time favorite cooks who worked with me for years. He hails from Salt Spring Island and is as big and bold as his name: Thor Magnusson. A big ole Viking kind of dude. He met his wife, Becca, here at SoBo when she was a server. They now have an adorable son, Soren. Come to think of it, SoBo is responsible for a *number* of relationships resulting in babies. Thor's dish makes for a fabulous brunch item when topped with Poached Eggs (page 99). It's equally good as an appetizer or served with a fresh green salad.

MAKES 8 FRITTERS

½ cup plus 1 Tbsp canola oil, divided, for frying

1 cup farro

2 cups Vegetable Stock (page 252) or water

2 tsp salt, divided

2 bay leaves

1 Tbsp lemon zest

½ cup chopped fresh parsley

½ lb smoked salmon, diced

½ cup plus 2–4 tsp flour, divided

2–3 eggs, divided

¼ cup milk

4 cups fresh sorrel leaves

2 cups fresh spinach leaves

2 Tbsp freshly squeezed lemon juice

½ cup sour cream (see Cook's Note on page 94), for garnish

2 Tbsp chopped fresh chives, for garnish

In a large heavy-bottomed saucepan, heat 1 Tbsp of the oil. Add the farro and toast until golden, with a nutty aroma. Add the stock, 1 tsp of the salt and the bay leaves. Stir with a wooden spoon. When the mixture reaches a gentle boil, turn the heat to low, cover and simmer for about 25 minutes, until all moisture has been absorbed. Remove the farro from the heat and let it stand, covered, for 5 minutes. Drain any remaining liquid. Remove and discard the bay leaves.

In a large bowl, place the cooked farro, lemon zest, parsley, smoked salmon and ½ cup of the flour.

In a blender, place 2 eggs, the milk, sorrel leaves, spinach leaves, lemon juice and remaining 1 tsp salt and blend on medium speed until you have a smooth, greenish, liquidy mixture.

Fold the wet mixture into the dry mixture. The fritter batter should resemble a medium-thick pancake batter. If it seems too dry, whisk another egg and add it to the mixture; if it looks too wet, add the remaining 2 to 4 tsp flour. Fritter batter can be unpredictable: sometimes you just need to adapt and go with the fritter-flow.

In a cast-iron pan over medium heat, heat ¼ cup oil to its smoking point. Using a ladle or an ice cream scoop, scoop the fritter batter (with all the herby goodies that sank to the bottom of the bowl) into the pan, making each fritter about 4 inches in diameter, being careful not to overcrowd the pan. If the oil is the right temperature, you will hear a sizzle when the batter touches the pan.

Once the edges start to brown and bubbles begin to form, about 2 minutes, gently flip the fritters with a spatula. Continue to cook for 2 to 3 minutes. Repeat the process, adding more oil to the pan as needed, until all the batter is used up. These are ready to eat right away or, if making ahead, reheat on a baking sheet in a 400°F oven for 5 minutes. Serve topped with sour cream and chives.

GRILLED PATTYPAN SQUASH, GREEN POLENTA AND GARLIC AIOLI

This recipe was conceived when we were making our signature polenta fries one lunch service and realized we had loads of polenta left over. I decided to turn it into a light vegetarian meal, heavy on the herbs. It is now a staple dish in our kitchen. It also looks beautiful on a plate, so you'll get lots of oohs and aahs from your guests.

SERVES 6

Green Polenta Cubes

1 cup whole milk

2 tsp salt

½ cup coarse-ground cornmeal, plus extra for dusting

3 Tbsp butter, cubed

½ cup grated Asiago cheese

1 cup coarsely chopped mixed fresh herbs (I use flat-leaf parsley and basil)

1 Tbsp olive oil

2 cups canola oil, for frying

Garlic Aioli

1 egg yolk

1 tsp capers, rinsed

1 tsp minced garlic

1 tsp apple cider vinegar

¾ cup olive oil

Pattypan Squash

1 lb pattypan squash

¼ cup olive oil

¼ red onion, sliced ultra-thin, for garnish

1 radish, thinly sliced, for garnish

A few sprouts of watercress, for garnish

Prepare the polenta: Preheat the oven to 300°F.

In a medium ovenproof saucepan over medium-low heat, put 1 cup water, the milk and the salt. Cover with a lid and allow the mixture to come to a frothy, latte-like state. This will likely take 10 to 15 minutes. Do not let the milk bubble up and seep out under the lid. (If this happens it means the milk is scalded and the flavor will, um, not be so good.)

Very slowly whisk in the cornmeal until it's smooth. No lumps allowed! The polenta will start to bubble in little eruptions—I call this the volcano stage. You *must* get your mixture this hot to ensure that the cooking process will continue in the oven. Cover and bake for 15 minutes. Remove from the oven and stir with a wooden spoon so that no part of your mixture is sticking to the bottom of the pan. Return to the oven and bake for another 10 minutes.

Carefully remove from the oven and stir in the butter, using a wooden spoon. (Some of my worst burns are from accidentally spilling polenta when removing it from the oven. It sticks like glue and burns like hell.) Add the Asiago, then the herbs, and stir again until everything is well incorporated.

Pour the polenta into a 9- × 9-inch baking sheet and let cool to room temperature, about 1 hour. The polenta should then be cool enough to put in the fridge to set for a few hours.

Remove from the fridge and cut into 3- × 3-inch pieces. Lightly dust with cornmeal to prevent sticking.

When ready to serve, heat the oils in a heavy-bottomed pot suitable for frying until it reaches between 325°F and 350°F—test it with a deep-fry thermometer, or do the bread cube test (see sidebar page 257).

continued on next page

Carefully add the polenta cubes to the hot oil. (Cook in two batches to avoid overcrowding the pan.) The cubes will get crispy, but don't expect them to get golden brown (the herbs will have turned the polenta green, and you can't get golden brown from green, if you know what I mean). Drain on paper towel.

Prepare the garlic aioli: In a small bowl, place the egg yolk, capers, garlic and vinegar. Mix well with a whisk, then slowly add the oil, whisking until the mixture is emulsified. The aioli should be refrigerated if not used within the hour and will keep for up to 5 days.

Prepare the pattypans: Preheat the grill to medium-high.

Wash and cut the squash in half lengthwise. Toss with the olive oil. Grill for 2 to 3 minutes, then turn over and cook on the other side for another 2 to 3 minutes, until cooked through. *Alternatively, you can roast the pattypans:* Preheat the oven to 400°F. Place the oil-coated pattypans in a baking dish and roast for 10 minutes or until caramelized.

To serve: Spoon a few tablespoons of garlic aioli on each of six plates, then arrange the polenta and squash on top. Garnish with red onions, radishes and sprouts.

CRAB LOUIS

I'll never forget the first time I was introduced to this dish. I lived in South Florida in the '80s and worked at some skookum seafood restaurants. One in particular served this classic dish. It was love at first bite. Traditionally, this recipe uses asparagus, but I have substituted avocado to take it to another level of creamy deliciousness. Look for Dungeness crabmeat from the Pacific Northwest, highly recommended over canned lump crab. But please—don't be fooled into buying that fake crab stick product you sometimes see in stores. Just. Don't.

Crab Louis Sauce
¾ cup mayonnaise
¼ cup ketchup
2 Tbsp Dijon mustard
1 avocado, pitted and smashed
2 tsp freshly squeezed lemon juice
1 tsp salt

Crab Louis
2 cups lettuce of choice (I like iceberg)
1 lb Dungeness crabmeat
4 eggs, hard-boiled, peeled and quartered
1 large heirloom tomato, cut in 8 wedges
1 avocado, sliced
1 tsp finely chopped fresh chives, for garnish
2 tsp fresh tarragon leaves, for garnish

Prepare the Crab Louis sauce: In a bowl, whisk together all the ingredients. Refrigerate for up to 2 hours before assembling the Crab Louis.

Assemble the Crab Louis: Divide all the ingredients equally among four bowls. Lettuce is the bottom layer, followed by the Crab Louis sauce, crabmeat, eggs, tomato and avocado. Garnish with the chives and tarragon.

COOK'S NOTE: Keep all the ingredients well chilled until moments before serving. If crab is not available, shrimp will work very well in its place.

COOK'S NOTE: Kombu is a type of edible kelp and can be found at Asian grocers or natural food stores. I freeze the leftover tomato pulp, to use when making vegetable stock. Nothing gets wasted!

Seared Halibut Cheeks and Tomato Dashi

Umami is a popular term nowadays, and dare I say this elegant (yet surprisingly simple) dish really packs an umami double punch. Finding halibut cheeks at the fish market is a bit like winning a summertime lottery—they're a rare find and highly prized by those in the know. So if you can't find any, you can substitute halibut fillet or even scallops for solid results.

SERVES 4

Dashi Broth
2 pieces dried kombu (see Cook's Note)
2 cups bonito flakes

Tomato Water
4 cups diced tomatoes
2 tsp salt

Halibut Cheeks
3 Tbsp olive oil
1 Tbsp salt
1 lb halibut cheeks, patted dry with paper towel
2 cups cherry tomatoes, halved
2 Tbsp extra virgin olive oil, to finish

Prepare the dashi broth: Put the kombu in a medium stockpot, then pour in 4 quarts cold water. If time allows, let this sit for 4 to 6 hours in the fridge or at room temperature—it will make for a significantly richer broth.

Bring the broth to a simmer over medium heat. Add the bonito flakes and continue to simmer for 10 to 20 minutes. Once the bonito flakes have settled to the bottom, strain the broth through a fine-mesh strainer into a large bowl and set aside, allowing it to cool.

Prepare the tomato water: In a blender, blend the tomatoes and salt on high speed until smooth. Line a fine-mesh strainer with cheesecloth and place over a medium bowl. Pour the blended tomatoes into the strainer and allow them to sit until most of their water has drained, about 1 hour. To expedite the process, press down on the tomatoes with the back of a ladle.

Once the tomatoes are no longer dripping, pour the tomato water into the dashi broth, whisking to incorporate (see Cook's Note).

Prepare the halibut cheeks: In a heavy-bottomed saucepan over medium-high heat, heat the olive oil to its smoking point.

Salt the halibut cheeks, then gently place in the pan, about 4 to 5 inches apart. Do not overcrowd: the cheeks carry a lot of moisture and will not sear properly if there are too many in the pan at once.

After 3 to 4 minutes, the cheeks will start to naturally release from the pan. Use a spatula to carefully flip them over, then cook on the other side for another 3 to 4 minutes.

To serve: Five minutes before serving, heat the dashi and tomato water in the stockpot, bringing the mixture to a gentle simmer (but do not boil).

Divide the cheeks among four soup plates. Distribute the cherry tomatoes among the plates, then pour in the simmering broth. To finish, drizzle with extra virgin olive oil.

Halibut, Cucumber and Grapefruit Ceviche

Ceviche, the national dish of Peru, is known there as "heaven on a plate." Your fish must be uber-fresh since the "cooking," or curing, is achieved by marinating it in freshly squeezed lime. Halibut, bountiful in the waters off Tofino, is the perfect fish for this heavenly dish. In this crowd-pleasing take, the twist of grapefruit juice amps up the cool zippiness of the dish. Keep it refrigerated until you're ready to serve as an appetizer or even as a salad or light summer entrée on a hot, hot day, channeling those Equator-adjacent vibes.

SERVES 4–6

1 lb halibut fillet, boneless, finely diced

1 cup freshly squeezed lime juice

½ cup freshly squeezed grapefruit juice

1 Tbsp salt

3 red jalapeños with seeds, finely diced

1 small cucumber, peeled, seeded and finely diced

2 green onions, thinly sliced

½ cup packed fresh mint leaves, finely chopped

½ cup packed fresh cilantro leaves, finely chopped

1 head little gem lettuce leaves, washed, dried and separated, or corn tortilla chips, for serving

In a medium bowl, place the halibut, lime juice and grapefruit juice. Gently stir with a spoon so the fish is evenly coated with the fruit juices. Cover and place in the fridge for 2 hours.

Remove from the fridge and drain off any excess liquid. Season with the salt. Add the jalapeños, cucumber, onions, mint and cilantro. Very gently, toss together until all ingredients are well incorporated.

Serve chilled, use the lettuce leaves or tortilla chips to scoop and enjoy.

SHARON WHALEN AND CHRIS TAYLOR

It's not every chef who can call up friends for a next-day seaweed delivery. Luckily, because of Sharon Whalen and Chris Taylor, I can. We met not long after I first arrived in Tofino—they ate one of my Thanksgiving turkey dinners back when I served them at the food truck, and right from the get-go made it clear they preferred their food from close to home. With my local sourcing, I must have passed their test because they followed me to the food truck and then to the restaurant in town—customers first but quickly friends.

The couple live on Clayoquot Island, just off Tofino, where they've been the island's stewards for over 30 years. In that time, they've unearthed and rejuvenated plants like historic rhododendrons, built massive gardens with flowers, shrubs and vegetables, and protected the island's native forests and shorelines.

On the island, Sharon collects ingredients for Sea Wench Naturals, her line of natural products, harvesting calendula, St. John's wort, rosemary and more from her garden, and gathering ingredients like cedar and spruce buds, seaweeds and lichens from the wild. We try to limit non-food scents in the restaurant, but Sharon's Sea Wench Naturals are an exception: we use her lightly fragranced hand soap in SoBo's washrooms and her pain relief salve in our kitchen. Sharon and Chris are so generous with the Sea Wench products, showering our staff with gift bags and goodies, and donating products to fundraisers for all sorts of environmental causes. They also supply the restaurant with seaweed, spring nettles and herbs—often, Chris even brightens my day with a surprise bouquet.

Any time I've asked to shoot photography or television shows against Clayoquot Island's perfect West Coast backdrop, Sharon and Chris have been gracious hosts. We've had some epic evenings around their huge firepit, cooking crab in Sharon's oversized wok and grilling over the open fire.

Best of all, though, is when I can help Sharon and Chris harvest the seaweed or gather plants from their gardens. Life in the kitchen can be hectic, but time on Clayoquot Island with my friends provides peace and calm.

COOK'S NOTE: Sidestripe shrimp or spot shrimps are excellent in this recipe. The tomatoes should be crispy and hot when you serve them, so if they cool down too much while you're cooking the shrimp, place them on a parchment paper–lined baking sheet and reheat in the oven at 400°F for 5 minutes.

FRIED GREEN TOMATOES
WITH SPICED SHRIMP AND HERBED MAYONNAISE

It's impossible for me not to think of the food-fight scene in the movie *Fried Green Tomatoes* when I'm making the real thing. There are times in the SoBo kitchen when I'm tempted to slap a custard pie or a handful of blackberries onto a coworker's face—in jest, of course. But I resist—too much cleanup! If you're lucky enough to grow tomatoes, you've probably noticed how they dig their heels in at the end of the season, refusing to ripen all the way. Well, you just got even luckier. Now is the perfect time for fried green tomatoes! Using them before they overripen means they won't leak while frying. These are excellent as a solo snack or fancied up by serving with sautéed shrimp.

SERVES 4

Herbed Mayonnaise

½ cup mayonnaise

¼ cup sour cream (see Cook's Note on page 94)

2 Tbsp minced shallot

2 tsp minced garlic

2 Tbsp chopped fresh dill

2 Tbsp finely chopped fresh parsley

2 Tbsp freshly squeezed lemon juice

½ tsp salt

Fried Green Tomatoes

2 eggs

1 cup coarse-ground cornmeal

1 cup flour

2 tsp salt

1 tsp ground cayenne pepper

2 large green tomatoes

1 cup canola oil

Shrimp

2 Tbsp olive oil

1 Tbsp minced onion

1 lb shrimp, peeled and deveined (see Cook's Note)

1 tsp salt

1 Tbsp hot sauce (I like Frank's RedHot or Louisiana)

2 Tbsp sliced chives, for garnish

Prepare the herbed mayonnaise: In a bowl, whisk together all the ingredients. Refrigerate until ready to serve.

Prepare the fried green tomatoes: In a shallow bowl, whisk the eggs.

In a separate shallow bowl, mix together the cornmeal, flour, salt and cayenne.

Slice the tomatoes into ¾-inch rounds. Dip the tomato slices into the eggs, coating thoroughly. Dredge them, one by one, in the flour mixture. Place the tomatoes on a baking sheet in a single layer to prep for frying (do not stack them or the breading will fall off). You have to work fast so the tomatoes don't get soggy.

Heat the oil in a cast-iron frying pan over medium-high heat. When the oil starts to sizzle, carefully add the tomatoes, being careful not to overcrowd the pan. When the tomatoes start to turn golden brown, about 3 to 4 minutes, use a spatula to turn them over, and brown the other side, about 3 to 4 minutes.

Transfer the fried tomatoes to paper towel and set aside. Repeat the process with the remaining tomatoes (see Cook's Note).

Prepare the shrimp: Heat the oil in a frying pan over high heat until it starts to smoke. Add the onions and shrimp, using tongs or a spatula to toss them until cooked, about 2 minutes, depending on their size. Salt the shrimp and fold in the hot sauce.

To serve: Spoon a few spoonfuls of herbed mayo onto each of four plates. Arrange 2 tomatoes on each plate and top with the shrimp. Garnish with the chives.

Soups and Sandwiches

CLASSIC TOMATO GAZPACHO

In her 1942 book enticingly titled *How to Cook a Wolf*, M.F.K. Fisher called gazpacho the "perfect summer soup . . . a soul-satisfying thing to drink, chilled, midway in a torrid morning." The soup has continued to be very hot—that is, cold—ever since. Real gazpacho—August's scarlet, tomatoey salad-soup—is a simply perfect dish whose whole is much greater than the sum of its parts. Banish any thought of dumping in canned tomato or V8 juice—use only the ripest tomatoes (heirlooms, if you have them! You know how I feel about these beauties). The soup's body and bite stem from the base of bread and garlic. Sherry wine vinegar gives a little zing; for soul, use a high-quality, fruity olive oil.

SERVES 4-6

4 cups cored and diced tomatoes

2 cups peeled, seeded and diced cucumber

1 cup diced onions

2 cups seeded and diced red bell peppers

1 jalapeño, seeded and diced

2 Tbsp minced garlic

1 cup 1-inch-cubed day-old bread

½ cup sherry wine vinegar

¼ cup freshly squeezed lemon juice

½ cup packed fresh basil leaves

1 Tbsp salt

1 tsp fresh cracked black pepper

1 tsp sugar

1¼ cups extra virgin olive oil or good fruity olive oil, if you can find it, plus extra for serving

¼ cup fresh basil leaves, for garnish

1 cup finely diced toasted bread croutons, for garnish

½ cup seeded and finely diced cucumber, for garnish

In a bowl and using an immersion blender, or in the bowl of a traditional blender or food processor, place all the ingredients except the oil and garnishes (see sidebar). Purée the soup until smooth. Drizzle in the olive oil and use a whisk or blender to incorporate. Chill in the fridge for at least 6 hours, or for up to 24 hours.

To serve, slice the basil and scatter it, along with the croutons and diced cucumber, on top of the chilled soup. Drizzle with olive oil and serve.

SUMMERTIME SOUPS

For a great summertime chilled soup, all you need is perfectly ripe produce, fresh herbs, an acidic ingredient and a bit of fat, like coconut milk or extra virgin olive oil. Even if your fruit or vegetable looks as if it has seen better days, the inside might be at the peak of its career. My chilled soup recipes often have a spicy element to counterbalance the sweetness of the tomatoes or fruit. Using a powerful blender (like a Vitamix) or food processor is a must with a chilled soup. Straining after blending is up to the cook. I prefer all the fiber that's in my food to land in my belly, for health reasons, but if I were going all out and putting on the Ritz, as they used to say, I might want to strain the soup through a fine-mesh strainer.

WATERMELON GAZPACHO

You know it's officially summer when juicy, sweet, refreshing fruit hits the farm stands. Along country roads in the Southern states, you'll find numerous fruit and vegetable stands. In the old days, there would be metal cattle-watering troughs filled with cold water, ice and freshly picked watermelons. We would stop daily to grab a melon, sometimes barely making it to the back of the station wagon before slicing one open and devouring it right then and there. It wasn't until I was an adult that I came to learn about gazpachos, so this recipe combines my childhood memories with my adult need to elevate those taste memories. But, really, does it get any better than a farm-stand snack?

SERVES 8

3 cups peeled, seeded and diced watermelon

1 cup seeded and diced tomatoes

1 cup seeded and diced cucumber

1 clove garlic, minced

1 jalapeño, seeded and finely diced

½ cup fresh mint leaves

½ cup fresh basil leaves, plus 6–8 chopped leaves, for garnish

2 tsp salt, plus extra to taste

¼ cup freshly squeezed lemon juice

¼ cup orange juice

½ cup extra virgin olive oil

Salt

In a large bowl and using an immersion blender, or in the bowl of a traditional blender or food processor, place the watermelon, tomato, cucumber, garlic, jalapeños, mint and ½ cup basil (see sidebar page 49). Sprinkle with the salt.

Blitz until smooth. (You may have to do this in batches if you are using a food processor or if your traditional blender is small.) Once the mixture is smooth, add the juices and blend on medium speed. Drizzle in the olive oil and blend to combine (you could do this with a whisk). Add the salt to taste.

Chill the soup in the fridge for at least 4 hours, or for up to 24 hours. Garnish with the remaining basil.

COOK'S NOTE: This soup does not keep for days: it will likely fall apart and separate after 36 to 48 hours. I like to make it in the evening and let it sit overnight to enjoy on a picnic lunch. If you make it first thing in the morning, then dinner is a snap.

MELON AND COCONUT MILK SOUP

This is a great way to use up those summer melons that are reaching maximum ripeness. When the melons I have start to ripen faster than I can eat them, they become destined for soupdom. I seed them, peel them and freeze them so that they're ready to pluck out and become a chilled soup any time of year. Who says you can't have cold soup in winter? You can! As long as you thought ahead to tuck away some of these summer delights.

SERVES 6

4 cups melon (any sweet variety, like cantaloupe, honeydew, muskmelon)

2 cups coconut milk (see Cook's Note)

½ cup freshly squeezed lemon juice

½ cup fresh mint leaves, plus a few extra for garnish

½ cup fresh Thai basil

¼ cup fresh lemongrass, tender bottom of stalk only

1 tsp minced Thai chili

2 tsp salt

½ cup olive oil

In a bowl and using an immersion blender, or in the bowl of a traditional blender or food processor, place all the ingredients except the olive oil (see sidebar page 49). Drizzle in the olive oil and blend to combine (you could also do this with a whisk).

Chill in the fridge for at least 6 hours, or for up to 24 hours.

Just before serving, garnish the chilled soup with the remaining mint leaves.

COOK'S NOTE: While some types of coconut milk come completely blended, I prefer buying cans, where the milk has separated into water and fat. The top fat layer is great for any sautéing you might get up to.

CHILLED PEA AND MINT SOUP

Shelling peas has become a family affair. SoBo is always so busy that time-consuming tasks like this don't always get done on restaurant time. So, long ago, I started to bring peapods home and teach my littles, Ella and Barkley, how to shuck. It's now become a time that I really look forward to with my no-longer-littles: the three of us around the dinner table, all shucking together. Sometimes I would set up a camcorder and let it roll, to capture the kids just interacting. We often have a great laugh over the time Barkley and I "fired" Ella, only a wee lass, for tossing the shelled peas all around the room. And every spring, we still find ourselves yelling, "ELLA, YOU'RE FIRED!"

SERVES 6

2 tsp salt, divided

1 cup sugar snap peas, stringy stems removed

4 lb shelled fresh English peas, pods and peas separated (see Cook's Note)

1 cup thinly sliced leeks, whites and greens separated

2 Tbsp olive oil

1 cup finely diced celery

1 bay leaf

3 black peppercorns

1 clove garlic, crushed or coarsely chopped

1 cup fresh mint leaves

1/2 cup fresh parsley leaves

1/4 cup freshly squeezed lemon juice

4 drops hot sauce (I like Frank's RedHot or Louisiana)

Fresh cracked black pepper

1 1/2 cups heavy cream (see Cook's Note on page 57)

Lemon zest, for garnish (optional)

In a 10-quart stockpot over high heat, bring 6 quarts water and 1 tsp of the salt to a boil. Add the sugar snap peas and blanch for about 3 minutes, then add the shelled English peas and blanch for another 3 minutes. Scoop out the peas using a slotted spoon (reserving the water) and plunge into an ice bath to stop the cooking process.

Bring the reserved blanching water back to a very light boil and add the English peapods and leek greens. Turn the heat to low and let simmer, uncovered, for 15 minutes. Meanwhile, remove the cooled peas from the ice bath and set aside. Strain the blanching water, discarding the peapods and leek greens.

Pour the reserved blanching water into a large heatproof glass or metal container, and set into a separate ice bath to chill.

Meanwhile, heat the olive oil in a large heavy-bottomed stockpot. Add the leek whites, celery, bay leaf, peppercorns and garlic. Stirring every few minutes, sweat down the mixture, about 15 minutes. Careful not to let it brown. Remove from the heat and let it come to room temperature.

In a blender, combine all the peas, 1/2 cup of the pea blanching water, the vegetable mixture, mint, parsley, lemon juice, hot sauce, pepper (just a crack) and the remaining 1 tsp salt. Purée until ultra-smooth. For best results, blend in batches, filling the blender only halfway each time. Strain the mixture through a fine-mesh strainer for a silkier soup (see sidebar page 49).

Add the cream and the remaining blanching water, 1/2 cup at a time, only enough to achieve your desired thickness. I usually end up only using half and freezing the rest (for up to 3 months) to use on another occasion.

Chill the soup in the fridge for 2 to 4 hours. Garnish with the zest of lemon, if desired. Serve chilled.

*Watermelon
Gazpacho, page 50*

Melon and Coconut Milk Soup, page 53

*Chilled Pea and Mint Soup,
page 54*

Classic Tomato Gazpacho, page 49

COOK'S NOTE: If fresh peas
are unavailable, by all means use
frozen. You will just need to use
veggie stock (page 252) in place of
the reserved pea blanching water.

CHANTERELLE MUSHROOM AND CORN CHOWDER

One of my all-time favorite soups is the love child of summer and fall coming together. I often refer to this time of year as the perfect storm: sweet tomatoes are still in their prime, hard acorn squashes are ready for harvest. After the intense heat of summer, the rains start in just enough to bring the forest back to life. The days are warm and humid, and the evenings start to grow cooler. That's when the chanterelles start to pop up all over the dense rain-forested areas of the Pacific Northwest. Meanwhile, the late-summer crops of corn are as high as an elephant's eyes, and so it is heaven on earth in my kitchen. Sweet corn and earthy mushrooms—my tummy and my heart are full.

SERVES 6-8

¼ cup olive oil

¼ cup butter

1 lb chanterelle mushrooms, cleaned and torn into bite-sized pieces (see sidebar page 184)

1 Tbsp minced fresh garlic

2 large onions, diced

2 large carrots, diced

1 rib celery, diced

1 lb potatoes, diced (I like red bliss or young yellow)

1 Tbsp salt

4 cups Vegetable Stock (page 252)

1 tsp dried thyme

1 head Roasted Garlic (page 259)

½ tsp red chili flakes

1 tsp fresh thyme leaves

2 cups corn kernels, roasted (page 258)

4 cups heavy cream (see Cook's Note)

Heat the oil and butter in a large heavy-bottomed soup pot over high heat until they start to smoke. Add the mushrooms and fresh garlic.

After 2 minutes, turn the heat to medium and cook the mixture for about 5 minutes, until the mushrooms are tender. Using a slotted spoon, remove the mushroom mixture and set aside.

There will be quite a bit of liquid left with some of the garlic in the pan. Add the onions, carrots and celery and cook for 10 minutes (still over medium heat). Add the potatoes, stirring frequently with a wooden spoon to prevent sticking. Add the salt, stock, dried thyme, roasted garlic, chili flakes and reserved mushrooms.

When the chowder comes back up to a lazy bubble, turn the heat to low and continue to cook until the potatoes are tender, about 20 to 25 minutes.

Add the fresh thyme, corn kernels and cream. Turn the heat to medium, heating the chowder until it is very hot but not boiling. Ladle into bowls, serve and enjoy.

COOK'S NOTE: Some of the soups in this book call for heavy cream, but you can always substitute that with a nondairy "milk" like oat, almond or soy, or use vegetable stock instead. Just remember to buy unsweetened milk products, and do note that flavors will vary.

WHITE BEAN AND CHICKEN CHILI

When I think chili, I think coziness. A dish for a long, wet, dark (did I say stormy?) night, when you want something hearty to reassure you that the light at the end of the tunnel is not the light of an oncoming train. Speaking of trains, it's said that legendary train robber Jesse James refused to rob the Loan Star Bank in McKinney, Texas, because his favorite chili parlor was in the hood. I wonder if he would have given Tofino's credit union a pass had he dropped by SoBo first for a bowl of our chicken chili.

SERVES 4–6

Beans

2 cups dried cannellini beans, rinsed and soaked in cold water in the fridge overnight, then drained

1 bay leaf

1 tsp salt

Chicken

6 chicken thighs

½ cup diced onion

2 cloves garlic

1 bay leaf

2 tsp salt

Chili

¼ cup cooking oil

1 Tbsp ground cumin

2 cloves garlic, coarsely chopped

1 cup diced onion

1 cup diced carrot

1 Tbsp fresh Mexican oregano (see Cook's Note on page 61)

1 tsp dried thyme

1 tsp salt

1 Tbsp fresh thyme leaves

1 cup diced fire-roasted green chilies (see Cook's Note)

4 Tbsp Roasted Garlic, puréed (page 259)

Crispy tortilla strips (optional)

Shredded Cheddar cheese (optional)

Prepare the beans: In a large soup pot, bring the beans, bay leaf and 8 cups cold water to a boil, then immediately turn the heat to low and simmer, covered, for 45 minutes to 1 hour. The beans should be tender but should not split. Add the salt in the last few minutes of cooking time. Reserve 2 cups of the bean broth, and drain the remainder, setting the beans aside.

Prepare the chicken: In a large stockpot, bring the chicken thighs, onions, garlic, bay leaf, salt and 8 cups cold water to a lazy bubble. Simmer for about 30 minutes, until the chicken is just barely cooked and the flesh is not red.

Remove the chicken, setting aside to cool. Once cooled, remove and shred the meat, returning the bones to the cooking liquid to simmer for 1 hour. Then skim off any excess fat off the stock and strain. Set the stock aside.

Now, put the chili together: In a heavy-bottomed, 8-quart stockpot over medium-high heat, heat the oil, cumin, garlic and onions. Sweat down this mixture for 10 to 15 minutes, until tender, stirring occasionally to prevent sticking. Add the carrots, oregano, dried thyme and salt and cook for 10 minutes. Add the cooked beans, bean broth, chicken stock, shredded chicken, fresh thyme, green chilies and roasted garlic and simmer for 15 minutes. Serve with tortilla strips and Cheddar, if desired. (I recommend it. Desire.)

This chili freezes beautifully and will keep for up to 6 months.

COOK'S NOTE: If you're pressed for time, you can modify this recipe by using canned beans, an in-store roasted rotisserie chicken, and store-bought chicken stock. Canned diced green chilies are widely available in supermarkets, but if you have the opportunity to roast your own chilies, they will add a truly wonderful flavor (page 260).

FALL HARVEST VEGETABLE SOUP

Fall in the Pacific Northwest—everything's cooking! Tomatoes, corn, summer squash—all at their peak of loveliness. I use this harvest time to fill my freezers with soups and stocks to get me through the winter, when my choices of anything fresh, especially produce, will be limited. If you don't like any ingredient in this recipe, leave it out! It's like the bumper sticker says: Non-Judgment Day Is Near. You can add whatever you please—mushrooms, butternut squash, turnips, celeriac or potatoes. This is just a good base-soup recipe that you can easily make at home.

SERVES 8

1 large head cauliflower

¼ cup olive oil

¼ cup canola oil

1 onion, diced

3 cloves garlic, minced

2 carrots, diced

2 ribs celery, diced

1 tsp dried thyme

1 tsp fresh Mexican oregano (see Cook's Note)

2 cups diced tomatoes

1 zucchini, diced

1 Tbsp salt

3 quarts Vegetable Stock (page 252)

1 cup corn kernels, roasted (page 258) or frozen

Preheat the oven to 400°F.

Slice the cauliflower (core and all) into bite-sized florets. Drizzle with the olive oil and place in a large baking dish or on a baking sheet (I like to use a baking vessel with sides so the oil has no chance of spilling onto the oven floor). Roast the cauliflower, flipping about halfway through, until it is dark brown and well caramelized, about 20 minutes in total. Remove from the oven and set aside to cool.

Heat the canola oil in a large heavy-bottomed stockpot over medium heat. Add the onions, garlic, carrots and celery. Sauté until tender, about 15 minutes, until the vegetables sweat and start to become tender, stirring occasionally with a wooden spoon to prevent sticking.

Add the thyme, oregano, tomatoes, zucchini and roasted cauliflower and sauté for 5 minutes. Stir in the salt and veggie stock.

Bring to a boil, then turn the heat to low and simmer for about 10 minutes. Add the roasted corn kernels, adjust the seasoning to your taste and serve (if using frozen corn, simmer for 3 to 5 minutes before serving).

COOK'S NOTE: Mexican oregano is a completely different plant from the Mediterranean oregano found in most Western cuisine. It's stronger in flavor and less sweet.

ROASTED CAULIFLOWER AND GARLIC SOUP

Cauliflower has become a vegetable star in the last few years, but it's been a favorite of mine since forever. I remember roasting it to a deep brown, just verging on blackening, to serve with my daily fish specials 20 years ago, and people sending the dish back to the kitchen saying that the cauliflower was burnt. Well, that was then and this is now. I think we are all used to seeing the benefits of good cauliflower caramelization. It adds so much depth to this simple soup.

SERVES 6–8

1 large head cauliflower

¼ cup olive oil

¼ cup canola oil

1 onion, diced

2 ribs celery, diced

1 carrot, diced

2 bay leaves

1 Tbsp salt

½ tsp ground cardamom

½ tsp ground coriander

½ cup Roasted Garlic, puréed (page 259)

½ cup dry white wine

2 Tbsp freshly squeezed lemon juice

8 cups Vegetable Stock (page 252)

½ cup chopped fresh parsley leaves

2 cups heavy cream (see Cook's Note on page 57)

Chive oil or thinly sliced fresh chives, for garnish

Preheat the oven to 400°F.

Slice the cauliflower (core and all) into 1-inch-thick slabs. Drizzle with the olive oil and place in a large baking dish or on a baking sheet (I like to use a baking vessel with sides so there's no chance of the oil spilling onto the oven floor). Roast the cauliflower, flipping about halfway through, until it is dark brown and well caramelized, about 20 minutes in total. Remove from the oven and set aside.

Meanwhile, in a heavy-bottomed stockpot over medium heat, combine the canola oil, onions, celery, carrots, bay leaves, salt, cardamom and coriander and sauté for 20 minutes or until the vegetables are tender, stirring frequently with a wooden spoon.

Stir in the roasted garlic, wine and lemon juice. Continue to cook for 5 minutes, then turn the heat to high. Add the stock and bring to a boil. Turn the heat to low, add the roasted cauliflower and simmer for 10 minutes. Add the parsley and cream, then simmer for 5 minutes more. Remove from the heat. Remove and discard the bay leaves.

With an immersion blender or in a traditional blender, blend the soup until smooth (see Cook's Note).

Garnish with a drizzle of chive oil.

COOK'S NOTE: If you are using a traditional blender for hot soups, fill it only halfway, hold the lid down tightly with a tea towel and pulse to keep the hot soup from splattering out of the blender.

Silky Parsnip, Apple and Celeriac Soup

Where others might call winter root vegetables wrinkly and weird, I call them sexy and satisfying. I can't get enough of them! I once read a study on how to get folks to eat more root vegetables (totally perplexing to me as to why anyone would need convincing, but in any case) that found that laying on indulgent descriptors helped seal the deal. You might tell them something like: "We have early-harvest white turnips in a soft-ripened bloomy-rind cow- and sheep-milk cheese mélange . . ." Well? Did I sell you on this soup?

SERVES 8

¼ cup canola oil

6 parsnips, peeled and diced

3 cloves garlic, minced

2 ribs celery, diced

1 celeriac, rinsed, peeled and diced

1 carrot, diced

2 bay leaves

1 Tbsp salt

1 tsp caraway seeds

1 tsp dried thyme

1 tsp ground cumin

2 apples, peeled, cored and diced

½ cup dry white wine

6 cups Vegetable Stock (page 252)

2 cups heavy cream (see Cook's Note on page 57)

Olive oil, for garnish (optional)

In a large heavy-bottomed soup pot over medium heat, combine the oil, parsnips, garlic, celery, celeriac, carrots, bay leaves and salt. Sauté for 10 minutes, stirring frequently with a wooden spoon. Stir in the caraway seeds, thyme, cumin and apples and sauté for 5 minutes. Add the wine and reduce for 2 to 3 minutes.

Turn the heat to high, add the stock and simmer for 30 minutes or until everything is tender. Do not boil. Add the cream (see Cook's Note) and simmer for 5 more minutes. Remove and discard the bay leaves.

Using an immersion or traditional blender (see sidebar page 62), purée until silky and smooth. Garnish with a drizzle of olive oil.

COOK'S NOTE: As you've probably gathered by now, my soups yield between 6 and 8 servings, because I wouldn't dream of making a pot of soup and not having lots left over to freeze for a later date when time is an issue and I need a bowl of soup RIGHT BLANKETY BLANK NOW. I recommend freezing your soup *before* adding any dairy. Once it's thawed and you are reheating, *then* add the cream.

CREAM OF MUSHROOM SOUP

Mushrooms: where to start? Which type best suits your personality? If you're a heavy meat eater or are just craving that umami, meaty taste, portobello mushrooms are the way to go. Carboholic? A single white button mushroom has 3 grams of carbs, so this one's for you. Into fitness, with a super healthy lifestyle and a desire to live forever? Shiitake are rich in selenium and vitamin C. Vegan or vegetarian: creminis are fantastically rich and flavorful in a veggie and mushroom soup or in mushroom bourguignon, vegan stroganoff or alfredo sauce. If you have a poet's soul: chanterelles. This soup gives you a chance to create your own style. I try to use at least two mushroom varieties in my soup, but three or four are even better.

SERVES 8

½ cup olive oil

½ cup butter

2 lb mushrooms of choice, cleaned and sliced (see sidebar page 184)

2 leeks, whites only, rinsed well and sliced

1 onion, diced

1 Tbsp minced garlic

2 ribs celery, diced

1 carrot, diced

1 tsp dried thyme

1 Tbsp salt

¼ cup soy sauce

1 tsp ground Aleppo chili

1 cup dry white wine

6 cups Vegetable Stock (page 252)

1 tsp fresh thyme leaves

1 Tbsp freshly squeezed lemon juice

2 cups heavy cream (see Cook's Note on page 57)

Heat the olive oil and butter in a large heavy-bottomed stockpot over medium-high heat. As soon as the butter starts to brown, add the mushrooms, leeks, onions, garlic, celery, carrots, dried thyme and salt. Sauté for about 20 to 25 minutes, stirring frequently, until all the vegetables are very tender. Remove a few of the mushroom slices and set aside for garnish.

Turn the heat to high and add the soy sauce, Aleppo chili and wine. Reduce for about 2 to 3 minutes, then add the stock and thyme and bring the mixture to a boil. Turn the heat to low and simmer for about 30 minutes. Pour in the lemon juice and cream, and continue to simmer for 5 more minutes.

Remove from the heat and blend until smooth with an immersion blender or in a traditional blender (see Cook's Note on page 62). Garnish with the reserved mushroom slices and serve.

KATRINA PETERS

Katrina Peters came into my life at a crucial time. We had just moved the SoBo food truck from its original location behind the Live to Surf shop to the Tofino Botanical Gardens, and I was pregnant with my daughter, Ella. Katrina was one of our frequent customers, working at a local coffee shop at the time. I'd noticed her when grabbing my morning coffee and right away could sense her reliability and sturdiness. One day we got to talking, and she told me she was interested in learning more about cooking. With this perfect timing, I took her on, training her on all the bases and prep for our chowder, polenta, shrimp cakes, pinto beans and tofu pockets. So, I was able to take time having Ella, and Katrina stepped in and stepped up to support our hot line chef.

Our shared love of good food—high quality, sourced ethically—brought and has kept us together. I admire Katrina's extensive knowledge about nutrition, and I depend on her to find reputable sources for products—I ask for organic coconut flour, she'll find it.

Katrina is also the recycling whiz—she not only helped set up SoBo's recycling system but makes sure everything tossed actually makes it to its proper bin. Heaven help you if she sees you throw something recyclable into the garbage can! Even before Tofino had much of a recycling infrastructure, she'd bundle up the shop's recycling and bike it up to the depot at the top of Industrial Way's steady incline.

Along with recycling, cycling is one of the many ways Katrina cares for the environment. She's a committed biker year-round, no matter the weather, and she also gives her time and energy to many environmental causes, keeping Tofino moving in such a positive direction.

The versatile and thoroughly reliable Katrina has now been with me at SoBo for almost 17 years. Now she works part time, filling in on the baker's days off, but I know that if I asked her to make tofu pockets or polenta, she would jump to it.

HOT AND SOUR CHICKEN NOODLE SOUP

Sometimes a comforting bowl of soup is all you need. The most time-consuming part of this yumsome (that's yummy and then some) soup is the prep work. My inspiration for this Thai-influenced recipe? Traveling abroad. Tofitians like to travel, and when we return home, we sometimes like to chow down on a dish that reminds us of that best-holiday-ever. But sometimes it's a case of rose-colored sunglasses, isn't it? Catching and missing flights, long days of walking, going back to a bed that just isn't yours . . . Seriously, there is no place like home, so why not just stay home and enjoy a bowl of soup without losing your money or your mind? Holidays: they might not be for everyone.

SERVES 6–8

The Broth

¼ cup canola or grapeseed oil

1 cup coarsely chopped ginger

2 Tbsp minced garlic

12 green onions, thinly sliced (white part for the broth, green part for garnish)

4 stalks fresh lemongrass, smashed and halved lengthwise

4 Thai chilies, fresh or dried

2 cups diced carrots

10–12 shiitake mushrooms, cleaned (see sidebar page 184) (stems for the broth, caps for garnish)

Makrut lime leaves

2 lb chicken bones

1 cup freshly squeezed lemon juice

½ cup fish sauce, preferably Thai

¼ cup sambal oelek, or to taste (optional, see Cook's Note on page 146)

The Chicken

1 lb chicken thighs

2 tsp salt, divided

1 lb vermicelli rice noodles (usually 1 package)

Prepare the broth: In a large stockpot over medium-high heat, place the oil, ginger, garlic, the whites of the green onions, the lemongrass, chilies, carrots, mushroom stems and lime leaves. Sweat down for about 10 minutes, until tender.

Add the chicken bones and stir for a few minutes. Add 10 quarts cold water, bring to a boil, then turn the heat down to a lazy bubble and let the mixture simmer for at least 2 hours to extract all the goodness from the bones. Remove the broth from the heat and strain. Add the lemon juice and fish sauce and, if you'd like, the sambal oelek to taste. I offer sambal on the side, too, for those who like it . . . hotter.

Prepare the chicken: In a medium saucepan over low heat, add 2 cups cold water, chicken and 1 tsp of the salt. Simmer for 20 to 30 minutes, until the chicken is just cooked through. Remove the chicken and allow the poaching water to cool, then add this water to the broth in the stockpot. Why throw it out? Debone the chicken, shred the meat and set aside.

In a medium pot, bring 8 cups water to a boil. Add the remaining 1 tsp salt and the rice noodles. Gently stir to separate the noodles, then boil for 2 minutes. Remove from the heat and drain. Run cold water over the noodles to cool them down.

Prepare the garnish: Heat the oil in a small frying pan over high heat. As soon as it starts to smoke, add the mushroom caps and cook for 3 to 4 minutes, until tender. Remove from the heat and lightly season with a pinch of salt. Have the other garnishes ready for plating.

continued on next page

The Garnish Goodies

3 Tbsp canola oil

Pinch salt

1 carrot, peeled and thinly julienned

2 cups thinly shredded cabbage

¼ cup each fresh cilantro, mint and
Thai basil leaves

To serve: Divide the rice noodles among six or eight large soup bowls, then add the shredded chicken. Fill three-quarters of each bowl with steaming broth. Garnish with the mushroom caps, vegetables, fresh herbs and the greens of the green onions.

COOK'S NOTE: This dish is all about a well-balanced broth that gets its richness from the chicken bones, but if you want to shorten the process or do not have access to bones, it's okay to buy premade broths. Many are quite good these days. The broth can be prepared a day or two in advance. What you don't use will freeze beautifully for up to 6 months.

FALAFEL POCKETS
WITH SUMAC ONIONS AND HERBED YOGURT DIP

Making falafel can be tricky. I have always been attracted to its flavor profile of warm spices and aromatic herbs but am oftentimes disappointed in the execution at North American restaurants, where I've found falafel can be heavy and overly greasy. This recipe is light and full of warm spices and herbs. You can fry these up in a flash—and make them in advance to quickly reheat in the oven. Makes a lovely little appetizer as well. (Note that you'll need to soak the chickpeas in cold water a day ahead of making this recipe.)

SERVES 4

Falafel Balls

2 cups dried chickpeas

1 bay leaf

2 tsp salt

2 tsp ground turmeric

1 tsp ground cumin

1 tsp ground coriander

2 tsp garam masala or madras curry powder

½ tsp ground cinnamon

Pinch ground cayenne pepper

Pinch ground cardamom

¾ cup rice flour (I like brown rice flour), plus extra as needed

¼ cup ground flaxseed

1 shallot, minced

12 cloves garlic, roughly chopped

½ bunch fresh parsley

½ bunch fresh cilantro

¼ cup freshly squeezed lemon juice

¼ cup olive oil

2 tsp maple syrup

3 cups grapeseed oil, for frying

Prepare the falafel balls: Place the chickpeas in a medium bowl, cover with water and refrigerate for 24 hours.

The next day, drain the chickpeas. Place half the chickpeas and the bay leaf in a large saucepan with 6 cups water, allowing space for movement and so that they don't burn dry, and bring to a boil. Cook until the chickpeas are very tender, about 1 hour. Add the salt and stir. Drain, remove and discard the bay leaf, and let cool to room temperature.

While the chickpeas are cooling, toast the turmeric, cumin, coriander, garam masala, cinnamon, cayenne and cardamom in a small saucepan over medium-high heat for about 2 minutes to release the powerful oils. Stir constantly so as not to burn it—never turn your back on spices while they are toasting.

In a food processor, pulse the cooled, cooked chickpeas until mostly smooth, with just a touch of texture left. Scoop into a large bowl and set aside. Add the toasted spices, rice flour and flaxseed to the puréed chickpeas, and mix until the spices are evenly distributed.

Place the remaining soaked, uncooked chickpeas in the food processor and pulse. It's important to pulse these separate from the cooked chickpeas to keep the proper texture, as the uncooked ones need longer to break down.

continued on next page

Sumac Onions

½ cup thinly sliced red onion

1 Tbsp red wine vinegar

2 tsp dried sumac

1 tsp salt

Herbed Yogurt Sauce

½ bunch fresh parsley, finely chopped

½ bunch fresh cilantro, finely chopped

2 Tbsp fresh mint, finely chopped

2 Tbsp Roasted Garlic, puréed (page 259)

Juice of 1 lemon

¾ cup plain yogurt

Salt

Falafel Pockets

4 pita

2 cups torn lettuce leaves

1 cucumber, thinly sliced

Transfer the puréed uncooked chickpeas to the bowl with the cooked chickpeas. Pulse the shallot, garlic, parsley and cilantro in the food processor and pulse until smooth. Transfer the mixture to the bowl with the chickpeas.

Pour in the lemon juice, olive oil and maple syrup. Using a wooden spoon, mix everything together. To gauge the proper consistency, form some chickpea mixture into a ball about 2 inches in diameter: it should hold together firmly. If they're turning out too dry, add 1 tsp more water; if they're too wet, add 1 tsp more flour. Once the proper consistency is achieved, form the mixture into 2-inch balls. At SoBo, we use a small ice cream scoop to make portioning easy.

Heat the grapeseed oil in a medium heavy-bottomed saucepan over medium-high heat to about 350°F—test it with a deep-fry thermometer, or do the bread cube test (see sidebar page 257). Using a slotted spoon, gently place three or four falafel balls at a time in the saucepan and cook until they are golden brown. Remove the balls and set on paper towel to soak up any excess oil.

Prepare the sumac onions: In a small bowl, mix all the ingredients and let sit for at least 1 hour. These onions keep in the fridge for up to 2 days.

Prepare the yogurt sauce: In a food processor, blend the herbs with the roasted garlic. Add the lemon juice, yogurt and salt to taste. Process again to combine.

Assemble the pockets: Preheat the oven to 350°F. Warm the pita in the oven for 3 minutes, until soft but not toasted. Divide the lettuce, cucumber slices and sumac onions evenly among the pita pockets. Add three or four falafel balls and a dollop of herbed yogurt sauce to each pita and enjoy.

COOK'S NOTE: Sumac is a Middle Eastern spice made from dried berries ground into a dark red burgundy powder. It has a crisp lemony flavor and can be used as a seasoning or condiment—to be sprinkled over hummus, for example—and is one of the main components of the spice blend za'atar. The sumac tree is related to the cashew family, so avoid if you suffer from cashew allergies.

SHRIMP, AVOCADO AND TOMATO ROTI WRAP

This is my go-to picnic dish anytime I can bring a cooler. It's cucumber-cool, crunchy and refreshing, so that when you take a hike on the wild side (or along a sandy beach or a well-marked trail), you don't feel bloated or weighed down after your break. In British Columbia, we have a fishery with sidestripe shrimp, a particularly sweet species. Spot prawns, king shrimp or humpback shrimp also work beautifully. Please, though, whatever you do, don't buy black tiger prawns grown in warm, brackish waters. Don't get me started on this—unless you want to stop by SoBo for a stiff drink and a sidestripe shrimp wrap with a side of rant.

SERVES 4

Roti

2½ cups flour, plus extra for kneading

2 tsp salt

The Dressing

¼ cup mayonnaise

3 Tbsp sour cream (see Cook's Note on page 94)

1 Tbsp freshly squeezed lemon juice

1 Tbsp chopped fresh dill, no stems

1 Tbsp thinly sliced shallot

Pinch salt and pepper

Parsnip Fries

1 lb parsnips, peeled

2–3 Tbsp olive oil

½ tsp salt

The Wrap

2 Tbsp olive oil

1 lb sidestripe shrimp, peeled and deveined

Salt

1 cucumber, thinly sliced

1 avocado, sliced

1 cup cherry tomatoes, halved

1 cup arugula

Prepare the roti: Preheat a 12-inch cast-iron pan, griddle or grill pan.

Pour 1 cup lukewarm water into a large bowl. Stir in the flour and salt using a wooden spoon. Turn the dough onto a floured work surface. Knead until smooth to the touch. If it is sticky, add 1 Tbsp more flour. If it's dry, wet your hands before continuing to knead. Return the dough to the bowl, cover and let rest for 10 minutes. Divide the dough into four pieces.

On a generously floured work surface, use a rolling pin to roll out each piece of dough so that it is thin but not see-through.

Place the dough pieces, one at a time, in the heated pan. When you see air bubbles start to form and the dough starts releasing from the pan, 30 to 45 seconds, flip the dough and continue to cook on the other side for 30 seconds. The idea is to end up with a soft, pliable, tortilla-like wrap.

Prepare the dressing: In a medium bowl, whisk together all the ingredients.

Prepare the parsnip fries: Preheat the oven to 450°F. Line a baking sheet with parchment paper.

Cut the parsnips into 4- to 5-inch-long sticks the shape of traditional french fries. In a bowl, toss the parsnips with the olive oil.

Spread the parsnips on the prepared baking sheet, leaving space between each so that they don't touch one another. Bake for about 8 to 10 minutes, then turn them over and bake for another 10 minutes or until they're crispy on the outside but still tender inside. Salt them while still hot.

continued on next page

Assemble the wrap: In a frying pan over medium-high heat, heat the oil to its smoking point. Add half the shrimp, lightly salt to taste, and cook for 1 minute. Flip the shrimp and cook on the other side until they're no longer translucent, about 1 minute more. Don't overcook: overcooked shrimp become mushy. Set aside. Repeat with the remaining shrimp, then set aside with the first batch.

Scoop some of the cucumber and avocado slices, cherry tomatoes and arugula onto one side of each roti, drizzle with the dressing and top with the shrimp. Roll each up and enjoy.

GRILLED HALLOUMI AND SUN-DRIED TOMATO TAPENADE ON FOCACCIA

If you have yet to discover Halloumi, brace yourself: this heavenly cheese (semi-hard, unripened, made from goat and sheep milk) may present as mozzarella, but it's much saltier and has a high melting point, so it's one of the few cheeses you can grill or fry. When I eat this sandwich, I imagine myself lounging by the Mediterranean, wearing big sunglasses and nothing else. (Well, okay, some sunscreen and a kaftan.) Halloumi comes from the island of Cyprus—the tomatoes and olives from that part of the world are to die and be reborn for—and focaccia is an Italian favorite. (It's also a great way to use excess pizza dough.) As soon as my royalties start pouring in, I am going to book a trip!

MAKES 4 SANDWICHES

Focaccia

½ recipe Pizza Dough, Tofino Style (page 119)

1 tsp extra virgin olive oil

Sun-Dried Tomato Tapenade

¼ cup sun-dried tomatoes in oil, drained

¼ cup green or Kalamata olives, pitted

¼ cup packed fresh parsley

1 anchovy fillet

1 Tbsp minced garlic

1 tsp capers, rinsed

1 tsp freshly squeezed lemon juice

½ tsp crushed red chili flakes

Halloumi Sandwich

17½ oz Halloumi, sliced ½ inch thick

2 Tbsp olive oil

1 large heirloom tomato, sliced

8 Kalamata olives, pitted and halved

1 cup mizuna greens or other salad greens of choice

Potato chips, for serving (page 256)

Prepare the focaccia: Follow the instructions for the pizza dough until it has done its second rest. Instead of dividing the dough, leave it as one ball and gently press the ball into a 7- × 11-inch baking sheet. The dough should be about ½ inch high.

Press your fingers into the dough to make dimples across the whole surface. Be mindful not to push so hard that the dimples become potholes.

Drizzle the olive oil on top and cover with plastic wrap. Set in a warm place, free of drafts, and let rise for about 1 hour, until the dough has doubled in size. If it doesn't rise enough, you'll get flatbread, not focaccia. We want lighter bread, with a few air pockets in it.

Preheat the oven to 400°F.

Uncover the dough and bake for 20 minutes or until the top is golden brown. Remove from the oven and use a spatula to immediately transfer the bread to a wire rack to cool, about 20 minutes.

Cut the focaccia into four pieces. Slice each piece in half crosswise, like you would a burger bun.

Prepare the tapenade: Place all the ingredients in a food processor and blend until the mixture is spreadable.

Prepare the Halloumi sandwich: Lightly oil the grill and preheat to medium.

continued on next page

Brush the Halloumi slices with the oil and place on the grill. Grill for 2 minutes, then flip and grill on the other side for 2 minutes.

Alternatively, you can bake the Halloumi: **Preheat the oven to 400°F** and place the Halloumi in a parchment paper–lined baking dish (leave some space in between slices, as the cheese tends to weep a little). Bake for 4 to 5 minutes, until the cheese starts to brown. Halloumi really doesn't melt in the same way that Cheddar or mozzarella does; it turns darker and dries out if cooked too long, so be careful not to overcook.

To serve: Spread the tapenade on the bottom of a slice of focaccia. I only do one side because, with the Halloumi, this can be a very salty sandwich. The tomato and greens will help balance this out. Divide the Halloumi, tomato slices, olives and greens evenly among each focaccia bottom. Top with the focaccia top, serve with potato chips and enjoy.

The Ponaks and Southcotts, Mitch's Catch

Well, by the time you're reading these words, my secret project will be out. Maybe you've even seen it out in the wild, if you're in British Columbia: SoBo's Wild Smoked Salmon Chowder. This is the venture, in the works for many, many years, that led me to Mitch's Catch. While chatting with a friend (I am known to chat quite a bit) about my challenges of finding a fisher who could keep up with the demands we would need to produce the soup, they mentioned this family-run seafood supplier from Vancouver. When I heard the story of how the company came to be, I knew I needed to meet with its crew.

As they tell it, Mitch's Catch started as a cocktail conversation on Hornby Island between two families, the Ponaks and the Southcotts. With their shared desire to connect people to where their food comes from, the group wanted to make it simple and easy for everyday people to get Pacific Northwest seafood directly from their local fishers, with careful sustainability as a top priority.

Hearing the Mitch's Catch crew's passion for supporting local stores, I knew they'd be a perfect partner for SoBo and my chowder endeavors. We share the values of celebrating and protecting the Pacific Northwest's abundance, sparked by collaboration and friendship. That's how we came to work together: the Ponaks, the Southcotts and the Ahiers, and now, SoBo is busy bringing incredible offerings to life using Mitch's Catch mercury-tested albacore tuna (it makes great sashimi) and wild-caught salmon and prawns.

I'm forever grateful for our connection. If you're ever at False Creek Fishermen's Wharf in Vancouver or West Vancouver's Dundarave Village, say hello to them for me. (Oh, and feel free to pick up some SoBo chowder!)

TUNA MELT

When this little classic hits SoBo's specials board, we expect a stampede of locals. While you mustn't feel guilty about buying canned albacore tuna, we have Mitch's Catch from Vancouver to supply us with some of the shiniest, freshest, cleanest, tastiest fish. The albacore tuna is hook-and-line caught, then immediately bled and frozen at sea to maintain its high quality. We tend to trim these loins to their prime center for our raw or lightly seared tuna recipes, giving us an excellent catch of trim, which we turn into these delicious Tuna Melts for zero tuna waste.

SERVES 4

1½ lb tuna loin

2 cups olive oil

1½ Tbsp salt, plus extra for seasoning

1 cup mayonnaise

½ cup Dijon mustard

1 cup finely diced red onion

1 cup finely diced red bell pepper

¼ cup finely diced jalapeño

½ cup finely chopped fresh parsley

½ cup finely chopped fresh mint

8 thick slices of rustic bread, like Sourdough (page 245)

2 cups shredded Cheddar cheese

1 cup radish sprouts or arugula, for garnish

Preheat the oven to 350°F.

Cut the tuna loin into 8 to 10 evenly sized chunks and place them in a medium baking dish. Cover with the olive oil and bake for about 10 minutes, until the loins are no longer pink.

Carefully remove the dish from the oven and allow the tuna to cool, about 20 minutes. Once cooled, transfer the tuna to a medium bowl, leaving the oil behind. Flake the tuna, using your fingers. Stir in 1½ Tbsp salt. The oil can be strained and refrigerated for up to 1 week, to be used the next time you cook tuna, or for frying fish (do not use it more than twice). I tend to use my tuna oil for Caesar salad dressing (my first cookbook has a my recipe).

In a medium bowl, combine the mayonnaise and mustard, then fold in the tuna, onions, bell peppers, jalapeños and herbs. Season with more salt to taste, as desired, but remember: the incoming cheese will add saltiness as well.

Toast the bread.

On a baking sheet lined with parchment paper, place the toasted bread and top with the tuna mixture. Top with the Cheddar and bake for about 10 minutes, until the cheese is golden and bubbly. Garnish with the radish sprouts—or with peppery arugula, if you'd like—and serve.

CRAB SALAD
ON FRENCH BAGUETTE

With crab as the star, this is the Pacific Northwest's take on a lobster roll. Honestly, I enjoy crab more than lobster, but let's be real—to use crab, lobster, shrimp or all three mixed together: we should be so lucky, right?

SERVES 4

French Baguette

1 Tbsp active dry yeast

1 Tbsp honey

1 cup bread flour

1 tsp salt

1 tsp olive oil

Crab Salad

1 lb crabmeat (I use Dungeness)

¼ cup finely diced red onion

¼ cup mayonnaise

1 Tbsp chopped fresh chervil

1 Tbsp chopped fresh chives

2 tsp freshly squeezed lemon juice

1 tsp hot sauce (I like Frank's RedHot or Louisiana)

1 tsp salt

1 cup salad greens

Pickled Kohlrabi (page 263), for serving

Prepare the baguette: In a medium metal bowl, combine the yeast, honey and 1 cup lukewarm water, gently mixing by hand for about 5 minutes. Cover with plastic wrap or a plate and let it sit for 10 minutes.

Add the flour and salt. Gently knead the dough. After a few minutes, it will become sticky and smooth on the surface. Continue kneading until it starts to pull away from the sides of the bowl, about 5 minutes.

Grease a separate medium bowl with the oil. Place the dough ball in this bowl and cover with plastic wrap. Set in a warm place, free of drafts, and let it ferment until it has tripled in volume, about 1 hour.

Punch down the dough. Cover it and let it rise a second time, another hour.

Let the shaping begin. Generously flour your work surface. Use the flat side of a dough scraper to divide the dough in half. Shape the dough by gently pressing it into a rectangle with your hands. Then use your hands like a rolling pin to roll the dough into a long, symmetrical cylinder, rolling it back and forth until it's the size you want for your final loaf.

Preheat the oven to 375°F. Line a baking sheet with parchment paper.

Place the dough on the prepared baking sheet. (Alternatively, use a French bread cradle, if you are lucky enough to have one.) Cover the dough loosely with a clean tea towel. Let it rise again for 30 minutes. Use a very sharp knife to slice a few slits widthwise across the top of the loaf, to allow steam to escape during baking.

Bake the loaf for 20 minutes. Remove from the oven and let it sit for at least 15 minutes.

continued on next page

Prepare the salad: In a medium bowl, gently fold together the crabmeat, onions, mayonnaise, chervil, chives, lemon juice, hot sauce and salt. Keep refrigerated until ready to serve.

To serve: Slice the baguette into four portions. Cut each open horizontally. Line the bottom of the baguette with the greens, then top with the crab salad and baguette top. Enjoy with a side of pickled kohlrabi.

SMOKED TURKEY, BACON, TOMATO AND ARUGULA
ON SOURDOUGH

This might seem like a simple sandwich, but if you're going to the effort of brining and smoking the turkey breast, you might as well also seek out the finest-quality bacon, an ultra-ripe, in-season heirloom tomato and peppery arugula—and make a silky avocado mayo, plus great bread to transform this into a flavorbomb. For me, this sandwich's ultimate partner is Waldorf Salad (page 94).

SERVES 4

½ cup salt

¼ cup molasses

4 black peppercorns

2 bay leaves

1½ lb boneless turkey breast, skin on (about 1 breast)

8 slices premium bacon

1 avocado, sliced

2 Tbsp mayonnaise

8 slices Sourdough Bread (page 245)

1 large heirloom tomato, sliced

1 cup arugula

In a large saucepan over high heat, combine 8 cups water, the salt, molasses, peppercorns and bay leaves and bring to a boil. Whisk the mixture until the salt has completely dissolved, then remove from the heat. Transfer to a large container and let cool to room temperature.

Place the turkey breast in the brine, making sure the brine completely covers the turkey. Cover and refrigerate for 24 hours.

Preheat the oven to 400°F. Line a baking sheet with parchment paper.

Remove the turkey from the brine. Rinse and pat the turkey dry with paper towel, then set aside.

Prepare the smoker according to the manufacturer's instructions (if you don't have a smoker, see the sidebar on page 86 for how to set up a homemade smoker) and smoke the turkey. I usually smoke turkey breasts at about 250°F for 30 to 45 minutes, until the internal temperature is 165°F when tested with an instant-read thermometer.

Remove the turkey from the smoker and let it rest, uncovered, for 30 minutes, then slice to your desired thickness.

While the turkey is resting, place the slices of bacon on the prepared baking sheet and bake for about 4 to 5 minutes. Flip the bacon and cook until crisp. Remove the bacon from the oven and transfer to paper towel to soak up any excess oil.

In a bowl, mash the avocado with the mayonnaise to combine.

continued on next page

To assemble the sandwiches, spread a dollop of avocado mayo onto one side of four slices of sourdough bread, then layer on the turkey, bacon, tomato and arugula. Top each with a slice of sourdough. Serve with Waldorf salad.

STOVETOP SMOKING

I realize most people do not have a smoker, but it's as easy as one-two-three to put together a stovetop device. All you need is a medium heavy-bottomed stockpot with a tight-fitting lid that you don't mind blackening inside (just pick up an inexpensive one from a thrift store), as well as a steaming basket, aluminum foil and smoking chips.

Line the pot with the aluminum foil. Place 1 cup smoking chips on top of the foil. If you can't find any, put regular-sized chips in your food processor and pulse a few times. You want wood shavings more than chips: applewood and alder are two of my favorites. You can usually find smoking and regular-sized chips at grocery or hardware stores.

Cover the chips with a piece of foil to prevent the meat drippings from getting all over them. Place a steamer basket or a small strainer in the pot, then place the turkey breast in it. Do not allow the turkey to touch the foil or chips. Cover the pot tightly with a third piece of foil. Finally, cover the pot with a tight-fitting lid. Turn the heat to medium-high and, when the shavings catch fire, turn the heat to low. The chips will produce smoke. The more smoke there is, the more flavorful the turkey will be. Be sure to turn your exhaust fan to high!

COOK'S NOTE: If you're going to eat bacon, or any meat for that matter, take the time to seek out an ethical and sustainable source, where animals are able to graze or gambol. Our naturally smoked and cured bacon comes from Port Alberni's Hertel Meats. The vegetarian in me likes to believe that the pigs that gave up their lives so that we could have high-quality bacon gamboled with lambs in chemical-free pastures, too.

Salads

Kale, Farro and Grilled Halloumi Salad
WITH LEMON PARSLEY VINAIGRETTE

When kale started to appear on so many menus, I thought, why not really pump up the volume? Which resulted in this extremely satisfying and nutritious entrée-style salad. It's full of chewy texture with a refreshing afterglow. Prepare the farro and lemon parsley vinaigrette in advance, but do not cook the Halloumi until moments before serving; it needs to be really hot when it hits the salad.

SERVES 4

The Salad

½ cup farro, rinsed

½ tsp salt

1 tsp olive oil

One 8-oz block Halloumi, sliced ½ inch thick

1 head black kale, rinsed and torn into bite-sized pieces (see Cook's Note)

1 English cucumber (see Cook's Note), thinly sliced

4 radishes, thinly sliced

Lemon Parsley Vinaigrette

1 shallot, minced

3 cloves garlic, minced

½ cup freshly squeezed lemon juice

2 Tbsp apple cider vinegar

1 tsp salt

1 Tbsp maple syrup

1 Tbsp nutritional yeast

1 cup packed fresh parsley leaves, coarsely chopped

1 cup extra virgin olive oil

Prepare the farro: In a small saucepan over high heat, put 1 cup water, the farro and salt. Bring to a boil, then cover and turn the heat to low. Simmer for 25 minutes. Turn off the heat and allow the farro to stand, covered, for 5 minutes, then strain off any excess water. Let cool to room temperature while making the dressing and preparing the salad.

Prepare the vinaigrette: In a blender, combine the shallots, garlic, lemon juice, vinegar and salt. If you have the time, let this sit for about 20 minutes to macerate. Add the maple syrup and nutritional yeast, then the parsley, and blend on medium speed until the parsley begins to break down. While the blender is on, drizzle in the olive oil. You are aiming for a thin-ish dressing. The vinaigrette can be stored in a mason jar in the fridge for up to 2 weeks.

Cook the Halloumi: Lightly oil the grill with the olive oil and preheat to medium. Gently place the sliced Halloumi directly on the grill. Grill for 2 minutes, then flip and grill on the other side for 4 minutes.

Alternatively, you can bake the Halloumi: Preheat the oven to 400°F and place the Halloumi in a parchment paper–lined baking dish (allow some space in between the slices, as the cheese tends to weep a little milk). Bake for 4 to 5 minutes, until it starts to brown. Halloumi really doesn't melt in the same way that Cheddar or mozzarella does; it turns darker and dries out if cooked too long, so be careful not to overcook.

Prepare the salad: While the Halloumi is cooking, put the kale, cooled farro, cucumbers and radishes in a large bowl. Dress with 1 cup of the lemon parsley vinaigrette and toss. Divide the salad among four bowls, and top with the hot Halloumi.

COOK'S NOTE: If the spine or rib of kale offends you, cut it out. You can now find cucumbers labeled "burpless." Researchers have developed cucumbers with reduced or eliminated cucurbitacin—that bitter stuff that may irritate the digestive system and make you burp. (I wonder if they'll make tearless onions and sourless lemons next? Or maybe they already do and I'm the last one to know!)

WEDGE SALAD
WITH ROQUEFORT DRESSING

Growing up in the '60s, there was very little choice in salad greens. It seemed to begin with iceberg and end with romaine. The crunch of iceberg is an essential component of the wedge salad—I remember going to the Forum Cafeteria chain in Kansas City with my mom and seeing the revolving glass display case filled with hefty wedges of iceberg, chunky blue cheese tumbling over it. Being a "composed salad," the ingredients are built on the plate, rather than tossed. It became my all-time favorite salad growing up. This is my way of paying homage to the much-maligned iceberg.

SERVES 4

Roquefort Dressing

½ cup crumbled Roquefort cheese or blue cheese of choice (see Cook's Note)

1 shallot, minced

½ cup mayonnaise

2 Tbsp white wine vinegar

½ tsp salt

½ tsp fresh cracked black pepper

The Salad

1 head iceberg lettuce, cut in 4 wedges

4 slices crisp bacon, crumbled

½ red onion, thinly sliced

¼ cup crumbled Roquefort cheese or blue cheese of choice

Fresh cracked black pepper (optional)

Prepare the dressing: Combine all the ingredients in a medium bowl, whisking together until the dressing has emulsified. Alternatively, purée in a blender. The dressing can be stored in a jar with a tight-fitting lid in the fridge for up to 2 weeks.

Assemble the salad: On four plates, place one lettuce wedge each. Sprinkle the crumbled bacon and red onions on top. Drizzle ¼ cup of the Roquefort dressing over the center of each salad, and top with the crumbled Roquefort. If you're like me, you'll want a few cranks of black pepper to finish.

COOK'S NOTE: Roquefort is a classic blue-mold cheese made in southern France from sheep milk, but you can easily substitute another blue cheese, like Italy's Gorgonzola or the English Stilton.

Waldorf Salad

Growing up, my family's Thanksgiving dinner menu never changed. Not one thing on it. The Waldorf salad was always our salad course—there's something to be said about tradition. I can't look at a Waldorf salad without it taking me back to sitting around the oak dining room table with my mom, dad and brother. Sometimes my dad's mom, too, but usually just us four. And even if it *was* just us four, my mom took out the crystal glasses, fine bone china and gold-plated cutlery. (Yes, gold-plated cutlery was a thing!) Mom made a point to have enough leftovers for epic turkey sandwiches with a side salad the day after the holiday. I highly recommend pairing this salad with the Smoked Turkey, Bacon, Tomato and Arugula on Sourdough (page 85).

SERVES 4

¼ cup sour cream (see Cook's Note)

¼ cup mayonnaise

2 apples, unpeeled and finely diced

1 rib celery, finely diced

1 cup halved seedless grapes (Concord is perfect for this salad)

¼ cup walnut pieces, toasted (see sidebar page 216)

2 Tbsp freshly squeezed lemon juice

½ tsp salt

4 gem lettuce leaves, for serving (optional)

In a medium bowl, whisk together the sour cream and mayonnaise.

Fold in the apples, celery, grapes, walnuts, lemon juice and salt.

Cover and refrigerate for a few hours. To serve, you can use the gem lettuce leaves as bowls, if desired.

COOK'S NOTE: You can substitute crème fraîche for sour cream, or even make your own. Mix together 1 Tbsp sour cream and 1 cup heavy cream, then let it sit for 12 to 18 hours at room temperature. Or, for another tasty substitute, blend low-fat cottage cheese with a dash of milk and lemon.

SANDY BARBER

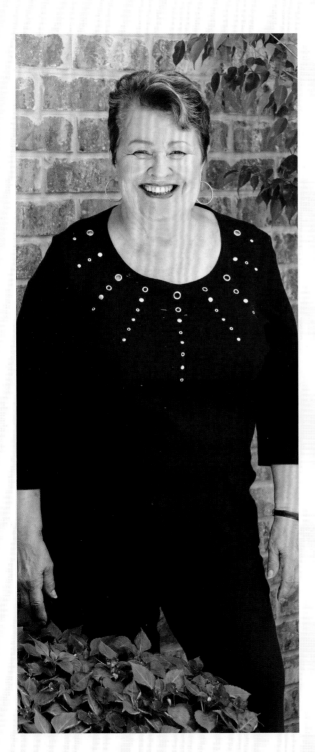

Without Sandy Barber, there would be no SoBo—and not just because she was the only one we trusted to make our signature tofu pockets in those early days. It's because she is my mother. She's the only person I could ask to do absolutely anything, from chopping vegetables to washing dishes to putting a baby to bed. People need their mothers at the best of times, but when you're simultaneously starting a new business and a family, having a mom like mine makes all the difference.

At the beginning, SoBo was very much a family affair. I was in the kitchen and my mom was right there —watching my kids, making our meals at home and working the register. Mom charmed everyone with her Texas accent and, more often than not, customers would come for a bowl of chowder and leave also loaded up with a slice of cornbread and a cookie.

Mom lorded over those tofu pockets. "Nobody did the rice like Grandma," she likes to say. That's still true —Grandma's tofu pockets are the best. I didn't much like to make them once I figured out the recipe because they're so finicky, so Mom took over and, before long, you'd hear her shouting, "Don't touch my pockets, don't touch my stuff!" We toned down her use of wasabi—she's a Texan, she likes things hot—and we let her get to it.

Mom was the reason I ever started working in restaurants. When I was growing up, she managed restaurants and even sang in nightclubs. I tagged along occasionally throughout the years, and I was 17 years old when I was thrown into cooking. That Christmas Day, the chef at Mom's restaurant quit, so she called me in and we ran the entire place, front and back. We made bread and crepes, we cooked and served the food, poured the beer, and even did the laundry. Clearly, Mom was never one to walk away from a challenge.

We've both had a lot thrown at us, but my mother is the circle, the life that keeps things going.

GREEN GODDESS SALAD

Here I go on a trip down memory lane again. My love of salads began at a very early age. I just loved to eat whole cucumbers and snatch everyone's parsley-sprig garnish off their plates. In those days, bottled dressings were all the rage: while my brother always grabbed the Catalina, I went for creamy green goddess. I feel like green goddess was the original ranch dressing, but I'm not here to start that fight . . . (I will just say: It's way better! Sorry, Texas, I know how attached you are to your ranch!) Most green goddess salads only have green vegetables, but I love tomatoes, carrots, beets and radishes in mine. Do whatever suits your mood.

SERVES 4

Green Goddess Dressing

¼ cup coarsely chopped parsley leaves

¼ cup thinly sliced fresh chives

¼ cup coarsely chopped fresh tarragon leaves

¼ cup freshly squeezed lemon juice

¼ cup white wine vinegar

1 cup mayonnaise or plain Greek yogurt

1 avocado, peeled and pitted

½ tsp salt

½ tsp fresh cracked black pepper

1 anchovy, chopped (if you like them)

The Salad

4 cups mixed lettuces

2 cups spinach

1 cup arugula

1 small red beet, peeled and julienned

1 carrot, peeled and julienned

1 tomato, sliced

1 radish, thinly sliced

½ red bell pepper, julienned

½ cucumber, thinly sliced

½ cup croutons or toasted seeds (see sidebar page 216), for garnish

Violas and kale tops (optional, for garnish)

Prepare the dressing: In a blender, place all the ingredients. Pulse a few times, then blend on low until smooth and creamy. This recipe will make more than you need for one sitting, but hey, it never hurts to have extra dressing on hand in case the mood strikes. Store in a container with a tight-fitting lid in the fridge for up to 2 weeks.

Prepare the salad: In a large bowl, toss together all the ingredients. Dress with the green goddess dressing and garnish with croutons or roasted seeds and edible flowers, if desired.

COOK'S NOTE: Don't salt your poaching water. That would create poached eggs with wispy sides. Use small eggs for poaching because they have thicker whites and are less likely to split apart than larger eggs. Poaching the perfect egg comes with experience. Be mindful not to add all the eggs to the pot at once—that would cause the water to cool down, and make it harder to keep the eggs separate.

CURRIED WHEAT BERRY AND LENTIL SALAD
WITH POACHED EGGS AND TURMERIC CAULIFLOWER

This is a mega-nutrient-rich bowl. Pulses and grains are an excellent source of protein and fiber, so I often make this as a brunch when I need extra fuel to get me through my day. Everything for the base salad can be made a day or two in advance. The addition of a poached egg means more protein, more energy, but lose the egg and it's a vegan-friendly meal! Vegans looking for some get-up-and-go can always toss in a bit of smoked tofu.

SERVES 4

The Salad

1 cup dried French or beluga lentils, rinsed (see Cook's Note on page 146)

3 tsp salt, divided

1 cup wheat berries

3 Tbsp olive oil, divided

3 Tbsp Madras curry powder (or blend turmeric, cumin, cloves, mustard seeds, chilies and nutmeg)

1 Tbsp ground cumin

1 Tbsp ground coriander

1 Tbsp ground turmeric

2 cloves garlic, minced

1 shallot, minced

1 cup coconut cream

½ head cauliflower, cut in bite-sized pieces

1 small carrot, grated

1 bunch rapini, cut in bite-sized pieces

Poached Eggs

4 small eggs

Prepare the salad: In a medium saucepan, bring the lentils and 4 cups cold water to a boil, then cover and turn the heat to low. Simmer for 15 minutes. Drain the lentils and season with 1 tsp of the salt. Set aside.

In a medium saucepan, bring the wheat berries and 4 cups cold water to a boil, then cover and turn the heat to low. Simmer for 30 to 45 minutes. Cooking time varies according to the freshness of the wheat berries. You want your wheat berries to be chewy but not tough. Drain the wheat berries and season with 1 tsp salt and 1 Tbsp of the olive oil. Set aside.

Heat the remaining 2 Tbsp olive oil in a heavy-bottomed frying pan over medium-high heat. Add the curry powder, cumin, coriander, turmeric, garlic and shallots and sauté, stirring frequently with a wooden spoon to avoid burning. Add the coconut cream, cauliflower, carrots and rapini. Turn the heat to low and bring the vegetable mixture to a simmer. Cook for 5 minutes.

Poach the eggs: Fill a heavy-bottomed poaching pot or a tall frying pan with cold water and bring it to a steady simmer over medium-high heat (so there is movement but the water is not aggressively boiling). (See Cook's Note.)

Crack 1 egg into a small bowl or ramekin, then slide it into the water. (This makes it easier to gently slide the egg into the water.) Repeat with the remaining eggs. Cover and poach the eggs for 2 to 3 minutes for a semisoft yolk; for a firmer-set yolk, cook the eggs for 3 to 4 minutes.

Using a slotted spoon, carefully transfer the eggs to a pie plate or shallow brimmed dish. If necessary, you can reheat with a quick dunk back in simmering poaching water for 30 seconds, using a slotted spoon. Season with the remaining 1 tsp salt.

To serve: Gently reheat the grains and vegetables in a saucepan on the stovetop. Divide among four plates and top each portion with a poached egg.

SEAWEED, SEA ASPARAGUS AND BRASSICA SHOOTS SALAD

This salad is a tribute to the beginning of spring here on the West Coast, celebrating the early tender growth of kale, broccolini and cabbage. Even the shoots of the cabbage family, called brassica shoots, are becoming more and more popular. Their natural bitterness pairs well with the saltiness and sweetness of sea vegetables in this salad. If the short season of brassica shoots shoots by (no pun intended), then either roasted broccoli or cabbage is a fine substitute. A bonus from this recipe: dried seaweed is a wonderfully nutritious staple to keep in your pantry.

SERVES 4

The Dressing
¼ cup peanut oil

2 Tbsp freshly squeezed lemon juice

2 Tbsp rice vinegar (I prefer the Japanese variety)

2 Tbsp tamari sauce

1 Tbsp agave syrup

2 Tbsp minced shallot

1 Tbsp finely chopped ginger

1 tsp minced garlic

Seaweed Salad
1 cup quinoa, rinsed well in a fine-mesh strainer (see Cook's Note on page 146)

1 Tbsp plus 1 tsp salt, divided

1 piece fresh or dried seaweed (see Cook's Note), thinly sliced

1 lb brassica shoots, trimmed and halved widthwise

1 lb broccolini, trimmed and halved widthwise

2 Tbsp olive oil

¼ lb fresh sea asparagus, rinsed and trimmed

4 Tbsp plain yogurt

Prepare the dressing: Combine all the ingredients in a jar and mix with a whisk or seal and shake well.

Prepare the salad: In a small saucepan, bring 2 cups water to a boil. Add the quinoa and 1 tsp of the salt and cook, uncovered, on a gentle simmer for about 10 minutes. Remove the pot from the heat, cover, and let the quinoa steam for 5 minutes. This gives the quinoa time to pop open into little curlicues, so it's nice and fluffy. Remove the lid and use a fork to fluff the quinoa.

Transfer the quinoa to a fine-mesh strainer and rinse with cold water while draining. Set aside and let cool to room temperature while preparing the rest of the salad.

In a medium saucepan, bring 4 cups water seasoned with the remaining 1 Tbsp salt to a vigorous boil.

Add the seaweed to the boiling water and blanch for 3 to 4 minutes. (If using dried seaweed, rehydrate according to the package instructions.) Scoop out the seaweed using a slotted spoon and immediately plunge into an ice bath to chill it quickly and so it retains its vibrant green color. If the seaweed has a center rib, use kitchen scissors or a paring knife to remove.

Turn the oven to 400°F.

In a large bowl, toss the brassica shoots and broccolini in the olive oil, then transfer to a baking sheet and roast for about 10 minutes, until the florets start to crisp. Remove from the oven and set aside.

continued on next page

Garnish

8 fresh kale flowers

2 radishes, thinly sliced

½ cup toasted almonds (see sidebar page 216)

In the same bowl used for the broccolini, toss together the blanched seaweed and sea asparagus. Add the dressing and toss again to coat.

Assemble the salads: Spread 1 Tbsp yogurt across each of four plates. Divide the quinoa, dressed vegetables, brassica shoots and broccolini evenly among the plates. Garnish with the kale flowers, radishes and toasted almonds.

COOK'S NOTE: For this recipe, I have used Egregia (feather boa kelp) before, but Naas Foods in Tofino is an excellent source that ships a variety of fresh and dehydrated seaweeds.

VINAIGRETTE VS DRESSING

Comparing vinaigrette to dressing is like comparing fettucine to pasta. Vinaigrette is a *type* of salad dressing.

Vinaigrettes have one identifying component that sets them apart from other, often creamier, dressings: they are a mixture of oil and something acidic. The oil is often olive oil; I like extra virgin in most of my dressings, but will occasionally use grapeseed, sunflower, peanut, avocado, flaxseed or pumpkin seed oil. Be creative and explore the different nuances of these products. The acidic ingredient is usually a citrus juice (often lemon or lime) or a vinegar (hence the name), like a deep sherry, red or balsamic vinegar, or a rice vinegar for Asian-influenced salads, or for something more subtle, a lighter vinegar like champagne, white wine, or apple cider.

The traditional, simple form of the recipe suggests three parts oil to one part vinegar, plus some salt and pepper to taste. The new standard is equal parts oil and vinegar—but it's entirely up to you. No rules, only effects! Just put everything in a lidded jar and shake vigorously.

Salad dressing, meanwhile, is a more general, all-encompassing term. It's a sauce—usually cold—used to coat or top salads and some cold vegetable, fish or meat dishes. It can be a base of mayonnaise, buttermilk, oil and vinegar, avocado or yogurt.

To make a dressing, you can use a traditional blender, an immersion blender or simply a bowl and whisk. I always make a full batch and refrigerate the leftovers for future quick, easy salads.

Warm Asparagus, Farro and King Oyster Mushroom Salad
WITH POACHED EGGS

This is such a satisfying spring/early summer salad. Asparagus season is much anticipated in our neck of the woods, since asparagus is the first green vegetable to pop out of the ground after being dormant all winter. Its timing is perfect, showing up right when we are getting bored with our winter root-vegetable selection. (I apologize for my human-centric perspective. There are no boring vegetables, only bored humans with their endless quest for variety, for something green after a long winter hibernating, like the asparagus plant itself, underground. Well, in our case, indoors.) With the addition of a sturdy grain, meaty mushrooms and a protein blast from the egg, this makes for a terrific light dinner.

Salad

4 Tbsp olive oil, divided

1 cup farro

2 cups Vegetable Stock (page 252) or water

2 bay leaves

2½ tsp salt, divided

1 Tbsp butter

1 lb king oyster mushrooms, cleaned and sliced (see sidebar page 184)

¼ cup dry white wine

1 lb asparagus spears, cut in 1-inch pieces

4 Poached Eggs (page 99)

Basic Vinaigrette

2 Tbsp white wine vinegar

Juice of 1 lemon

2 cloves garlic, minced

2 Tbsp minced shallots (see Cook's Note)

1 Tbsp Dijon mustard

¼ cup extra virgin olive oil

Garnish

2 radishes, thinly sliced

¼ cup sliced almonds, toasted (see sidebar page 216)

Prepare the salad: Heat 2 Tbsp of the oil in a heavy-bottomed saucepan over medium heat. Add the farro and toast until it's golden and you start to smell its nutty aroma. Add the stock, bay leaves and 1 tsp salt to the saucepan. Stir with a wooden spoon, then bring to a gentle boil. Turn the heat to low, cover and simmer for 25 minutes.

Remove from the heat and let stand, still covered, for 5 minutes. If there is any liquid left in the pan, drain it off. Set the farro aside and let cool to room temperature. Remove and discard the bay leaves.

In a large heavy-bottomed frying pan over medium-high heat, combine the remaining 2 Tbsp olive oil and the butter. As soon as the mixture starts to smoke, add the mushrooms in a single layer. Cook on one side for about 3 minutes, until golden brown. Flip the mushrooms and cook for another 3 minutes on the other side. I like a crispy, firm king mushroom, not a sweaty, limp version.

Remove from the heat. Use a slotted spoon to transfer the mushrooms to a side plate. Season with 1 tsp salt. In the same pan, add the wine and reduce for 1 minute. Turn the heat to medium, add the asparagus and for about 2 minutes, until slightly tender, but not limp (I like a little crunch to my asparagus). Remove the asparagus and set aside. Season with ½ tsp salt.

Prepare the dressing: In the same pan, place the vinegar and lemon juice, followed by the garlic and shallots. Turn the heat to low and cook until the shallots start to sweat. Whisk in the mustard, then slowly whisk in the olive oil. The vinaigrette can be stored in a mason jar in the fridge for up to 2 weeks.

Assemble the salad: Return the farro, asparagus and mushrooms to the pan, gently toss with the dressing and reheat over medium heat.

Divide the salad mixture among four plates. Garnish with the radishes and almonds. Finish by topping each portion with a poached egg.

COOK'S NOTE: If you don't have shallots on hand, substitute equal parts garlic and red onion.

PANZANELLA WITH FRESH MOZZARELLA

For this salad to really be at its best, you must have all four components just right. The toasted bread should have just a little softness left in the center. The croutons should rest in the vinaigrette just long enough to absorb the flavors, but not so long that they get soggy. Of course, the tomatoes have to be perfectly ripe and in season, so they taste like the sun, and the mozzarella has to be hot when it hits the salad. That's what makes this salad especially, well, special—the hot mozzarella.

SERVES 4

Tomato Vinaigrette

1 tsp olive oil

1 plum tomato

1 small shallot, halved

1 Tbsp garlic

¼ cup sherry vinegar

1 Tbsp aged balsamic vinegar (splurge on a good one)

½ tsp salt

½ cup extra virgin olive oil

Panzanella

1 cup big chunks Sourdough Bread (¼ loaf, page 245)

1 Tbsp olive oil

12 cherry tomatoes halved or quartered and divided

10–12 fresh basil leaves, torn, divided

2 large heirloom tomatoes, sliced

2 balls fresh mozzarella cheese (about ½ lb), thinly sliced

Fresh cracked black pepper (optional)

Prepare the vinaigrette: Preheat the oven to 425°F.

In a small ovenproof baking dish, drizzle the olive oil over the tomato. Roast for 5 to 7 minutes, until the tomato starts to blacken. Add the shallots and garlic to the baking dish and bake for 3 to 4 minutes. Remove from the oven and let cool to room temperature, then skin the tomato. Turn the oven to 350°F.

In a blender, blend the tomato, shallots, garlic, vinegars and salt to combine. With the blender on low speed, drizzle in the olive oil and blend until emulsified. The vinaigrette can be stored in a mason jar in the fridge for up to 2 weeks.

Prepare the panzanella: Preheat the grill to high.

In a medium bowl, toss the chunks of bread with the olive oil to coat.

Place the bread directly on the grill and toast until lightly charred in spots, about 1 minute per side (turn before the chunks have a chance to catch on fire!). Let the bread cool slightly, then tear into bite-sized pieces and set aside.

Alternatively, you can bake the bread: Tear the sourdough chunks into bite-sized pieces, then toss with olive oil to coat. Transfer the bread to a baking sheet and toast for 3 to 4 minutes in the 350°F oven.

In a small bowl, toss the sourdough croutons with half of the vinaigrette. Let sit for about 10 minutes. Gently stir 8 cherry tomatoes and half of the basil in with the croutons.

continued on next page

Assemble the salad: On four plates, arrange the heirloom tomato slices in whatever fashion you'd like. Drizzle the remaining vinaigrette on top. Top with the crouton mixture.

Line a pie pan with parchment paper. Place the mozzarella slices on the lined pan, allowing several inches of space between each slice. Bake for 3 to 5 minutes in the 350°F oven, until the mozzarella is half melted.

Drape the warm, semi-melted mozzarella over the tomatoes. Artfully assemble the remaining basil leaves and cherry tomatoes on top. Finish with a few cracks of black pepper, if desired.

COOK'S NOTE: Using a grill for the bread of this panzanella (bread salad) adds a slight smokiness and a satisfying crunch. But if you are bereft of a grill, you can make do by toasting the bread in an oven.

ROASTED BRUSSELS SPROUTS AND SUNCHOKES
WITH PARMESAN DRESSING

Sunchokes, also known as Jerusalem artichokes, have one of my very favorite flavors—like a nutty potato, with just the right contrast of sweet and earthy—but they're not for everybody. They're rich in inulin, a form of starch that our bodies don't easily digest, so eating a lot at once can get a little "beans, beans, the magical fruit." But that's easy to solve! Boiling them in an acid like lemon juice hydrolyzes the inulin to fructose and small amounts of glucose, removing the gas. So, no more excuses!

SERVES 4

The Garnish

1 sunchoke, scrubbed with an unused toothbrush or vegetable brush

2 cups peanut oil

Salt

Parmesan Dressing

¼ cup balsamic vinegar

Juice of 1 lemon

4 Tbsp Roasted Garlic, puréed (page 259)

4 Tbsp finely grated Parmesan cheese

2 Tbsp minced shallot

1 tsp fresh cracked black pepper

¼ cup olive oil

The Base

1 lb Brussels sprouts, cut lengthwise

½ red onion, sliced

¼ cup olive oil, divided

1 lb sunchokes, scrubbed well, cut to the size of the Brussels sprouts

½ tsp salt

¼ cup grated or shaved Parmesan cheese

Prepare the garnish: Cut the sunchoke into thin slices, like potato chips.

Heat the peanut oil in a heavy-bottomed, medium pot over medium-low heat to 300°F—test it with a deep-fry thermometer or by gently placing a piece of sunchoke in it. The sunchoke should float to the top and start to curl; if it sinks to the bottom, wait for the oil to get a bit hotter; if it browns instantly, the oil is too hot and you will need to turn down the heat.

Using a slotted spoon, add the sunchoke slices to the hot oil, being careful not to overcrowd the pot. Use a slotted spoon to gently move the chips around; when the chips start to turn a deep golden brown, use the spoon to transfer them to paper towel to soak up any excess oil. While the chips are still hot, sprinkle them with salt. They will not be super crisp straight out of the fryer but will crisp up in about 10 minutes.

Alternatively, if you suffer from fear of frying, you can bake the sunchokes: Preheat the oven to 300°F. Place the sunchoke slices on a parchment paper–lined baking sheet. Bake for about 20 minutes, flipping the chips halfway through.

Prepare the dressing: In a bowl or a blender, combine all the ingredients except the olive oil. Mix well with a whisk or purée. While whisking or with the blender on low speed, slowly drizzle in the oil.

Prepare the base: Preheat the oven to 400°F.

In a medium bowl, toss the Brussels sprouts and red onions in half of the olive oil, coating evenly. Spread in an even layer on a baking sheet lined with parchment paper.

continued on next page

In the same bowl, combine the sunchokes with the remaining olive oil and mix to coat evenly. On a second parchment paper–lined baking sheet, spread the sunchokes in an even layer.

Put both sheets in the oven and roast the veggies for about 20 minutes. The sunchokes should be tender all the way to the center, and the Brussels sprouts should be deeply caramelized. If either needs to cook longer, continue to roast for 5 minutes at a time. Season with the salt.

To serve: Toss the warm roasted Brussels sprouts, onions and roasted sunchokes with the dressing, then top with the Parmesan and sunchoke chips.

COOK'S NOTE: Why the misnomer? Jerusalem artichokes do not come from Jerusalem, nor are they artichokes. They're a species of sunflower grown for their underground tuber, which is the root vegetable we eat. The plant was originally called *girasol* and *girasole* (the Spanish and Italian words, respectively, for sunflower) because of its resemblance to the flower, and "artichoke" was added because of the similar taste. "Jerusalem artichoke" could possibly have been an English corruption of the Italian *girasole articiocco*. In the 1960s a specialty produce marketer, Frieda Caplan, decided that Jerusalem artichokes needed a sexier name. She came up with "sunchokes". (Why does she get to be boss of the world?)

COOK'S NOTE: For an added treat, you could remove the scallop's small side muscle, top it with a little salt and olive oil and down the hatch it goes! Like a crudo. If you're keen on exceptionally fluffy quinoa, you could steam it after boiling. Place the sieve full of your rinsed quinoa over a few cups of boiling water and steam for 7 to 10 minutes. Some final tips: the quinoa should not be touching water, and don't let the water run dry.

Seared Scallop and Quinoa Salad

While it's considered an "ancient grain," quinoa has lately become a staple in home kitchens —including mine. When I'm in the mood for something lighter, but still want to give myself or my guests a treat, this is a frequent go-to. It's extremely refreshing and healthy with its high vitamin and mineral content, while still feeling luxurious. The quinoa salad is meant to be served cold or at room temperature, while the scallops should be seared at the very last minute and served hot. I quite like the contrast of hot proteins on cold salads. It is a recurring theme in my kitchen.

SERVES 4

Quinoa Salad

3 beets

¼ cup plus 2 Tbsp olive oil, divided

2 Tbsp salt, divided

Fresh cracked black pepper

2 cups quinoa, rinsed well in a fine-mesh strainer (see Cook's Note on page 146)

1 red bell pepper, finely diced

1 bunch green onions, sliced

2 cups orange segments

½ cup freshly squeezed orange juice

¼ cup fresh mint leaves, torn in half

2 cups mixed lettuces

Scallops

½ cup olive oil

8 large scallops (see Cook's Note)

2 tsp salt

Prepare the salad: Preheat the oven to 375°F.

Place the beets on a large piece of aluminum foil (enough to envelop them). Sprinkle with 2 Tbsp of the olive oil, 1 tsp of the salt and pepper, then wrap the beets in foil and seal. Roast for 1 hour. Remove from the oven and open the foil to let cool. Once cool enough to handle, rub the skins off using your hands or a paper towel and finely dice.

While the beets are roasting, bring 5 quarts water to a boil in a large stockpot. Add 1 Tbsp of the salt and boil on high for 11 minutes (see Cook's Note). Drain in a fine-mesh sieve, rinsing with cold water. Set aside and allow to cool while preparing the salad.

In a large bowl, gently toss the beets and quinoa with the remaining ingredients (including the remaining olive oil and salt) until everything is evenly coated. Divide among four plates.

Prepare the scallops: Heat the olive oil in a frying pan over medium-high heat.

Season the scallops with the salt, then place flat side down in the frying pan, careful not to overcrowd the pan. Sear for 2 to 3 minutes on one side, until they release easily from the pan (keep watch—scallops cook quickly), then flip and sear the other side for 30 to 60 seconds. The scallops should be caramel brown on the outside, and tender, juicy and translucent on the inside. It's really important to not overcook them!

To serve, immediately divide two hot scallops per plate of salad and enjoy.

Pizza

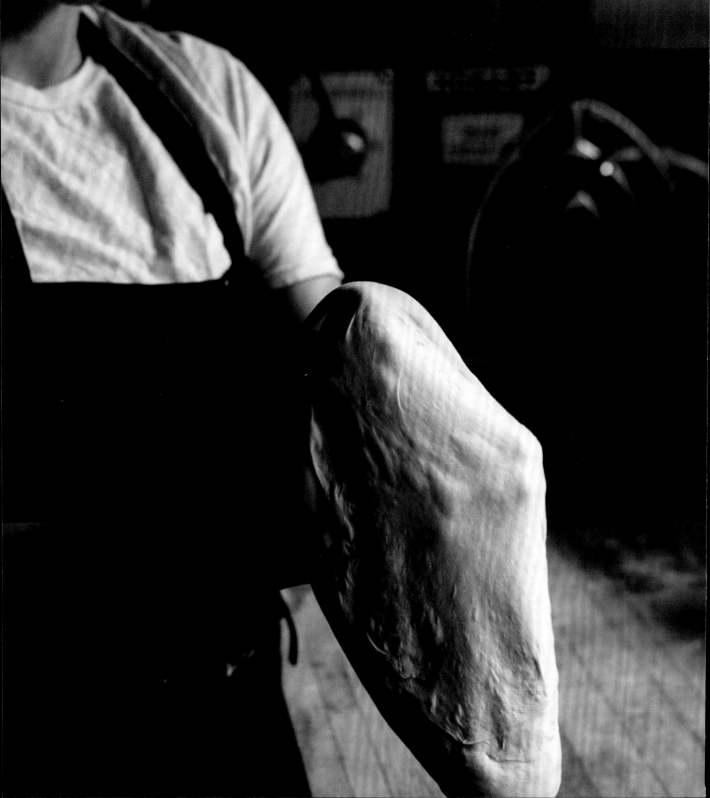

Pizza Dough, Tofino Style

At SoBo, our own Marco Procopio takes an almost spiritual approach to pizza, using an overnight fermentation process. He was born and raised in southern Italy's Calabria region, where he inherited his love of food—particularly pizza, which he then traveled the world for, spending hours, days and years in search of the perfect recipe. Here in Tofino, he surfs and works and says, "When I know there is a pizza dough fermenting in my house, everything is better—I surf better, I walk happier. The round shape of a pizza symbolizes unity. It brings everyone together in harmony." He could write a book about his technique, if he ever decides to hang up his surfboard.

MAKES FOUR
10-INCH PIZZAS

2 cups lukewarm water (about 110°F, from the tap), plus extra as needed

½ tsp active dry yeast

¼ cup dark beer (I like Hoyne Brewing Co.'s Dark Matter)

3 Tbsp olive oil

3¾ cups 00 flour (see Cook's Note)

3¾ cups all-purpose flour, plus extra as needed

1½ Tbsp salt

First mix: In a stand mixer fitted with the dough hook attachment, combine the water, yeast, beer, oil and 00 flour and mix for 5 minutes on low speed or until well incorporated. If you don't have a stand mixer with a dough hook, you can mix the ingredients in a large bowl by hand: Use one hand to mix the dough until it forms a ball and all the dough has pulled away from the sides of the bowl. Transfer to a clean, dry work surface (marble or granite is fabulous) and knead, using the heels of your palm, for about 5 minutes, then stretch and flip. Repeat, until the dough can't be stretched any more. Cover and let rest for 10 minutes. (Never let your dough get a crust from the air.)

Second mix: Return the dough to the stand mixer or bowl and add the all-purpose flour and salt. Mix for 5 minutes on medium speed. If mixing by hand, it will take about 7 minutes. The dough should form a cohesive ball and pull away cleanly from the sides of the bowl. If it is too wet and sticking to the bowl, add more flour, 1 tsp at a time. If it is too dry and not all the flour is incorporated, add more lukewarm water, 1 tsp at a time, until you have a smooth, shiny dough.

Cover the bowl with plastic wrap or a plate and let rest for 20 minutes.

Divide the dough into four pieces. One at a time, cup each piece of dough in your hand and roll it around in a circle on a clean, dry work surface until you've formed a smooth, round ball. Place the dough balls in a large container, spaced about 4 inches apart, to allow them room to expand.

Seal the container tightly with its lid or plastic wrap and let the dough rest at room temperature for 1 hour. Then place in the fridge for at least 24 hours, and up to 72 hours. One hour before shaping and assembling the pizzas, remove the dough from the fridge and let it come to room temperature.

continued on next page

Form the dough: Flour your hands and transfer one ball of dough to a lightly floured work surface. Sprinkle more flour onto the dough and your hands to prevent sticking.

Starting at one side of the ball, press down with your fingertips and gently stretch it with a circular motion until it expands into a disk about 6 to 8 inches in diameter. Continue massaging the dough, shaping it with your palms and fingers until the disk is about 10 inches across. Don't worry about making a perfect circle, or making a doughy rim (aka the cornicione); this will naturally form when baking. Just go for a completely flat disk. Whatever you do, don't overhandle the dough: be gentle with the blisters and bubbles that air will create in the crust; they will add texture and character to your final creation. Remember: no rolling pin!

Flop the dough onto a lightly floured, perforated 14-inch pizza pan (or a regular pizza pan or an inverted baking sheet, if that's what you have) and gently pull the edges outward, leaving some space so as not to cover the pan completely. I do this so that when transferring to and from the oven, the outer crust remains undisturbed

Assemble and bake: Follow each recipe's method for assembly and baking instructions, topping your dough immediately with your desired toppings. Timing is critical here! Waiting too long before topping your stretched dough can result in dry dough.

COOK'S NOTE: In Italy, flour is classified either as 1, 0 or 00, referring to how finely ground the flour is, and how much of the bran and germ have been removed. For instance, 00 flour is the most refined, similar to unbleached all-purpose/plain flour, which is a mix of hard and soft wheat, though somewhat finer. Invest in a bag of Tipo 00 flour (aka *doppio zero*, meaning "double zero" in Italian) and fall in love (a light crust that's crisp on the outside but tender to the bite? That's *amore*). Or try the grand don, the Godflour: the Caputo 00 made from a selection of the finest grains sourced by the Naples-based Caputo family—and have been for three generations.

Pizza Sauces

I always make more sauce than I need for the pizzas, storing it in the fridge for up to 1 week, or in the freezer for up to 6 months. If I have some sauce stored away, I can bring it out for sandwich spreads, pasta dishes or soup garnishes, or even to add to scrambled eggs.

Red Sauce

MAKES 4 CUPS

One 28-oz can San Marzano tomatoes or whole plum tomatoes

1 Tbsp salt

¼ cup olive oil

2 Tbsp red wine vinegar

¼ cup Roasted Garlic, puréed (page 259)

1 cup fresh basil leaves

¼ cup fresh oregano leaves

In a food processor or a blender, purée all the ingredients to your desired smoothness (I like mine smooth enough to spread really well).

Pumpkin Seed Pesto

MAKES 4 CUPS

½ cup toasted pumpkin seeds (see sidebar page 216)

¼ cup minced garlic

1 cup fresh basil leaves

1 cup spinach leaves

½ cup arugula or watercress

¼ cup freshly squeezed lemon juice

1 tsp crushed red chili flakes

1 tsp salt

½ cup olive oil, plus extra as needed

¼ cup grated hard aged cheese, like Parmesan, pecorino, Asiago or Romano

In a food processor or blender, combine the toasted seeds, garlic, basil, spinach, arugula, lemon juice, chili flakes and salt.

Pulse until the herbs are finely chopped, then, with the food processor running, drizzle in the olive oil and blend to your desired texture (I like it smooth and creamy. If you want a thinner sauce, add a bit more olive oil). Transfer to a bowl and fold in the cheese.

White Garlicky Sauce

MAKES 3 CUPS

2 cups ricotta cheese

½ cup Roasted Garlic, puréed (page 259)

Juice of 1 lemon

2 Tbsp olive oil

1 Tbsp minced garlic

1 tsp crushed red chili flakes

1 tsp salt

1 cup packed spinach, black kale or fresh parsley or a combination (optional, for a Green variation)

In a food processor or blender, blend all the ingredients (including the spinach for a Green variation) until smooth.

Acorn Squash Sauce

MAKES 6 CUPS

1 small acorn squash (about 2 lb)

3 Tbsp olive oil, divided

1 Roasted Chili, coarsely chopped (page 260)

1 head Roasted Garlic (page 259)

1 cup ricotta cheese

Juice of 1 lemon

1 tsp crushed red chili flakes

1 tsp salt

Preheat the oven to 375°F. Line a baking sheet with parchment paper.

Cut the squash in half and scoop out the seeds. Rub 1 Tbsp of the olive oil on the squash's flesh and prick all over the outer skin with a fork or paring knife. Place the squash cut side down on the prepared baking sheet and bake for 40 minutes or until the flesh is tender and easy to scoop out of its skin. Set aside to cool, then scoop out the insides.

In a food processor, combine three-quarters of the squash with the chili, roasted garlic, ricotta, lemon juice, chili flakes, salt and remaining 2 Tbsp olive oil and blend until smooth.

Dice the remaining quarter of squash, and set aside to garnish the pizza.

COOK'S NOTE: When you're assembling your pizzas, do not overload the crust with the saucy stuff. Make your first pizza with the recipe's smallest suggested amount of sauce, then work your way up if you're finding it's just not enough. Your mantra is *Think scant, think scant*. It will result in a better pie.

CLASSIC MARGHERITA PIZZA

When Raffaele Esposito created the first Margherita pizza for the Queen of Italy in 1889, the pizzaiolo (the awesome title for a pizza maker) used tangy tomato sauce, stretchy mozzarella and peppery basil to showcase the colors of the national flag. Back then, the toppings were kept sparse to make the economical dish last for a few meals. The toppings we use today are still simple and minimal, although if you wish to elevate the complexity to an utterly divine flavor, you are permitted—Queen's orders—a light grating of Parmesan cheese. I even sprinkle a little coarse salt on my pizza at the end.

MAKES FOUR
10-INCH PIZZAS

Pizza Dough, Tofino Style (page 119)

1–2 cups Red Sauce (page 122, see Cook's Note on page 123)

4 cups sliced or torn bocconcini (see Cook's Note)

½ cup grated Parmesan cheese

12–16 fresh basil leaves

Preheat the oven to 450°F.

Form the dough for one pizza at a time on its floured pan, following the method on page 120.

Once you have shaped one piece of dough, immediately spoon ¼ cup red sauce on top. Use a spatula or the back of the spoon to spread it out evenly. Sprinkle with 1 cup bocconcini pieces and 2 Tbsp Parmesan.

Repeat the shaping and topping process with the remaining balls of dough.

Bake for 10 to 12 minutes, until the crust is golden brown and the cheese is bubbly.

Remove from the oven and top with basil (this is done after baking so that the basil stays green).

COOK'S NOTE: Margherita pizza is defined by its fresh bocconcini (small balls of mozzarella), which has more moisture than the loaf-style of mozzarella we might usually shred.

ROASTED ACORN SQUASH AND KALE PIZZA

What really elevates this pizza to the next level are the kale chips on top—that sweet and spicy base coalescing with the crunchy, savory chips . . . I need to go make one right now. The kale chips can be prepared a day ahead of assembling the pizza, and they make a fantastic snack on their own.

**MAKES FOUR
10-INCH PIZZAS**

8–16 pieces black kale (see Cook's Note), center rib removed

4 Tbsp olive oil

½ tsp salt

1 Tbsp nutritional yeast

Pizza Dough, Tofino Style (page 119)

3–4 cups Acorn Squash Sauce, including diced squash, for garnish (page 123)

4 cups shredded mozzarella cheese

Preheat the oven to 300°F. Place a wire rack on a baking sheet.

In a medium bowl, coat the kale with the olive oil and gently massage. Spread the kale on the rack. Do not overlap the pieces or they will not crisp up.

Bake for 10 minutes, then flip each piece of kale over and bake for another 10 minutes. Remove from the oven and season with salt and nutritional yeast. Let cool to room temperature. The kale chips can be made up to 24 hours before assembling the pizza: store in a tightly sealed container at room temperature.

Turn the oven to 450°F.

Form the dough for one pizza at a time on its floured pan, following the method on page 120.

Once you have shaped one piece of dough, immediately spoon ¾ cup squash sauce on top. Use a spatula or the back of the spoon to spread it out evenly. Sprinkle with 1 cup shredded mozzarella.

Repeat the shaping and topping process with the remaining balls of dough.

Bake for 8 to 12 minutes, until the crust is golden brown and the cheese is bubbly.

Remove from the oven and top with kale chips and the diced squash.

COOK'S NOTE: Black kale (also known as Lacinato or dinosaur kale) works best for chips, as they have less grooves, allowing them to lie flat and cook more evenly. But curly kale will work in a pinch. A tip: Kale chips are a standout side to grilled cheese, or even crushed up to give an extra kick to popcorn.

Mushroom, Caramelized Onion and Goat Cheese Pizza

One of the great perks of living in British Columbia's rainforest is the abundance of wild forest mushrooms. Chanterelles, pine, chicken of the woods, porcini . . . I encourage you to experiment with the different varieties and find what best suits you. The key to this pizza is the earthiness of the mushrooms and the sweetness of the caramelized onions. And the acidic nature of the goat cheese really perks it up.

**MAKES FOUR
10-INCH PIZZAS**

2 Tbsp butter

¼ cup plus 2 Tbsp olive oil, divided

2 onions, thinly sliced

½ lb shiitake mushrooms, de-stemmed, cleaned and sliced ½ inch thick (see sidebar page 184)

2 large portobello mushrooms, cleaned and diced

½ lb cremini mushrooms, cleaned and sliced ½ inch thick

½ tsp salt

Pizza Dough, Tofino Style (page 119)

1–2 cups Red Sauce (page 122)

1 cup Pumpkin Seed Pesto (page 122)

3 cups shredded mozzarella cheese

1 cup crumbled soft goat cheese

2 cups baby arugula

In a medium heavy-bottomed frying pan over medium-high heat, add the butter and 2 Tbsp of the olive oil. As soon as the butter melts, add the onions and turn the heat to medium-low, stirring the onions frequently to prevent them from burning, until they reach a rich, dark brown, about 20 to 30 minutes. By cooking low and slow, you are creating so much flavor, bringing out the onion's natural sweetness without any sharp, bitter taste. If the onions start to stick or burn, turn the heat to low and add 1 Tbsp water. Stir too much and the onions won't brown; stir too little and they burn. Remove from the heat and set aside to cool.

Heat the remaining ¼ cup olive oil in a separate medium heavy-bottomed frying pan over high heat. As soon as it starts to smoke, add all the mushrooms and cook until tender, about 5 minutes. Remove from the heat and season with the salt.

Preheat the oven to 450°F.

Form the dough for one pizza at a time on its floured pan, following the method on page 120.

Once you have shaped one piece of dough, immediately spoon ¼ cup red sauce and ¼ cup pesto on top. Use a spatula or the back of the spoon to spread them out evenly. Sprinkle with one-quarter of the onions, ¾ cup mozzarella, one-quarter of the mushrooms, and ¼ cup goat cheese.

Repeat the shaping and topping process with the remaining balls of dough.

Bake for 10 to 12 minutes, until the crust is golden brown and the cheese golden.

Remove from the oven and garnish with arugula.

MYSTIC CLAM PIZZA

Well, I'm truly showing my age here! This recipe is inspired by the little ole '80s rom com *Mystic Pizza*, starring Julia Roberts. For anyone unfamiliar, it's about a small-town, hole-in-the-wall pizzeria that makes a splash when a renowned food critic sings the praises of its unique blend of spices and seafood for its pies. This is my little spin on what I imagine such a pizza would be like. Rustic, mystic and unidentifiably superb!

**MAKES FOUR
10-INCH PIZZAS**

4 Tbsp butter, divided

2 Tbsp shallots, minced

¼ cup fresh garlic, minced

½ cup dry white wine

2 lb fresh clams, purged (see Cook's Note on page 157)

2 cups ricotta

¼ cup Roasted Garlic (page 259)

1 cup packed chopped kale, de-stemmed

1 tsp red chili flakes

1 tsp cumin powder

½ tsp black pepper

½ tsp fennel seeds

2 Tbsp lemon juice

Lemon zest

2 tsp fresh oregano leaves

1¼ tsp salt, divided, plus extra for seasoning

1 leek, sliced, whites and tender part of greens

Pizza Dough, Tofino Style (page 119)

4 cups shredded mozzarella

¼ cup grated Parmesan

In a medium saucepan over high heat, place 2 Tbsp of the butter, the shallots and the fresh garlic. Sauté for 2 minutes and stir with a wooden spoon to prevent burning.

Add the wine and the clams. Cover and steam until clams are just opened, about 2 minutes. Turn off the heat, uncover and use a slotted spoon to scoop the clams into a shallow vessel (a baking pan will do perfectly) to cool.

Turn the heat down to medium and reduce the clam juice to about a third of its original volume. Remove from the heat and let cool to room temperature.

While the clam juice is cooling, remove the clams from their shells. Discard the shells and put the clam meat in a small bowl. Refrigerate until you're ready to build the pizzas.

In a medium mixing bowl, make the mystic sauce by mixing together the clam juice, ricotta, roasted garlic, kale, chili flakes, cumin powder, pepper, fennel seeds, lemon juice, lemon zest, oregano and salt until well incorporated. Alternatively, you can use a food processor for a smoother texture.

In a small sauté pan over medium-low heat, melt 2 Tbsp of the butter. Add the leeks and sweat down for 4 minutes or until tender, stirring occasionally with a wooden spoon. Remove from the heat and season with salt.

Preheat the oven to 450°F.

Form the dough for one pizza at a time on its floured pan, following the method on page 120.

continued on next page

Once you have shaped one piece of dough, immediately spoon ¾ cup mystic sauce on top. Sprinkle with ¾ cup of the mozzarella. Repeat the shaping and topping process with the remaining balls of dough.

Bake for 8 to 10 minutes, until the crust is golden brown and the cheese is bubbly.

Remove from the oven and top with the clams, leeks and Parmesan. Return to the oven for 2 to 3 minutes or just enough to reheat the clams.

BRENDA SCHWAB

I love flowers, but at SoBo they're largely kept outside the restaurant so that scents don't interfere with the food. Brenda Schwab has been tending our gardens and creating a magnificent welcome for our guests for more than six years. She's one of the hardest-working people I know, and at least three days a week either she or one of her crew is in our gardens.

Brenda understands that a building's exterior reflects its interior. A tidy, attractive outside gives a visitor confidence that the business owners care about what they're doing. Tofino has a tough growing climate —it's very wet, often overcast or foggy, and even on warm summer days it cools right off at night. So there's a fairly limited selection of plants that thrive here, and still, Brenda finds a way to create visual interest year-round. And, thanks to its fireplace, our patio has a remarkable microclimate that extends the growing season. At first, Brenda couldn't figure out why our planters there were so happy—then she came to the restaurant one night when the fire was going. The patio stones were warm and radiating heat, creating a lovely, warm habitat for the plants on an otherwise cool night.

In spring, there are the bulbs and, in summer through to the fall, begonias, fuchsias, lobelia and other flowering plants give vibrant color. Brenda grounds those colors with the foliage and greens of native plants, such as ferns and huckleberries, which are not only pleasing to the eye but happy in the damp climate. I appreciate that she injects SoBo's signature purple here and there, too. Like an interior designer, Brenda uses plants to help define the space on our patio, using taller plants like dahlia and lilies to create privacy screens for tables.

Both Brenda and I have busy lives, so to wind down, we launch our paddleboards near my house and paddle up the inlet. We might see a boat or two, but otherwise it's quiet, just the two of us relaxing in the place we call home.

ASPARAGUS AND POTATO PIZZA

When springtime arrives and asparagus is being harvested in the fields, I binge on it. I love it raw as a snack, I toss it in salads, roast it for side vegetable dishes and, oh well, why not as a pizza topping? White pizzas have been gaining in popularity in recent years, often loaded with garlic and sometimes potatoes, too—so that's my inspiration here. Fontina adds a creamy, nutty component to this pizza. If asparagus is (tragically) not in season, broccoli rabe, broccoli crowns or broccolini are good substitutes. But you'd then have to change the name of the pizza.

MAKES FOUR 10-INCH PIZZAS

2 yellow potatoes

2 tsp salt

1 lb asparagus, trimmed of woody ends

1 Tbsp olive oil for roasting (optional), plus 2 Tbsp for drizzling

Pizza Dough, Tofino Style (page 119)

1 lb thinly sliced fontina or provolone cheese (see Cook's Note)

3 cups White Garlicky Sauce, Green variation (page 123)

1 Tbsp finely chopped fresh rosemary

Preheat the oven to 450°F.

In a medium saucepan, bring the potatoes, salt and enough cold water to cover the potatoes to a low boil. Cover and turn the heat to simmer; simmer for 15 minutes or until the potatoes are fork-tender but not mushy.

Drain the potatoes and let cool to room temperature. Slice thinly.

If the asparagus stalks are thick, I recommend roasting them first: Preheat the oven to 400°F. Place the asparagus on a baking sheet, drizzle with 1 Tbsp of the olive oil and roast for 5 minutes. If the stalks are slender, no need to precook.

Form the dough for one pizza at a time on its floured pan, following the method on page 120.

Once you have shaped one piece of dough, immediately place a few cheese slices directly on the dough, then spoon ¾ cup sauce on top. Use a spatula or the back of the spoon to spread it out evenly (see Cook's Note).

Add a single layer of potatoes, about 6 to 8 slices. Add another layer of cheese, and then arrange about 5 stalks of asparagus on top. Drizzle a little olive oil over the asparagus, then sprinkle a bit of rosemary on top of the pizza.

Repeat the shaping and topping process with the remaining balls of dough.

Bake for 10 to 12 minutes, until the crust is golden brown and the cheese is bubbly.

COOK'S NOTE: Since this sauce is so thick, using sliced cheese (rather than shredded) and laying these down first creates a shield to help prevent tearing while spreading the sauce.

LAMB PIZZA

I had the great privilege of doing my culinary externship at Old Chatham Sheepherding Company, where Melissa Kelly was the executive chef. Melissa is at the highest level of farm to table: and with fresh lamb weekly, I quickly learned everything lamb-related. The racks and loins sold out in a flash, but we'd turn the off-cuts into ground lamb for pizzas, burgers and sausages. Bones were prized for the rich broths they would yield. Oh, and how could I forget the fresh sheep's cheese—to die for. Melissa taught me so much about work ethics and honoring the animal by not wasting a single part. Melissa is a two-time James Beard Award winner, has been called "the real deal" by Anthony Bourdain and is possibly the hardest-working chef in the biz.

**MAKES FOUR
10-INCH PIZZAS**

1 lb ground lamb or leftover Braised Lamb (page 165)

½ cup minced onion

2 Tbsp minced garlic

1 Tbsp minced fresh rosemary

1 tsp fennel seeds

1 tsp salt

¼ cup olive oil

Pizza Dough, Tofino Style (page 119)

1–2 cups Red Sauce (page 122)

2 cups shredded full-fat mozzarella cheese

2 cups shredded provolone cheese

½ cup sliced Kalamata olives

¼ cup grated hard aged cheese, like Parmesan, pecorino, Asiago or Romano

¼ lb arugula leaves, for garnish

Preheat the oven to 450°F.

In a bowl, mix the lamb, onions, garlic, rosemary, fennel seeds and salt to combine well.

Heat the oil in a medium heavy-bottomed frying pan over medium-high heat, then add the lamb mixture. Cook for 3 to 5 minutes, stirring occasionally with a wooden spoon, until most of the red is gone from the meat but it's still super pink. Leaving it pink will allow it to withstand the pizza cooking time; if you overcook it in this first stage, it will likely be too dry after baking on the pizza. Set aside.

Form the dough for one pizza at a time on its floured pan, following the method on page 120.

Once you have shaped one portion of dough, immediately spoon ¼ cup red sauce on top. Use a spatula or the back of the spoon to spread it out evenly. Add one-quarter of the lamb mixture in clumps and one-quarter each of the mozzarella and provolone. Scatter 2 Tbsp olives on top, then sprinkle with 1 Tbsp grated hard cheese.

Repeat the shaping and topping process with the remaining balls of dough.

Bake for 8 to 10 minutes, until the crust is golden brown and the cheese is bubbly. Garnish with the arugula and enjoy.

Mediterranean Pizza

These pizza toppings transport me to a sunny rooftop patio overlooking the Mediterranean Sea. I can feel the sun warming my heart just thinking about it. Speaking of heart, we've all heard about the health benefits of the Mediterranean diet, so if I can feel healthy and eat my pizza, it's a win-win. I seem to naturally crave foods in their appropriate season, so this is my late-summer go-to. If you're one to salt your eggplant (see Cook's Note), you'll need to let it rest for an hour before baking the pizza.

MAKES FOUR 10-INCH PIZZAS

1 zucchini, sliced in ½-inch-thick rounds

1 red bell pepper, thinly sliced

1 medium tomato, finely diced

4 Tbsp olive oil, divided

1 medium eggplant, sliced in ½-inch-thick rounds

½ tsp salt (optional, see Cook's Note)

Pizza Dough, Tofino Style (page 119)

1–2 cups Red Sauce (page 122)

2 cups shredded mozzarella cheese

½ cup Macedonian feta cheese

½ cup sun-dried tomatoes packed in oil, drained

½ cup olives, pitted and halved (Kalamata or Sicilian green are two of my favorites)

16 leaves fresh basil, torn

Preheat the oven to 450°F. Line a baking sheet with parchment paper.

Place the zucchini and bell peppers on the prepared baking sheet, drizzle 2 Tbsp of the olive oil on top and bake for 5 to 7 minutes. The vegetables should be only cooked halfway; they will finish cooking while the pizza is baking. Remove from the oven, transfer to a bowl and let cool to room temperature.

On the same prepared baking sheet, place the eggplant and drizzle with 2 Tbsp of the olive oil. Bake for 5 to 7 minutes (the eggplant should be more tender than the zucchini and peppers). Remove from the oven and let cool to room temperature.

Form the dough for one pizza at a time on its floured pan, following the method on page 120.

Once you have shaped one piece of dough, immediately spoon ¼ cup red sauce on top. Use a spatula or the back of the spoon to spread it out evenly. Sprinkle with ½ cup mozzarella, followed by one-quarter of the vegetables, 2 Tbsp feta, 2 Tbsp sun-dried tomatoes and 2 Tbsp olives.

Repeat the shaping and topping process with the remaining balls of dough.

Bake for 8 to 12 minutes, until the crust is golden brown and the cheese is bubbly. Remove from the oven and top with basil.

COOK'S NOTE: To salt or not salt the eggplant? Salting eggplant is a way to remove its bitterness. But is it really necessary? In recent years, some farmers have been breeding the bitterness out of the plant. So, there's that. Some people continue to salt to remove excess moisture. I stopped doing it years ago, and if I experience the odd bitter one, well, that's cool, sometimes bitter's better!

Entrées

SUMMER RATATOUILLE AND POLENTA

When my mom would make this back in the '70s, I thought it was the most exotic dish imaginable. Even the word in my mouth—*rat-a-too-ee*—tasted delicious. Mom—who was, in my mind, the best cook ever—would cut up all the vegetables, toss them together and throw it all in a CorningWare dish (remember those? I still have a few tucked away) to bake. Nothing to it. For my recipe, I sauté the ingredients first, but either way works. I also like to use mushrooms, which is not traditional, and a creamy, soft, silky polenta. I adore the rich ragu of vegetables on top. If you have leftovers and want to try a different version, serve with crispy polenta croutons (see Cook's Note).

SERVES 6

Polenta
1 cup milk
1 tsp salt
½ cup coarse-ground yellow cornmeal
¼ cup butter, cubed
¼ cup grated Asiago cheese

Ratatouille
½ cup olive oil, divided
8 cloves garlic, minced
1 bay leaf
½ onion, diced
1 red bell pepper, diced
1 small eggplant, diced
1 yellow squash, diced
1 zucchini, diced
3 tsp salt, divided
1 portobello mushroom, diced
1 tsp dried thyme
1 tsp dried oregano
1 tsp dried marjoram
1 large tomato, diced

¼ cup fresh parsley leaves, for garnish
8–10 leaves fresh basil, for garnish
¼ cup shaved hard aged cheese, like Parmesan, pecorino, Asiago or Romano, for garnish

Prepare the polenta: Heat the oven to 325°F.

In a medium ovenproof saucepan over medium heat, add 1 cup water, the milk and salt. Cover with a tight-fitting lid and let simmer for about 15 minutes. Watch carefully to avoid the milk bubbling up and spilling over the sides. If it gets too hot, the milk scalds and will lose its natural sweetness.

Test the milk with a deep-fry thermometer. When it is 155°F (I call this the latte stage), slowly whisk in the cornmeal. Continue to whisk until a few bubbles appear. (I call this the volcanic stage.)

Cover and place in the oven for 20 minutes. Remove and stir with a wooden spoon, then return to the oven and continue to bake for 15 minutes. Remove from the oven, stir in the butter and cheese and serve as soon as possible. It sets up and hardens quite quickly.

Meanwhile, cook the ratatouille: Heat ¼ cup of the olive oil in a large heavy-bottomed pan over high heat. As soon as it's hot, add the garlic, bay leaf and onions. Sweat down for 2 to 3 minutes. Add the peppers, eggplant, yellow squash and zucchini and continue to cook for another 5 minutes. Season with 1 tsp of the salt. Remove the mixture from the pan and set aside.

Return the pan to the stovetop, again over high heat, and add the remaining ¼ cup oil. Once it's hot, add the portobello and cook for 5 minutes or until tender. Season with 1 tsp salt.

Return the vegetables to the pan and add the dried herbs. Turn the heat to low, add the tomatoes and remaining 1 tsp salt and use a wooden spoon to gently stir. Let the mixture simmer for a couple of minutes.

To serve: Dish out the hot polenta onto a serving plate, scoop the ratatouille on top and garnish with the fresh herbs and cheese.

COOK'S NOTE: Any leftover polenta can easily be made into crispy polenta cubes. Preheat the oven to 400°F. Line a baking sheet with parchment paper. Cut leftover polenta into small cubes and toss in a bit of olive oil. Bake on the prepared baking sheet for 15 minutes or until crispy and golden brown.

LENTIL VEGIBALLS
WITH CHIMICHURRI AND FRESH CHEESE

Why do some meat alternatives try to resemble actual meat? Sometimes, producers hope to sell to nonvegetarians/vegans as well, so it makes sense to create a product that looks . . . familiar. Think tofu dogs that look like hot dogs, Beyond Beef burgers bleeding beet juice (bit of a tongue twister there). Most other recipes would call the protein in this dish "lentil meatballs," which seems like a paradox. "Meatless balls" sounds a bit impotent; "lentil balls" still unnecessarily testicular. In Middle Eastern cuisine, you might've seen them called lentil kofta, but proper kofta are meatballs, so we are no further ahead. For this book, I have settled on "vegiballs"—but I'm always open to suggestions! These vegiballs also make for an excellent filling for a veggie burger or burrito.

SERVES 4, OR 8 AS AN APPETIZER, WITH 16 VEGIBALLS

1 cup beluga lentils, rinsed (see Cook's Note)

2 Tbsp salt, divided

1 cup quinoa, rinsed (see Cook's Note)

1 cup forbidden rice, rinsed (see Cook's Note)

½ cup plus 3 Tbsp olive oil, divided

½ cup finely diced onions

3 portobello mushrooms, cleaned and diced (see sidebar page 184)

½ cup Roasted Garlic, puréed (page 259)

1 Tbsp sambal oelek (see Cook's Note)

1 cup ground flaxseed

1 cup rolled oats

1 cup fresh cheese (see Cook's Note page 26)

Chimichurri Sauce (page 260)

In a medium heavy-bottomed saucepan, bring 4 cups cold water to a boil. Add the lentils and 1 tsp of the salt and simmer for about 20 minutes. Drain and set aside.

In a small heavy-bottomed saucepan, bring 2 cups cold water, the quinoa and 1 tsp salt to a boil. Turn the heat to simmer and cook for about 10 minutes. Remove from the heat, cover and set aside for 5 minutes. Like rice, quinoa benefits from standing, when the residual steam makes the grains a bit fluffier. Once cool, set a few tablespoons aside for the garnish.

In a small heavy-bottomed saucepan, bring 1¾ cups cold water, the forbidden rice and 1 tsp salt to a boil. Cover, turn the heat to low and simmer for 20 minutes. Remove from the heat and set aside, still covered, for 5 minutes.

Heat 3 Tbsp of the olive oil in a medium frying pan over medium-high heat until the oil starts to smoke, about 1 minute. Add the onions and cook for a couple of minutes, stirring occasionally, then add the mushrooms and remaining 1 Tbsp salt. Cook until the mushrooms are tender, about 5 minutes. If the mushrooms start to dry out, just add a few tablespoons of water to the pan. Remove from the heat and let cool to room temperature.

In a large bowl, add the lentils, quinoa, rice, mushroom mixture, roasted garlic, sambal oelek, flaxseed and oats. Stir with a wooden spoon to combine.

continued on next page

In a food processor, working in small batches, add the mixture and pulse until it holds together in a ball, much like (dare I say it?) a traditional meatball. Transfer the mixture to a medium bowl and mix by hand until well incorporated.

Line a baking sheet with parchment paper. Using an ice cream scoop, scoop balls onto the prepared baking sheet. Refrigerate until ready to bake, up to 3 days if tightly wrapped.

Preheat the oven to 400°F.

Drizzle the remaining ½ cup olive oil over the vegiballs and bake for 20 to 25 minutes, until crispy on the outside. On a separate parchment-lined baking sheet, lay out the reserved quinoa and bake for 5 minutes. Divide the vegiballs among four plates. Top with the fresh cheese, chimichurri and crunchy toasted quinoa.

COOK'S NOTE: To rinse lentils, quinoa and forbidden rice, place each ingredient in a fine-mesh strainer and run under cold water, keeping an eye out for any pebbles. Forbidden rice (or "black rice") is a medium-grain, non-glutinous heirloom rice with a nutty, slightly sweet flavor. Sambal oelek is an Indonesian spice made from pure chilies—no vinegar, no garlic, nothing else.

BUCKWHEAT CREPES

WITH RHUBARB, FIDDLEHEADS, ASPARAGUS AND FENNEL

After a long, cold, hard, dark, bitter, rainy, windy, wet (okay, I exaggerate a bit) winter of root vegetables and boiled cabbage overload (nothing wrong with root vegetables; everything wrong with boiled cabbage) comes spring. It's a hopeful time of the year for everyone, including chefs, who long for the world to turn green again and for the welcoming sight of the season's first vegetables—slender spears of asparagus, fiddleheads and bundles of bright red rhubarb. Rhubarb is most often paired with strawberries in pies, crisps or compotes, but it truly shines when combined with a vibrant green vegetable or three. You can use whichever speak to you; I recommend this spring combination. The coconut and rhubarb sauce's sweet, savory and creamy components perfectly balance each other out.

MAKES 6–8 CREPES

Coconut and Rhubarb Sauce

2 Tbsp coconut oil

Pinch ground cardamom

Pinch crushed red chili flakes

Pinch fresh cracked black pepper, plus extra as needed

2 sprigs fresh thyme (see Cook's Note)

2 cloves garlic, minced

1 cup diced onion

½ cup diced rhubarb

1 tsp salt, plus extra as needed

4 cups coconut milk (see Cook's Note on page 53)

¼ cup maple syrup

1 Tbsp freshly squeezed lemon juice, plus extra as needed

Prepare the sauce: Heat the coconut oil in a medium heavy-bottomed saucepan over medium heat. When the oil is warm, add the cardamom, chili flakes, pepper and thyme and cook for about 1 minute, stirring with a wooden spoon, until fragrant. (Careful! You don't want the pan too hot.)

Add the garlic, onions, rhubarb and salt. Cook until everything is tender—ideally, there will be no coloration or caramelization of the onions or garlic.

Stir in the coconut milk and maple syrup. Let simmer over medium heat, uncovered, for 20 to 30 minutes, to reduce the coconut milk a little bit. Remove from the heat. Pour the sauce along with the lemon juice into a blender and purée until smooth. Taste, and add salt, pepper or more lemon juice to taste.

Keep the sauce in the saucepan over low heat so that it stays warm while you prepare the crepes.

Prepare the filling: Preheat the oven to 350°F.

In a large pot, bring 2 quarts water seasoned with 2 Tbsp of the salt to a boil.

In an 8- × 8-inch baking dish, place the rhubarb and fennel and sprinkle the maple syrup, olive oil and the remaining 1 tsp salt on top. Add the bay leaves. Bake for 20 to 25 minutes, until the rhubarb is tender.

continued on next page

Filling

2 Tbsp plus 1 tsp salt, divided

2 cups chopped rhubarb

½ cup shaved fennel

1 Tbsp maple syrup

1 Tbsp olive oil

2 bay leaves

2 cups chopped trimmed asparagus

2 cups fiddleheads

Crepe

¾ cup buckwheat flour

¾ cup all-purpose flour

1 tsp salt

3 eggs

1½ cups milk, or nut or oat milk, plus extra as needed

2 Tbsp butter or coconut oil, divided

Blanch the asparagus in the pot of boiling water until slightly firm, but not mushy, 2 to 3 minutes, depending on their size. Immediately scoop out the asparagus using a slotted spoon and transfer to an ice bath for 1 minute to stop the cooking and retain the vegetable's brilliant green color.

In the same pot of salted water, blanch the fiddleheads until completely tender, 2 to 3 minutes, depending on their size. Immediately scoop out the fiddleheads using a slotted spoon and transfer to an ice bath for 1 minute.

Prepare the crepes: In a medium bowl, mix together the flours and salt.

In a separate medium bowl, whisk the eggs and milk. Gradually add the dry ingredients to the wet ingredients while mixing. Mix until there are no lumps.

Heat 1 tsp of the butter in a medium cast-iron or nonstick pan over medium-high heat. Using a ladle, pour one scoop of the batter into the center of your pan. Then take the pan by its handle and lift and tilt it to spread the batter around to form the crepe. The mixture should spread thinly. If you find it too thick, add a little milk to the batter remaining in the bowl.

Turn the heat to medium. Once the surface of the crepe is no longer wet, about 2 minutes, use a spatula to flip it to the other side. Cook for about 30 seconds, then transfer to an ovenproof, lidded dish. Repeat this process until you have used up all the batter. You can keep the crepes warm in a 250°F oven, covered so that they do not dry out, until you are ready to serve. Any leftover batter will keep stored in an airtight container in the fridge for up to 4 days.

To serve: If necessary, reheat the filling in a frying pan over medium heat with a few spoonfuls of the coconut rhubarb sauce to prevent it from sticking. Place a crepe on a plate and scoop some filling and sauce into the center. Roll up the crepe and garnish with more sauce.

COOK'S NOTE: Pick the thyme fresh from your spring garden. If you aren't lucky enough to have one, raid a neighbor's (after asking permission, of course)—or substitute 1 tsp dried thyme.

SPAGHETTI SQUASH PATTIES
WITH POACHED EGGS AND SALSA VERDE

This toothsome dish was created by my sous-chef, dear, sweet Laurence Fisette, who jogs, surfs, practices yoga and still manages to dedicate the whole of her heart to preparing, cooking and serving food to appreciative guests. There's a dash of my Southern inspiration in this recipe, blended with her commitment to eating fabulously well and healthily at the same time. When you wake up craving Eggs Benny but don't want all that buttery, heavenly, Hollandaisey, gluteny goodness to weigh you down as soon as you hit the sidewalk, catch a wave or practice your one-legged tree pose, try this nutritious—while still rich and satisfying—option. Especially in the fall, when our local tomatoes are still hot red with the memory of the bedazzling summer sun.

SERVES 4

Squash Patties

1 spaghetti squash
1 egg
½ cup grated Asiago cheese
1 Tbsp salt
1 Tbsp chili powder
2 tsp sweet paprika
½ bunch fresh parsley, finely chopped
1½ cups dried breadcrumbs
2 Tbsp flour
½ cup oil, for frying

Kale and Heirloom Tomato Garnish

4 cups fresh kale, de-stemmed and torn into 2-inch pieces
2 Tbsp olive oil
2 heirloom tomatoes

Prepare the squash patties: Preheat the oven to 400°F. Line a baking sheet with parchment paper.

Carefully cut the squash in half lengthwise and scoop out the seeds (you can freeze these for future vegetable stocks). With a paring knife, cut 8 to 10 small slits in the squash so the steam can vent. (You don't want an explosion in the oven.)

Place the squash flesh side down on the prepared baking sheet (alternatively, you can use a casserole dish). Put in the oven to bake, checking on it at the 30-minute mark: depending on its size, the squash may have softened and be finished cooking at this point. If it's not, you can flip it and continue baking for another 15 to 30 minutes. When the squash is softened all the way through, remove it from the oven and let cool to room temperature. When the squash is cool enough to handle, use a fork to pull the pulp out in strands. It will resemble cooked spaghetti.

In a large bowl and using two wooden spoons, toss together the squash, egg, Asiago, salt, chili powder and paprika. Gradually add the parsley, breadcrumbs and flour, continuing to toss.

Using your hands, form the mixture into patties the size of an English muffin.

continued on next page

Salsa Verde

1 cup Roasted Chilies (page 260), seeded and diced

½ cup minced red onion

1 bunch fresh cilantro, coarsely chopped

1 bunch fresh parsley, coarsely chopped

2 Tbsp minced garlic

½ cup lime juice

1 tsp salt

¼ cup extra virgin olive oil

8 Poached Eggs (page 99, double the recipe)

In a medium frying pan, heat ¼ cup of the oil, enough to liberally coat the bottom of the pan. When the oil is hot, add four patties to the pan at a time (avoid overcrowding the pan or it will be hard to flip the patties) and shallow-fry for 3 to 4 minutes. They should start to release from the pan and turn golden brown. Using a sturdy spatula, gently turn the patties so they crisp up on the other side, another 2 minutes or so. Drain the patties on a plate or baking sheet lined with paper towel. (Personally, I reuse the pan and parchment I roasted the squash on. Reduce, reuse, recycle, right?) Keep them warm in a 300°F oven while you prepare the rest of the recipe (now would be a good time to poach the eggs, too).

Prepare the kale and tomato garnish: In a bowl, toss the kale with the olive oil. Transfer to a small frying pan over medium-high heat and cook for 2 to 3 minutes, until the kale begins to soften. Return to the bowl. Cut the tomatoes into wedges and add to the bowl of kale.

Prepare the salsa verde: Place all the ingredients except the olive oil in a blender or food processor and pulse until blended but still a bit rough. Drizzle in the olive oil. The texture should be rustic—that is, not too refined!

To serve: Make sure the patties, kale and eggs are hot! Arrange 2 patties on each of four plates and top with 2 poached eggs each. Garnish with the kale and tomatoes. Spoon the salsa verde generously on top.

LAURENCE FISETTE

Mademoiselle Fisette joined the SoBo team in 2015, when she was barely 22 years old. I was instantly drawn to her—her pure love and dedication to seasonal, healthy food—*real food*, she calls it. "I cook," she says. "That is what I do, what I am meant to do. I have always had a crush on food. Even as a baby, my face would light up when a plate was placed in front of me."

Growing up, Laurence was inspired by her grandmother, Gigi, who owned a restaurant in a small town in Quebec. "She was passionate about cooking. I would serve tables for fun and 'help her out' in the kitchen where we made pies and spaghetti sauce together. She would always say, 'It tastes good because it's made with love.' As cheesy as it sounds, my cooking definitely embodies her words."

It tastes good because it's made with love. Perfect mantra for Laurence's transition to SoBo, where our tag line is "Taste the Love." I have watched Laurence grow over the last number of years into a confident and capable young chef, a fierce and stunning human who never backs down from a challenge. The healthy lifestyle she leads spills over into the dishes she creates. "It's about involving and making people happy. It is an art: you see, smell and taste."

When not baking heavenly sourdough or rolling to-die-for pasta dough, Laurence spends time in the ocean—surfing, paddling, diving. She lives with me and my family, not too far from the restaurant.

SEAFOOD SAFFRON RISOTTO

For a great risotto, you must have your ingredients prepped and ready—anyone who has spent time in a professional kitchen knows the term *mise en place*, French for "putting in place." This means you can stand in front of the stove and methodically become engaged. In the act. Of stirring. Opera cranked to the max, chilled white wine in hand. And you're stirring, stirring, stirring. I would never dream of using anything but a wooden spoon for this. Why? Because the Italian chef who taught me said so. He barely spoke a word of English, but his raised eyebrows spoke volumes of disappointment if I so much as *thought* of using a metal spoon. His risotto was the creamiest and most perfect risotto I have ever eaten, so I listened.

SERVES 4

½ cup olive oil, divided

1 cup arborio rice

4 cloves garlic, minced

1 small shallot, minced

1 tsp saffron threads

½ cup plus 2 Tbsp dry white wine, divided

4–6 cups hot Fish Stock or Vegetable Stock (pages 253 or 252)

8 large scallops

1 lb shrimp, peeled and deveined

Salt

1 lb clams, rinsed and purged (see sidebar page 157)

1 Tbsp butter

1 cup sea asparagus or baby arugula, for garnish

Heat ¼ cup of the olive oil in a heavy-bottomed pan over medium heat. Add the rice and gently stir with a wooden spoon. Toast the rice to a light golden brown, then add the garlic, shallots and saffron. Stir again and, after 2 to 3 minutes, add ½ cup of the wine, continuing to stir. The rice will immediately start to absorb the wine.

Before all the wine has evaporated, add 1 cup of the hot stock. Stirring constantly, add another 1 cup stock right before the last addition has all evaporated. Continue adding the stock in this way until it has all been used up and is fully absorbed, stirring constantly until you reach the desired consistency (see Cook's Note). You want the rice to still have texture and not be mushy, and for the risotto to be runny, not sticky (it would move around on a plate if the plate were tilted). This usually takes about 4 cups of stock and constant stirring for about 20 minutes. Remove the risotto from the heat while you prepare the shellfish.

In a large heavy-bottomed frying pan over high heat, heat the remaining ¼ cup olive oil to its smoking point.

Season the scallops and shrimp with salt. Add the scallops (not the shrimp) to the pan and sear for 2 to 3 minutes on one side, until they easily release from the pan to flip. Do not overcrowd the pan, as the scallops give off a fair amount of moisture, which stops them from getting caramelized, which is the goal. If needed, cook in batches. Remove the scallops from the pan, leaving all the tasty bits behind (you don't need to cook the other side; they'll finish cooking when mixed into the risotto).

continued on next page

Turn the heat to medium-high and add the clams, butter and the remaining 2 Tbsp wine to the pan. Gently stir, then cover and allow the clams to steam for 3 minutes. Add the shrimp, cover and steam for another 2 to 3 minutes, until the shrimp are fully cooked and all the clams have opened (discard any that are unopened).

Add the scallops, shrimp, clams with their nectar and any cooking liquid remaining in the pan to the risotto, gently toss together and then gently heat over medium-low heat. The clam nectar from the steaming process will add the extra moisture needed to enhance the rich flavor of the risotto.

Divide the risotto among four plates. If you have sea asparagus, it is a lovely addition on top for salt and crunch. Alternatively, fresh arugula is a nice finishing touch.

COOK'S NOTE: The constant stirring with the wooden spoon is what makes the risotto creamy; you're agitating the surface starches, combining them with the liquid. The scientific reason for the wooden spoon (assuming you don't have a chef standing over you, threatening you with his eyebrows!) is that wood is more porous than metal or silicone and is therefore more abrasive against the surface of the rice, removing more of the surface starch and increasing the creaminess.

How to Purge Clams

Purging is a crucial step when preparing clams, unless you like them à la sand. Most clams have spent their lives nestled on the ocean floor, minding their own business, mindlessly siphoning sand along with the rest of their diet, so if you dig for your clams, or buy wild or fresh ones, sand will especially be an issue. Farm-raised clams are usually cleaned and flushed before they're sold, but never assume your clams have been properly purged.

First, gently tap any clams with open shells against the countertop. Discard any clams that do not close their shells within a few minutes, and any with cracked or chipped shells. They are either dead or dying, and should not be consumed.

Place all the clams in a bowl and fill it with cold water. Let the clams sit for 30 minutes to 1 hour. During this time, they will spit out the sand from within their shells. Because sand is heavier than water, it will sink to the bottom of the bowl.

When you're ready to cook, lift each clam from the water using your hands or a slotted spoon, and transfer to a colander. Don't drain the clams directly into the colander, as you'll end up dumping any purged sand back on top of the clams.

CLAM AND CORN VONGOLE

A traditional vongole consists of clams with spaghetti, white wine, garlic, parsley and olive oil. In our SoBo version, the addition of roasted summer corn adds a little twist of sweet and smoky. I come from the land of corn—I love a good corn chowder, and that flavor profile doesn't stray too far from that of clam chowder. So why not marry them in a pasta? As the olive oil is a key flavor in this dish, this is a good time to use a high-quality one (read more on page 20). I remove the clams from their shells because it makes for much easier eating, but they can certainly be kept in their shells, just make sure to scrub them well—a little sand or grit can ruin the dish.

SERVES 4

¼ cup olive oil

½ cup butter

8 cloves garlic, minced

½ cup dry white wine

2 Tbsp heavy cream

1 Tbsp crushed red chili flakes

1 tsp salt

2 lb clams, purged (see sidebar page 157)

1 lb dried spaghetti or Egg Pasta Dough (page 250), shaped as spaghetti

4 ears fresh corn, roasted and kernels cut off cobs (page 258)

½ cup finely chopped parsley, for garnish

¼ cup grated Parmesan cheese, for garnish

In a heavy-bottomed pan over medium-high heat, add the oil and butter. As soon as it melts, add the garlic and sauté for 2 minutes. Add the wine and cream and reduce for 2 minutes. Add the chili flakes, salt and clams. Cover and cook until all the clams have opened. Remove from the heat (discard any unopened clams) and let cool to room temperature for about 10 minutes.

When the clams are cool enough to handle, remove the meat from the shells and place in a medium bowl, separate from the cooking broth, which will become your sauce.

Fill a large pot with 8 quarts water. Salt and bring to a boil. If you are cooking fresh pasta, it will take 3 to 4 minutes. If you're using dried pasta, cook according to the package instructions. Drain the pasta (do not rinse), reserving ¼ cup of the pasta water.

While the pasta is cooking, set the clam broth over low heat. Add the corn and clams and heat for 1 minute. Add the pasta and the reserved pasta water and toss everything together.

Serve up family style in a large serving bowl or divide among individual plates. Garnish with parsley and Parmesan.

Nettle, Clam and Shrimp Tagliatelle

In the spring, when nettles grow like weeds here in Tofino, I take the opportunity to stockpile. The foragers I work with all know that I will never turn nettles away. Some days my staff look at me as if to say, "Seriously, Chef, don't you think we have enough?" To that, I would reply: "How could anyone have *too many* nettles in their life?" I blanch, purée and freeze them in ice cube trays for soups, pastas and pizza toppings. I dry them for tea. Never have I ever had nettles left over from the previous year. All that said, if nettles are hard to come by, spinach is a good substitute here. This is such a quick dish that I steam my seafood at the same time as cooking the pasta.

SERVES 4

Egg Pasta Dough, Nettle Pasta Variation (page 251), shaped as tagliatelle

½ cup olive oil

2 Tbsp butter

10 cloves garlic, minced

1 tsp crushed red chili flakes

½ cup dry white wine

2 lb fresh clams, rinsed and purged (see sidebar page 157)

12 large shrimp (head on, if you are lucky enough for same-day harvest)

Hard aged cheese, like Parmesan, pecorino, Asiago or Romano, for garnish (optional)

Fresh cracked black pepper

Fill a stockpot with 8 quarts water. Salt and bring to a rolling boil.

Add the pasta and cook, using a wooden spoon to give it the occasional gentle stir (if you don't, it will stick together). Be careful not to break the pasta strands by stirring too vigorously. Cook for 3 minutes, then test the pasta. Cook until al dente. Drain the pasta (don't rinse), reserving ¼ cup of the pasta water.

In a large heavy-bottomed sauté pan over medium-high heat, melt the oil and butter. Add the garlic and chili flakes and sauté for 2 to 3 minutes, being careful not to let the garlic brown. Add the wine and reduce by half, then add the clams. Cover and cook for 2 minutes. Add the shrimp, cover and cook for 3 minutes or just until the shrimp turns pink and all clams are open. (The shrimp cook very quickly, so keep an eye on them!) Discard any clams that are unopen. Add the pasta and pasta water. Toss everything together.

Transfer to a serving bowl and sprinkle with the cheese, if desired, and a few cracks of black pepper.

Braised Chicken and Roasted Brussels Sprouts Pappardelle

This recipe calls for chicken, but you can use duck or almost any kind of braising meat. The rich braising liquid doubles as the pasta sauce. Although we make fresh pasta in this recipe, it is perfectly fine to use dried pasta. This recipe can be made a day in advance—except for the pasta.

SERVES 4

5 Tbsp olive oil, divided

4–8 bone-in chicken thighs

1 Tbsp salt, plus extra for seasoning

6 cloves garlic, minced

½ onion, finely chopped

2 bay leaves

¼ cup tomato paste

½ cup dry red wine

¼ cup sherry vinegar

6 cups chicken stock

4 sprigs fresh thyme

1 lb Brussels sprouts, halved

½ cup halved raw walnuts

Egg Pasta Dough (page 250), shaped as pappardelle (see photo)

A few sprigs parsley, for garnish

Preheat the oven to 325°F

Heat 3 Tbsp of the olive oil in a large heavy-bottomed, ovenproof frying pan over medium-high heat. Season the chicken thighs with the salt, then add to the pan and sear, skin side down, for 4 to 5 minutes, until the skin is golden brown. Remove from the pan and set aside while you prepare the braising liquid.

Add the garlic, onions and bay leaves to the oil left behind in the pan, and stir with a wooden spoon to prevent burning. Once the onions start to soften, add the tomato paste. Stir for about 2 to 3 minutes, then deglaze with the wine and vinegar. Reduce for about 3 to 5 minutes, then pour in the stock.

Bring the mixture to a boil. Return the thighs to the pan, skin side up. Add the fresh thyme sprigs. Cover with a tight-fitting lid and transfer to the oven to braise for 45 minutes or until the thighs are tender.

Remove the thighs from the braising liquid and let cool to room temperature. Remove and discard the skin and bones, and set the meat aside.

Turn the oven to 400°F.

Put the pan of braising liquid on the stovetop and reduce over low heat until it thickens into a sauce. This usually takes about 15 minutes.

In a medium saucepan, bring 4 cups water to a boil and season with salt. Blanch the Brussels sprouts in the boiling water for 2 minutes. This will ensure crispy and tender Brussels sprouts with a soft and delicious center after roasting.

continued on next page

Drain and then pat the Brussels sprouts dry with a clean tea towel. In a medium bowl, toss the Brussels sprouts with the remaining 2 Tbsp olive oil. Line a baking sheet with parchment paper. Spread the Brussels sprouts on the prepared baking sheet and roast for 5 minutes or until well caramelized. Remove and set aside, keeping the oven on.

Spread the walnuts on a separate baking sheet and toast in the oven for 3 to 4 minutes. Walnuts burn easily, so keep a close watch. Remove and set aside.

Fill a stockpot with 8 quarts water. Salt and bring to a rolling boil. Add the pasta and cook, giving it an occasional gentle stir, for about 4 minutes for fresh pasta. Drain the pasta, reserving one-quarter of the pasta water.

Return the chicken and Brussels sprouts to the pan with the braising-liquid sauce. Turn the heat to medium. Add the pasta and reserved pasta water, and toss everything together. Top with the walnuts and parsley sprigs.

ORECCHIETTE, BRAISED LAMB AND CAULIFLOWER

When we were growing up, pasta was called spaghetti and it came in a blue box. Fresh pasta would have been when the blue box hadn't yet been opened. (For a real treat, there was Chef Boyardee ravioli in a tin.) These days, there are so many superb brands and shapes of dried pasta available. Orecchiette is a great shape to buy dried. Originally from Puglia in southern Italy, its name translates to "small ears," and that's what it looks like. This tiny-ear shape lends itself to a thick sauce, or "gravy," as it's often referred to, as in this dish. When it comes to the lamb here, I like the sweet and flavorful shoulder cut, which becomes beautifully tender when braised.

SERVES 4

Braised Lamb

½ cup canola oil

1 lamb shoulder (see Cook's Note)

1 Tbsp salt

1 tsp fresh cracked black pepper

1 onion, chopped

10 cloves garlic, minced

2 bay leaves

4 sprigs fresh thyme

½ cup tomato paste

1 cup dry red wine

6 cups Beef, Chicken or Vegetable Stock (pages 252–254)

The Cauliflower

½ head cauliflower, cut in small florets

¼ cup olive oil

The Pasta

2 cups dried orecchiette

10–15 Kalamata olives, pitted and halved

½ cup grated Parmesan cheese, for garnish

¼ cup torn fresh basil leaves, for garnish

Braise the lamb: Preheat the oven to 350°F.

In a heavy-bottomed pan suitable for braising over high heat, heat the oil to its smoking point. Season the lamb all over with the salt and pepper. Sear the lamb in the hot pan for 5 to 10 minutes, until it starts to release from the pan, then flip over. The seared side should be very well caramelized but not burnt. Cook on the other side for about 5 minutes, until a golden crust appears. Remove from the pan and set aside.

Add the onions, garlic, bay leaves and thyme to the braising pan and sauté for 3 to 4 minutes. Stir in the tomato paste and continue to cook over medium heat for 3 minutes, then pour in the wine and reduce by half. Pour in the stock.

Return the lamb to the pan, turn the heat to medium-high and bring the mixture to a lazy bubble. Cover and transfer to the oven to braise for 1½ to 2 hours, until the meat pulls apart.

Remove the meat from the braising liquid and set aside to cool. Remove and discard the bay leaves and thyme. Set the braising liquid aside to cool, then scoop any excess oil off the top of the sauce and discard.

If you prefer a smooth sauce, you can blend it. We keep ours rustic. If it seems thin, reduce over medium heat until it thickens to your liking. Shred the lamb and add to the braising liquid.

Roast the cauliflower: Turn the oven to 400°F. Line a baking sheet with parchment paper.

continued on next page

Toss the cauliflower florets in the oil and place on the prepared baking sheet. Roast for 15 minutes or until very dark brown.

Prepare the pasta: Cook the orecchiette according to the package directions. Drain the pasta (do not rinse), reserving ¼ cup of the pasta water.

Toss the pasta with 2 cups of the saucy shredded lamb, the cauliflower, olives and reserved pasta water. Leftover lamb can be cooled completely, then stored in a freezer-friendly container for up to 6 months. Heat the mixture in a saucepan over low heat to warm the pasta. Divide among four plates, and garnish with the Parmesan and basil.

COOK'S NOTE: While the whole lamb shoulder may yield more than you need for this recipe, it freezes well for future use in tacos (page 189), on pizza (page 137) or in hearty soups. Or chat with your butcher about buying half a shoulder, and halve the braised lamb recipe.

HALIBUT CHEEKS
WITH MORELS, FIDDLEHEADS AND CELERIAC CREAM

This is a dish our family looks forward to in the late spring come halibut season—their cheeks are a treat. They have a unique texture, maybe closest to scallops or cooked and shredded crab meat, but there's really nothing like cheeks. It's a natural bridge between their delicate, buttery texture and delicious, buttery morels and fiddleheads—which both have very short seasons, so as soon as they're available, I toss them onto my plate at every chance I get. Morels, especially, are rock stars in the food world. They're hard to come by, adored by groupies who travel great distances, hike for miles, and camp remotely for weeks battling mosquitoes, blackflies, no-see-ums and gnarly weather, all to somehow transport these tasty forest treasures back in decent condition for folks like you and me to serve with—what else—fiddleheads and halibut cheeks.

SERVES 4

Celeriac Cream

1 small onion, quartered

1 celeriac, peeled and cut into chunks

1 cup milk

1 cup heavy cream

1 head Roasted Garlic (page 259)

2 tsp salt

Morels and Fiddleheads

2 Tbsp olive oil

4 Tbsp butter, divided

½ lb fresh morel mushrooms, cleaned and sliced (see sidebar page 184)

Salt

1 lb fiddleheads, trimmed of brown ends

Halibut Cheeks

4–8 halibut cheeks, depending on size

1 Tbsp salt

¼ cup olive oil

3 Tbsp Pickled Mustard Seeds (page 264), for garnish

Prepare the celeriac cream: In a dry medium cast-iron skillet or grill pan over high heat, place the onions and roast until blackened on one side. Turn and repeat on the other side. This entire process takes about 3 to 5 minutes.

Add the celeriac, milk and cream. Bring to a boil, then turn the heat down and simmer for about 30 minutes, until the celeriac is tender. Add the roasted garlic and the salt. Transfer to a blender and purée until very smooth. This can be made a day in advance and reheated when you're ready to serve.

Cook the morels and fiddleheads: In a heavy-bottomed frying pan over medium-high heat, add the olive oil and 2 Tbsp of the butter. As soon as the butter melts, add the morels and sauté for 4 to 5 minutes, until lightly caramelized and cooked through. Season with the salt.

Add the remaining 2 Tbsp butter and the fiddleheads. Cook until the fiddleheads are no longer crunchy but also not mushy.

Prepare the halibut cheeks: Using paper towel, pat the halibut cheeks as dry as you can get them. Season with the salt. In a heavy-bottomed saucepan over medium-high heat, heat the olive oil to its smoking point.

Carefully add the cheeks, two at a time, allowing 4 to 5 inches between cheeks. Do not overcrowd the pan, otherwise the cheeks won't sear properly. After 3 to 4 minutes, the cheeks will start to naturally release from the pan. Using a spatula, carefully flip them over (dare I say, turn

continued on next page

the other cheek) and repeat. Well-caramelized cheeks are the goal, and they must be thoroughly cooked all the way through.

To serve: In a small saucepan over low heat, reheat the celeriac purée. Put a dollop of the purée onto each of four plates and arrange the halibut cheeks on top. Serve with the fiddleheads and morels. Top everything with a few tablespoons of pickled mustard seeds.

COOK'S NOTE: Make sure fiddleheads and morels are thoroughly cooked. Possible side effect from undercooking: tummy upset. Besides, they just get tastier when they are completely cooked.

SHRIMP AND POLENTA GRITS

Shrimp and grits may have started out as a breakfast dish, but it tantalizes the taste buds and satisfies that craving for sweet, salty, spicy and comforting all day long. While most Southern home kitchens have relied on grits and eggs as an economical way to fill their families' bellies, these days the eggs are often replaced by "luxury" items such as shrimp, when in season. The style of gravy varies from one home to the next. Red-eye is common, as is one made of butter, Worcestershire and hot sauce. My version of this low-country classic is more modern-upscale, with classic polenta grits and barbecue sauce. For a satisfying stick-to-your-ribs kind of meal, serve with a handful of the wilted greens or a pile of onion rings—or both!

SERVES 4

Barbecue Sauce

¼ cup canola oil

2 cloves garlic, minced

½ cup finely diced yellow onion

½ cup finely diced green bell peppers

1 Tbsp salt

1 tsp ground cayenne pepper

2 cups diced tomatoes

¼ cup brewed coffee or espresso

½ cup apple cider vinegar

¼ cup Dijon mustard

¼ cup maple syrup

1 Tbsp Worcestershire sauce

Grits

2 cups Vegetable Stock (page 252) or water

2 tsp salt

¾ cup coarse-ground cornmeal or grits

½ cup milk

2 Tbsp cubed, cold butter

¼ cup shredded sharp Cheddar cheese

Prepare the barbecue sauce: Heat the canola oil in a medium heavy-bottomed pot over medium heat. Add the garlic, onions and bell peppers and sauté for about 15 minutes, until tender, stirring frequently with a wooden spoon to prevent burning. Add the salt and cayenne and continue to cook for another minute.

Turn the heat to low, add the tomatoes, coffee, vinegar, mustard, maple syrup and Worcestershire and stir frequently as you continue cooking the mixture for 30 minutes to 1 hour. Cook to taste, as it will get stronger the more it reduces—it will be perfect when it coats the back of the spoon. Remove from the heat. Blend with a hand immersion blender if you like a smooth sauce. Set aside until ready to serve.

Leftover sauce can be stored in the fridge for up to 2 weeks, or in the freezer for up to 2 months. This sauce freezes beautifully and can be used with a multitude of foods, like chicken, steak, grilled salmon or potatoes.

Prepare the grits: In a medium heavy-bottomed saucepan, bring the stock and salt to a boil. Using a whisk, stir in the cornmeal very slowly, to avoid lumps.

Turn the heat to low and continue stirring, frequently, with a wooden spoon. I adore cooking this dish—I crank up some Dixieland or zydeco tunes and it transports me to New Orleans—so I tend to hover over it.

Alternatively, you can bake the grits: Cover the mixture and transfer to a 325°F oven, taking it out to stir every 10 minutes. Either method takes about 30 minutes, until you can no longer taste the rawness of cornmeal. Remove from the heat and slowly add the milk while gently stirring.

continued on next page

Wilted Greens

2 Tbsp olive oil

8 large leaves kale, mustard greens or Swiss chard

1 tsp salt

Shrimp

2 Tbsp peanut oil, plus extra as needed

1 lb fresh shrimp, peeled and deveined

2 tsp salt

Onion Rings (page 257), for serving

Add the butter little by little, followed by the Cheddar, while continuing to stir. The result should be smooth and creamy, not stiff and dense. Keep the lid on the pot to keep the grits warm while you prepare the greens and shrimp.

Prepare the wilted greens: In a medium frying pan or saucepan over medium heat, heat the olive oil so that it is hot but not smoking. Add the greens and salt and, using tongs, immediately begin to toss, or they will quickly burn. When the leaves start to wilt, add 2 Tbsp water and continue to cook for 3 to 4 minutes, until the greens are tender and the water has evaporated.

Prepare the shrimp: Heat 2 Tbsp of the peanut oil in a medium heavy-bottomed frying pan over medium-high heat. When the oil starts to smoke, add the shrimp in batches, placing about ½ inch apart, being careful not to overcrowd the pan. Sprinkle with the salt. After 1 minute, the shrimp should start to release from the pan. Turn them over and sear for another 30 seconds to 1 minute, until they are no longer translucent. Transfer to a dish and set aside. Repeat the process with the remaining shrimp.

You might have to clean the frying pan between batches to remove any shrimp bits. As with any sautéed dish, the amount of cooking oil needed will vary: if the pan dries out, add more oil.

To serve: Pour 1 cup barbecue sauce into the frying pan you cooked the shrimp in. Once the sauce is warm, add the cooked shrimp and toss to coat liberally. Transfer the warm grits to a heated platter. Top with the greens, shrimp and sauce. Garnish with crispy onion rings.

COOK'S NOTE: The difference between grits and polenta basically comes down to the texture of the grind and the type of corn used. Traditionally, grits is coarse-ground corn that's then treated with lime or lye, referred to as hominy. Polenta starts with the yellow corn typically called flint corn, from Italy. I use coarse-ground cornmeal from North America, with great results.

Cosy Lawson

Tofino is filled with people devoted to the environment, and with the amount of work my friend Cosy Lawson does on behalf of the ocean, its shores and wild salmon, she has my total admiration. Born on the beach (seriously!) and growing up on an island surrounded by wilderness, it's no wonder she's so committed to Clayoquot Sound.

Cosy's love for salmon started at a young age. As a food staple for her family, "salmon literally provided for our family's growth," she says. Cosy's father was the family fisherman, but she would often accompany him to help out on his fishing trips and, by the age of eight, was doing a good share of the fishing herself, setting out in the family boat each morning at first light. "It was my happy place," she says. "Fishing and being in the boat were big responsibilities, and I took them seriously."

In 2010, when she heard of Get Out Migration, an organized march down the length of Vancouver Island in support of protecting wild salmon, she and her 11-year-old daughter, Laterra, walked from Tofino all the way across the island to join the main group near Qualicum. It was a Pacific Northwest spring, wet and cold, so it took a lot of stamina and determination. Whenever someone was driving that way, I'd send a care package of chowder and cornbread as a little pick-me-up. After walking 300 kilometers over two weeks, their voices joined over five thousand others on the lawn of the B.C. Legislature, rallying for wild salmon.

Few species have proven to be as central to the Pacific Northwest's foundation as wild salmon. Understanding the interconnectedness between the health of wild salmon populations and the survival of all living beings helps us recognize why this beautiful species must be protected. Yet, wild salmon populations have been drastically declining. Opposing open-net pen salmon farming is the first step in upholding the wild salmon economy that has formed the backbone of this region for centuries. Cosy's been a huge influence on me, completely impacting how we source sustainable salmon for SoBo's dishes.

CHINOOK SALMON
WITH CAULIFLOWER PURÉE AND PARSNIP PUFFS

The mighty king salmon is the star on this plate, but I like to complement it with vegetable sides —charred broccoli and cauliflower and cauliflower purée—and our parsnip puffs. The puffs come courtesy of our former sous-chef, Jeff Miller, when we were looking to create a savory doughnut, one without a hole, one that could change with the seasons. When he made these, we decided they weren't so much doughnuts as they were puffs. Puffs don't need to be explained—they are simply *puffy* and *delicious*. Their delicate nature working with the rustic qualities of the broccoli and cauliflower make for righteous yin and yang.

SERVES 4, WITH 12 PUFFS

Cauliflower Purée

½ head cauliflower, cut in small florets

½ small onion, diced

2 cups milk

2 Tbsp butter

1 tsp salt

Charred Cauliflower and Broccoli

½ head cauliflower, cut in bite-sized florets

1 lb broccoli, cut in bite-sized pieces with stalks

2 Tbsp olive oil

Salt

Parsnip Puffs

12 parsnips, peeled and diced large, or potatoes, butternut squash, celeriac or another starchy vegetable

1 Tbsp salt

⅔ cup butter, melted

1½ cups flour

3 cups canola oil, for frying

Prepare the cauliflower purée: In a medium saucepan over medium heat, bring the cauliflower, onions, milk, butter and salt to a lazy bubble and simmer for about 30 minutes, until the onions and cauliflower are tender.

Set aside to cool. I like to let the mixture cool down just because it's safer to handle. If you're short on time and need to blend right away, place a towel over the lid of the blender and hold it down tightly for extra security and pulse rather than blending continuously. Hot liquids like to blow the lid off blenders, and nobody wants the nickname Scarface. Besides, it's been used.

Char the cauliflower and broccoli: Preheat the oven to 400°F. Line a 9- × 13-inch baking dish with parchment paper.

In a medium bowl, toss the cauliflower and broccoli with the olive oil. In the lined baking dish, arrange the vegetables in a single layer, being careful not to overcrowd the dish. Roast for about 15 minutes, turning once halfway through, until charred. Remove from the oven (leaving at 400°F for the salmon) and lightly salt. Set aside until ready to serve.

Prepare the parsnip puffs: In a medium heavy-bottomed saucepan, bring the parsnips, salt and 6 cups cold water to a gentle boil. Cook for 10 to 15 minutes, until fork-tender. Drain.

Mash the parsnips using a food mill or potato masher. (You can use a food processor, but if you do, use the pulse setting and monitor, rather than just letting it blend. Like potatoes, parsnips can get gluey if you beat them for too long.) Set the purée aside.

continued on next page

Chinook Salmon

3 Tbsp canola oil

Four 6-oz portions wild Chinook salmon

1 tsp salt

1 lemon, halved

2 Tbsp butter

In a separate medium heavy-bottomed saucepan over medium heat, melt the butter. Add 1¾ cups water. When the mixture starts to boil, turn the heat to medium and whisk in the flour, a little bit at a time. As soon as all the flour is incorporated, stir vigorously with a wooden spoon. Continue stirring and cooking until the batter pulls away from the sides of the pan.

Add the parsnip purée and continue stirring until everything is well mixed. Remove from the heat. Once the batter is cool enough to handle, use a 4-oz ice cream scoop or your hands to roll it into smooth balls.

In a large heavy-bottomed saucepan, heat the canola oil to 325°F. Use a deep-fry thermometer or do the bread cube test (see sidebar page 257) to test the heat before carefully placing 3 or 4 balls in the pan. Fry for 3 to 4 minutes, until golden brown. Using a slotted spoon, transfer the puffs to paper towel to soak up any excess oil. Repeat this process with the remaining batter.

Tip: While you're getting used to the timing and technique, break the first puff open to make sure the batter is cooked all the way through; adjust cooking time accordingly.

Prepare the salmon: Heat the canola oil in a large ovenproof frying pan over medium-high heat. Season the salmon with the salt and place it in the hot pan. Do not overcrowd the pan. After 2 to 3 minutes, the salmon will start to naturally release from the pan. If it's still sticking, give it another minute or so.

Carefully turn the salmon pieces over. Squeeze lemon juice over the fish, add the butter to the pan and transfer to the oven for 3 to 5 minutes, depending on the thickness of the fish and desired doneness (see Cook's Note).

To serve: Spread the cauliflower purée on four plates and lay the salmon on top. Place charred broccoli and cauliflower around the fish, then drizzle the lemon butter from the pan on top. Finally, divide the parsnip puffs among the dishes (always add these last to keep them from getting soggy from the lemon butter). Enjoy!

COOK'S NOTE: Some salmon testing tips! I insert a metal skewer or thin knife into the cooked salmon for a couple of seconds, then withdraw it and feel the blade: if it's cold, the salmon needs to cook a few more minutes; if it's hot, the salmon is ready. I also lightly press down on the sides—like temperature-testing steaks: rare is super soft, and the flesh firms more as it cooks. Careful: if it's totally firm, you've likely overcooked it.

Seared Wild Salmon
WITH NEW POTATOES, BROCCOLINI AND PARSLEY SAUCE

Wild salmon is the life blood of many of our coastal families. The fight to protect wild salmon is a constant and ongoing campaign. I will always choose wild over farmed: wild is simply healthier for both our bodies and the environment. It's lower in saturated fats than farmed salmon, for one. What many consumers don't know is that packages labeled *Atlantic salmon* mean that the salmon was farmed. We are also starting to see farmed coho and Chinook, so do read the labels. This is a wonderfully basic and tremendously tasty dish. Parsley is full of nutritional value and is completely underused in most kitchens (but not in SoBo's!).

SERVES 4

Parsley Sauce

2 bunches fresh parsley

1 shallot, quartered

1 head Roasted Garlic (page 259)

½ cup white wine vinegar

¼ cup olive oil

1 tsp salt

Potatoes and Broccolini

1 lb new potatoes

1 bunch broccolini, cut in bite-sized pieces

Seared Wild Salmon

2 Tbsp olive oil

Four 8-oz fillets wild Chinook salmon

2 tsp salt

1 lemon, halved

2 Tbsp butter

Chive flower blossoms, for garnish (optional)

Prepare the parsley sauce: In a blender, blend all the ingredients until very smooth. Set aside until ready to serve.

Prepare the potatoes and broccolini: In a medium saucepan, bring 4 cups salted water to a boil. Add the potatoes, cover and turn the heat to medium-low. Simmer for about 15 minutes, until cooked through. Drain and let cool to room temperature. Slice into medallions.

In a separate medium saucepan, bring 4 cups salted water to a boil. Drop the broccolini into the water and cook for 2 minutes. Broccolini is quite nice nearly raw, so it doesn't need much cooking time. Remove from the water and set aside.

Cook the salmon: Preheat the oven to 400°F.

Heat the oil in a large ovenproof frying pan over medium-high heat. Season the salmon with the salt. Place the salmon in the pan, one piece at a time so that the pan stays hot enough for a good sear. Do not overcrowd the pan. After 2 to 3 minutes, the salmon will start to release from the pan (see Cook's Note). If it's still sticking, give it another minute or so.

Carefully flip the salmon pieces over. Squeeze the lemon on top, add the butter to the pan and transfer to the oven. Bake the salmon for 3 to 5 minutes, depending on the thickness of the fish and desired doneness (see Cook's Note on page 177).

To serve: While the fish is baking, reheat the vegetables in the oven alongside. (Don't reheat the parsley sauce: it's meant to be served room temperature and will turn brown if reheated.) Divide everything among four plates, garnish with the chive flowers, if desired, and enjoy.

COOK'S NOTE: A good sign that fish or seafood is ready to turn is that it has released from the pan. If you struggle to flip it over, the fish tears apart. I usually tell my cooks that the fish will tell you when it's time.

Seared Halibut, Black Beans, King Oyster Mushrooms and Almond Cream

When you want to serve a starch along with your fish, beans are an excellent option. When I crewed a private yacht around the Caribbean, I grew quite fond of this combination. Now I find it really helps my kitchen budget when I add beans to a dish with high-priced ingredients, such as king oyster mushrooms and halibut. As a bonus, the few dashes of premium olive oil give the luxurious mouthfeel often delivered by butter-laden sauces but with lower fat content.

SERVES 4

Black Beans

1 cup black beans, picked over and rinsed (see Cook's Note)

1 bay leaf

2 Tbsp chopped fresh chives

2 tsp salt

Almond Cream Sauce

1 onion, sliced

1 jalapeño pepper, finely diced

3 cups unsweetened almond milk

2 cloves garlic, minced

2 Tbsp cornstarch

1 Tbsp salt

¼ tsp ground mace

King Oyster Mushrooms

¼ cup olive oil

½ lb king oyster mushrooms, cleaned and sliced lengthwise in strips (see sidebar page 184)

1 tsp salt

Prepare the beans: In a medium saucepan over high heat, bring the black beans, bay leaf and 4 cups cold water to a boil, cover and turn the heat to low. Simmer for 1 hour or until tender. Drain and then immediately add the chives and salt, while the beans are hot. Set aside while you prepare the other recipe components.

Prepare the almond cream sauce: In a dry cast-iron skillet or grill pan over high heat, cook the onions for 4 to 5 minutes, until you achieve a dark char. Flip the onions and char the other side until very dark, but not burnt to a crisp.

In a medium saucepan over medium heat, add the charred onions, jalapeño, almond milk and garlic. Cook until the milk has reduced by about one-third.

In a small bowl, whisk the cornstarch with 2 Tbsp water, then pour into the milk mixture and whisk until combined. Bring to a boil, then turn the heat to simmer and cook for about 10 minutes, until the onions and jalapeño are completely tender. Season with the salt and mace. Remove from the heat and blend until smooth with an immersion blender or in a traditional blender. Return to the pot.

Cook the mushrooms: In a heavy-bottomed frying pan over high heat, heat the oil to its smoking point. Add the mushrooms in a single layer and cook like you would bacon: allowing the mushrooms to get crisp, then turning and crisping the other side. Season with the salt.

continued on next page

The Halibut

2 Tbsp canola oil

Four 6-oz portions halibut

1 tsp salt

1 lemon

Radish sprouts, for garnish (optional)

High-quality olive oil, for drizzling

Prepare the halibut: Heat the oven to 400°F.

In a large ovenproof frying pan over medium-high, heat the oil to its smoking point. Season the halibut with the salt. Place the halibut in the pan, one piece at a time so that the pan stays hot enough for a good sear. Do not overcrowd the pan. After 3 to 4 minutes, the halibut will start to release from the pan. Flip the pieces over, squeeze the lemon on top and transfer the pan to the oven. Bake the fish for 3 to 4 minutes, until slightly firm, with no translucent flesh.

To serve: Reheat the almond cream sauce over low heat. Add the mushrooms to the pot with the black beans and gently reheat. Arrange the beans and fish on four individual plates, then pour the almond cream sauce around the beans. Garnish with the radish sprouts, if desired, and a drizzle of the olive oil.

COOK'S NOTE: The last thing you need is to bite down on a pebble or rock. I put my dried beans on a rimmed baking sheet and shake it to separate out any stones. It just takes a keen eye and a tad of patience. I also always rinse dried beans in cool water just to remove any dust.

Pacific Halibut, Chanterelles and Corn Purée

I madly love, truly and deeply, the late summer/early fall here in the Pacific Northwest. The corn standing tall in the fields, the chanterelles popping up everywhere in the woods and shining an almost iridescent gold among all that green. A recurring theme of mine is to pair chanterelles with corn. Sweet and earthy—a divine combination that doesn't overpower the subtle nature of the halibut. (Did you know that a halibut's diet is mainly squid, clams and crab? With such a delicious diet, that's probably why it tastes so darn good.)

SERVES 4

Corn Purée

4 ears fresh corn, kernels cut off cob (page 258)

½ onion, finely diced

1 cup heavy cream

4–6 cloves Roasted Garlic (page 259)

1 tsp salt

The Halibut and Chanterelles

4 Tbsp olive oil, divided

Four 6-oz portions halibut

1 tsp salt

1 lemon, halved

2 Tbsp butter

1 shallot, minced

½ lb chanterelle mushrooms, cleaned and torn into bite-sized pieces (see sidebar page 184)

A few pea sprouts, radish slices or watercress sprigs, for garnish (optional)

Prepare the corn purée: In a medium saucepan over high heat, add the corn kernels, onions, heavy cream, roasted garlic and salt. Bring to a simmer and cook for 15 minutes. Set aside and let cool to room temperature.

Blend until smooth with an immersion blender or in a traditional blender.

Prepare the halibut and chanterelles: Preheat the oven to 400°F.

The halibut and chanterelles require the same amount of time to cook, so prepare their pans simultaneously.

In a large ovenproof frying pan over medium-high heat, heat 2 Tbsp of the olive oil to its smoking point.

Season the halibut with the salt. Place the halibut in the pan, one piece at a time so the pan stays hot enough for a good sear. Do not overcrowd the pan. After 3 to 4 minutes, the fish will start to release from the pan. Flip it over and squeeze the lemon on top. Transfer the pan to the oven. Bake the fish for 3 to 4 minutes, until slightly firm, with no translucent flesh.

Meanwhile, melt the remaining 2 Tbsp olive oil and the butter in a separate large frying pan over high heat. Add the shallots and mushrooms and cook for 5 to 10 minutes, until the mushrooms are cooked through. I like it when there is no butter or oil left in the pan and the mushrooms have a light caramelization. Season with the salt.

continued on next page

To serve: Place the corn purée on the plate, top with the chanterelles and halibut and, if desired, garnish with pea sprouts, radish slices or watercress sprigs.

CLEANING MUSHROOMS

Cleaning mushrooms is best done with a soft touch, in case they tear. Rinse under running water and use a soft, clean mushroom brush or tea towel. Some mushroom stems are edible, some are not. If choosing shiitakes, remove the stem and use in vegetable stock.

FRIED CHICKEN DINNER, SOUTHERN STYLE

Every time I make this fried chicken dinner, I can't help but smile thinking of my friend Andrew Morrison. Never met anyone in my life who loved the crispy, finger lickin' chicken as much as he did. When we worked together on the first SoBo cookbook, he could not stop rearranging all my chicken plates being photographed. I actually had to run him out of the kitchen so that our photographer, Jeremy, could get the shots. We would both yell "Andrew! Stop playing with the chicken!" A pure bird lover, he even took up birdwatching in the last few years of his life. This one is for him.

SERVES 4

Fried Chicken

3 cups buttermilk (see Cook's Note on page 248)

½ cup hot sauce (I like Frank's RedHot or Louisiana)

2 lb assorted chicken pieces (thighs, breasts, legs)

4 cups canola oil, for frying

1 cup cornstarch

3 egg whites, whisked

2 cups flour

2 Tbsp salt

1 Tbsp onion powder

1 Tbsp garlic powder

1 Tbsp sweet paprika

½ Tbsp fresh cracked black pepper

Brine the chicken: Whisk together the buttermilk and hot sauce. Place the chicken in the brining mixture and soak for 24 hours, in the fridge.

Prepare the coleslaw: In a medium bowl, whisk together the mayonnaise, orange juice, vinegar, olive oil, mustard seeds and ½ tsp of the salt.

In a separate medium bowl, toss together the cabbages, carrots, bell peppers, apples, mint and the remaining 1 tsp salt. Add the dressing and mix. The coleslaw can be stored in the fridge for up to 3 days.

Prepare the baked beans: Preheat the oven to 400°F.

In a small heavy-bottomed stockpot, bring 8 cups water, the navy beans and bay leaf to a boil. Turn the heat to low and cover. Simmer for 1 hour or until the beans are tender. Drain off about 90% of the water. Add the salt to the beans and set aside.

Heat the oil in a medium heavy-bottomed frying pan over high heat until it comes to its smoking point. Add the garlic, onions, bell peppers and chili. Sauté, using a wooden spoon to stir frequently to prevent sticking, until the mixture is softened. Deglaze with the bourbon. Allow the bourbon to fully evaporate, then stir in the tomato paste. Turn the heat to low and cook for 3 to 5 minutes, until the bourbon has evaporated.

Add the vegetable mixture to the cooked beans. Add the molasses and mustard, stirring well to incorporate all the ingredients. Pour the bean mixture into a large baking dish and bake for 30 minutes.

Fry the chicken: Remove the chicken from the buttermilk brine and pat very, very dry with paper towel.

continued on next page

Coleslaw

¼ cup mayonnaise

¼ cup orange juice

2 Tbsp apple cider vinegar

2 Tbsp extra virgin olive oil

1 tsp yellow mustard seeds

1½ tsp salt, divided

2 cups ultra-thinly-sliced green cabbage

½ cup ultra-thinly-sliced red cabbage

1 carrot, julienned

1 yellow bell pepper, julienned

1 apple, cored and julienned

½ cup torn fresh mint leaves

Southern Baked Beans

2 cups dried navy beans

1 bay leaf

2 tsp salt

¼ cup olive oil

3 cloves garlic, minced

1 onion, finely diced

1 green bell pepper, finely diced

1 serrano chili, minced

¼ cup bourbon

2 Tbsp tomato paste

¼ cup blackstrap molasses

¼ cup Dijon mustard

Biscuits and Honey Butter (page 248), for serving

Heat the oil in a deep cast-iron skillet or Dutch oven to 325°F—test it with a deep-fry thermometer.

Set up a breading station: Pie pans or large plates work well for this. Put the cornstarch in one pan and the egg whites in a second pan. Combine the flour, salt, onion powder, garlic powder, paprika and pepper in a third pan.

Working with one piece at a time, coat the chicken in cornstarch, then dip in the egg whites, and, finally, in the spiced flour mixture. Set aside.

Using a slotted spoon, very carefully lower a few pieces of chicken into the skillet and fry for about 15 minutes, until the internal temperature of the chicken registers as 165°F on an instant-read thermometer. Remove from the skillet and place on a wire rack or paper towel to cool. Repeat the process until all the chicken has been cooked.

To serve: This chicken is delicious either hot or cold. Serve with the baked beans, coleslaw, biscuits and honey butter.

COOK'S NOTE: Traditional Southern baked beans call for bacon. But I am not *that* traditional, and with so many folks eating a plant-based diet these days, who's going to get on my case for skipping the bacon? If you have an old-fashioned clay bean crock, this is the perfect time to dust it off and make it start working for a living.

BRAISED BEEF CHEEK TACOS

WITH BLACK BEAN SALSA

SoBo's first menu item was a fish taco with fresh fruit salsa. I remember, when I first came to Canada some 20 years ago, having to extoll the virtues of said taco. They just weren't on Canadian menus back then! And now this: Braised Beef Cheek Tacos with Black Bean Salsa. Are you ready for it? Beef cheeks, I should warn you, tend to be gelatinous. When they are cooked and then refrigerated, you might be alarmed by their slightly stiff consistency. Fear not. As soon as they are heated, they become tender again. You could certainly use a different cut of braising meat, such as pork shoulder or butt.

SERVES 4

Braised Beef Cheeks

¼ cup canola oil

2 lb beef cheeks (they typically weigh 1 lb each)

2 Tbsp salt

1 Tbsp ground cumin

1 Tbsp Ancho chili powder

1 Tbsp ground coriander

6 cloves garlic, minced

1 shallot, minced

½ onion, diced

1 bay leaf

1 cup dry red wine

2 cups coarsely chopped tomatoes

4 cups Beef Stock (page 254) or water

Black Bean Salsa

1 cup dried black beans

1 bay leaf

Salt

1 ear fresh corn, roasted and kernels cut off cob (page 258)

½ red bell pepper, finely diced

½ small white onion, finely diced

1 serrano chili, minced

2 Tbsp lime juice

A few sprigs fresh cilantro (optional)

Prepare the beef cheeks: Preheat the oven to 325°F.

Heat the oil in a large heavy-bottomed, ovenproof pan over medium-high heat. Season the cheeks with the salt, cumin, chili powder and coriander. Sear in the pan until golden brown, 3 to 5 minutes. Turn over and sear until the other side is deeply caramelized.

Remove the cheeks from the pan. Add the garlic, shallots, onions and bay leaf to the pan and sauté for 5 minutes or until everything is tender. Deglaze with the wine until the wine is reduced by half, then add the tomatoes and stock.

Return the beef cheeks to the pan and bring the mixture to a boil. Cover tightly and transfer to the oven. Cook until the cheeks are fork-tender, about 3 hours. Check halfway through to make sure the liquid hasn't evaporated; add 1 cup water if they are starting to dry out. Cheeks can take a very long time to get super tender, so patience is key. Remove from the oven, transfer the cheeks from the sauce to a plate and set aside to cool.

Transfer the pan of braising liquid to the stovetop and reduce by half over medium heat. If there are any little pools of fat, spoon these off. Remove from the heat. When the beef is cool enough to handle, shred it, then add the meat to the sauce.

Prepare the salsa: In a medium saucepan over high heat, bring the black beans, bay leaf and 4 cups cold water to a boil, cover and turn the heat to low. Gently simmer the beans for 1½ hours or until tender. Drain the liquid and season the beans with salt. In a bowl, combine the beans, corn, peppers, onions, chilies and lime juice. Add cilantro, if you like.

continued on next page

Tacos

12–16 fresh 6-inch corn tortillas
(see Cook's Note)

¼ green cabbage, shredded

Pickled Shallots (page 264)

To serve: In a cast-iron frying pan over high heat, heat 1 tortilla for about 30 seconds, until a few dark spots start to form but the tortilla is still pliable, before turning it over to warm the other side. (A cast-iron pan is perfect for this—no oil, just a hot, dry pan.)

Lay a clean tea towel on a plate and transfer the warmed tortilla to the plate. Fold the towel over to cover to keep warm. Warm the remaining tortillas, stacking one on top of the other on the plate. Return the sauce with the shredded beef to the stovetop and warm over medium heat.

Assemble the tacos: Spoon some of the shredded beef onto a tortilla and top with the salsa, cabbage and pickled shallots.

COOK'S NOTE: Here on Vancouver Island, we have a company called Abuelos Tortillas, in Comox, and its tortillas are *muy auténticos*, made with three simple ingredients: corn, lime and water. In general, for the freshest tortillas, you want to look for those with short shelf life!

Desserts

CHOCOLATE MASCARPONE COOKIES

This soft little delight is SoBo's fancy answer to the Oreo cookie question—assuming there even *was* a question in the first place!

Cookies

½ cup butter, room temperature

¼ cup granulated sugar

¾ cup flour

¼ cup cocoa powder

Mascarpone Filling

¾ cup mascarpone cheese

2 Tbsp icing sugar

¼ tsp pure vanilla extract (or for a variation, ¼ tsp coffee extract or ½ tsp instant espresso coffee granules)

Prepare the cookies: In a stand mixer fitted with the paddle attachment, cream the butter and sugar for 2 minutes.

Turn the stand mixer to low speed, and gradually add the flour and cocoa. Mix until just combined.

Using your hands, shape the dough into a flat 10-inch disk. Wrap tightly in plastic wrap and chill in the fridge for at least 30 minutes, or up to 4 days.

Preheat the oven to 325°F. Line a baking sheet with parchment paper.

On a lightly floured work surface, roll out the cookie dough to a ¼-inch thickness.

Using a 2-inch cookie cutter, cut out the cookies. Place the cookies on the prepared baking sheet, keeping them a few inches apart to help with heat circulation when baking, and put in the fridge to chill for 30 minutes. A fun idea: Just before baking, cut a small circle or other shape (maybe a crescent moon or a star) in the center of half of the cookies. This is purely for aesthetics.

Bake for 10 minutes or until the cookies are firm to the touch. Remove from the oven and let cool to room temperature on a wire rack while preparing the filling.

Prepare the filling: In a medium bowl, mix the mascarpone, icing sugar and vanilla together until smooth.

To serve: Spread a generous amount of the mascarpone filling on the bottom half of each cookie. Sandwich together by topping with another cookie.

COOKIE TIPS

At SoBo, I use a 4-oz ice cream scoop to portion my cookies, but my cookies are giant (and so are my portions of ice cream, come to think of it!). If you want smaller cookies, use a smaller scoop.

I whisk the dry ingredients, rather than sift, to ensure that the leavening agents are evenly distributed.

A stand mixer fitted with the paddle attachment works best for making cookie dough, but not every household has one. Standard electric beaters and a bowl will also work.

If you don't have, or want to use, cookie cutters, the cookie dough can also be rolled into cylinders and sliced.

SARAH DAVIES-LONG

To run a successful family restaurant, it helps to understand that you can't be good at everything. And while it's possible to search the internet to find people with the skills you need, it's so much better when a talented friend fits the bill. Sarah Davies-Long, who is a cherished friend and a designer, is one of those people for me. She came into my life early on, wanting to lend her design help back when I first had the SoBo food truck. It wasn't long before I was relying on her strong sense of style and design.

Sarah is a big part of the reason our first cookbook was such a success. Working alongside photographer (also her husband), Jeremy Koreski, she kept our shoots on schedule and in style. Her eye for particular details—linens, cutlery, dishes, backdrop—proved invaluable, especially on our first shoot in an off-grid cabin. We had to haul everything over by boat and through the forest—that takes a lot of organization (and a strong back)!

Sarah also always helps us with the challenge of softening a restaurant space that's based on glass and concrete. Her help with paint colors, furnishings and lighting injects soul and warmth into SoBo, and she continues to work to soften our noisy, echoey acoustics.

Sarah and Jeremy share a great love for the outdoors, healthy living and a commitment to eating well. They split their time between Tofino and the east coast of Vancouver Island, where Sarah is from and where they have a farm with horses and chickens and a large garden. Sarah's committed to growing a lot of her own food, which is something I can certainly get behind!

Friends like Sarah, with their numerous qualities and talents, have helped me survive running SoBo in all its incarnations these past 20 years. You can hire someone to cut onions or paint a room, but you can't hire someone to love you. I know that Sarah loves me.

SALTED CARAMEL CASHEW COOKIES

This cookie is sweet and salty and extremely tender. A melt-in-your-mouth kind of cookie. This is a three-part recipe: you start by making the cookie dough, then let it chill while you roast the nuts and prepare the caramel.

MAKES 8 COOKIES

Cookies

⅔ cup butter, room temperature

⅔ cup granulated sugar

⅔ cup brown sugar

1 egg

1⅓ cups cashew butter

1 tsp pure vanilla extract

2 cups flour

½ tsp baking soda

½ tsp salt

1 cup semisweet chocolate chips

Candied Cashews

1⅔ cups raw cashews, divided

½ tsp plus ⅛ tsp salt, divided

2 Tbsp plus 2 tsp granulated sugar

1 Tbsp butter

½ tsp pure vanilla extract

Caramel

⅓ cup whipping cream

2 tsp butter, melted

½ tsp pure vanilla extract

¼ tsp salt

1 cup granulated sugar

Prepare the cookie dough: In a stand mixer fitted with the paddle attachment, cream the butter and sugars on medium speed for 4 to 5 minutes. (See sidebar page 197.) Add the egg, cashew butter and vanilla. Mix for 1 minute on medium speed.

In a medium bowl, whisk together the flour, baking soda and salt. With the stand mixer on low speed, gradually add the dry ingredients to the butter mixture, being careful not to overmix. Fold in the chocolate chips until just incorporated.

Using a 4-oz ice cream scoop, portion the dough into balls. Line a baking sheet with parchment paper, and place the dough balls on the prepared baking sheet. Put in the fridge to chill for 1 hour.

Roast the cashews: Preheat the oven to 300°F.

On a baking sheet, arrange ⅔ cup of the cashews and sprinkle with ½ tsp of the salt. Roast in the oven for 8 to 12 minutes, until golden. Remove from the oven and set aside.

In a medium frying pan over high heat, bring the remaining 1 cup cashews, the remaining ⅛ tsp salt, the sugar, ⅓ cup water, the butter and vanilla to a boil. Turn the heat to medium-high and continue to cook, stirring occasionally, until the water has evaporated, about 5 to 10 minutes.

Line a baking sheet with parchment paper. Arrange the cashew mixture on the prepared baking sheet and bake for 10 minutes or until golden. Remove the candied cashews from the oven and let cool to room temperature on the sheet.

In a food processor, pulse the roasted cashews and candied cashews (or put them in a bag and roll over with a rolling pin). You are looking for a chunky texture. Set aside.

continued on next page

Prepare the caramel: In a large heat-resistant bowl, whisk the whipping cream, butter, vanilla and salt. Set aside.

In a small heavy-bottomed saucepan over low heat, dissolve the sugar in ⅓ cup water.

Turn the heat to medium-low and bring the mixture to a simmer. At this stage, you want to avoid stirring, otherwise the mixture will seize and become a big lump. If sugar crystals form on the side of the saucepan, gently dissolve them with a damp pastry brush. Cook the mixture until it is amber in color.

Remove from the heat. Place a tea towel under the bowl of whipping cream to protect your work surface and pour in the hot sugar water. Be very careful with this step! The mixture will foam up and expand before it becomes the thick caramel you are looking for. Let cool to room temperature before using.

Bake the cookies: Preheat the oven to 325°F.

Take the cookie dough out of the fridge. Using your hands, press the dough balls to flatten.

Spread the candied cashews in a pie pan or saucer. Working with one cookie at a time, press one side into the cashews, then return to the sheet, nut side up. Keep the cookies a few inches apart to allow for spreading. Bake for 12 minutes, rotating the sheet halfway through.

Remove from the oven. While the cookies are still warm, use the back of a spoon to gently press down in the center to make a small well. Spoon the thick, gooey caramel into the well.

Fruit and Nut Cookie, page 203

Vegan Chocolate Almond Cookie, page 202

Salted Caramel Cashew Cookie, page 199

VEGAN CHOCOLATE ALMOND COOKIES

Here's the thing: studies have suggested that people on vegan diets have lower body mass indexes than omnivores, and experience lower levels of total cholesterol, LDL-cholesterol and glucose when compared with nonvegans. If all that means you can happily indulge in a Vegan Chocolate Almond Cookie or two, or even three—that's music to my ears! All I know is that they're mighty tasty. *Pictured on page 201.*

MAKES 8 COOKIES

1½ cups spelt flour

½ cup all-purpose flour

¼ cup cocoa powder, sifted

1½ tsp baking soda

1½ tsp baking powder

½ tsp salt

¼ tsp cream of tartar

¾ cup maple syrup

½ cup plus 1 Tbsp canola oil

1 Tbsp apple cider vinegar

2 tsp pure vanilla extract

1 cup 70% dark chocolate chips

½ cup coarsely chopped toasted almonds (see sidebar page 216)

Preheat the oven to 325°F.

In a large bowl, mix together all the dry ingredients except the chocolate chips and almonds.

In a separate bowl, mix the wet ingredients together. Add the wet ingredients to the dry ingredients, mixing only until combined—try to mix as little as possible. Gently fold in the chocolate and almonds.

Line a baking sheet with parchment paper. Using a 4-oz ice cream scoop, portion the dough into 8 cookies and place on the prepared baking sheet. Keep the cookies a few inches apart to allow for spreading.

Bake for 12 minutes, rotating the sheet halfway through.

Remove from the oven and let cool to room temperature on the baking sheet for 15 minutes before trying to remove them, as they can be quite fragile until they are cooled.

FRUIT AND NUT COOKIES

This is a cookie packed with goodies and goodness. I have been known to take them with me camping and hiking—occasions where I might need to refuel in a hurry. Thanks to the xanthan gum in place of eggs as a binding agent, this recipe is vegan-friendly and can easily be made gluten-free by using gluten-free oats. *Pictured on page 201.*

MAKES 8 COOKIES

⅓ cup coconut oil

1⅓ cups rolled oats

1⅓ cups brown sugar

1 cup toasted almonds (see sidebar page 216)

⅔ cup toasted pumpkin seeds (see sidebar page 216)

⅔ cup toasted sunflower seeds (see sidebar page 216)

⅔ cup dark chocolate chips

⅔ cup chopped dried fruit (raisins, chopped figs and/or dates)

⅓ cup toasted coconut flakes (see sidebar page 216)

3 Tbsp ground flaxseed

1 tsp baking soda

1 tsp ground cinnamon

1 tsp salt

¼ tsp xanthan gum

⅓ cup soy, almond or oat milk

3 Tbsp canola oil

3 Tbsp molasses

3 Tbsp maple syrup

Preheat the oven to 325°F.

In a small saucepan over medium heat, heat the coconut oil until it melts. Remove from the heat and set aside.

In a large bowl, whisk together all the dry ingredients.

In a small bowl, whisk together all the wet ingredients.

Pour the wet ingredients into the dry ingredients and mix well, using a wooden spoon or rubber spatula.

Line a baking sheet with parchment paper. Using a 4-oz ice cream scoop, portion the dough into 8 cookies. Place on the prepared baking sheet. Keep the cookies a few inches apart to allow for spreading.

Bake for 12 minutes, rotating the sheet halfway through. Remove from the oven and transfer to a wire rack to cool before eating.

TRIPLE CHOCOLATE CHIP COOKIES

Tell me who in this world doesn't love a chocolate chip cookie? While semisweet chocolate chips are standard, I have grown fond of mixing different intensities of chocolate. The slightly bitter dark with the crunchy bits of cocoa nibs makes this cookie a standout instead of standard.

MAKES 8 COOKIES

⅓ cup butter, room temperature

1 cup brown sugar

½ cup granulated sugar

1 tsp pure vanilla extract

1 egg

2½ cups flour

1 tsp baking soda

1 tsp baking powder

1 tsp salt

⅓ cup cacao nibs

⅓ cup 70% dark chocolate chips

⅓ cup milk chocolate chips

⅓ cup white chocolate chips

Preheat the oven to 325°F.

Using a stand mixer fitted with the paddle attachment, cream the butter and sugars on low speed until smooth and pale, about 3 to 5 minutes.

Add the vanilla and egg. Mix for 1 minute more.

In a medium bowl, whisk together the flour, baking soda, baking powder and salt.

With the stand mixer on low speed, gradually add the flour mixture to the creamed butter, mixing until well incorporated.

Using a wooden spoon or rubber spatula, fold in the cacao nibs and chocolate chips.

Line a baking sheet with parchment paper. Using a 4-oz ice cream scoop, portion the dough into 8 cookies and place on the prepared baking sheet. Keep the cookies a few inches apart to allow for spreading. Using the heel of your palm, flatten the cookies a bit.

Bake for 12 minutes, rotating the sheet halfway through. Remove from the oven and transfer the cookies to a wire rack to cool for at least 10 minutes before eating.

CHOCOLATE MOUSSE TARTS

These decadent, chocolatey tarts are both gluten-free and vegan, so you can have your tarts and eat them too. Vegan butter is often available in grocery stores, but you can easily make your own (page 249) and get double the satisfaction from that first (and second, and third . . .) bite. These are ridiculously rich. Enjoy!

MAKES EIGHT TO TWELVE
3-INCH TARTS OR ONE
10-INCH TART

Tart Shells

2 cups ground almonds

1 cup unsweetened shredded coconut

½ cup gluten-free flour

½ cup cocoa powder

½ cup brown sugar

1 tsp baking powder

¼ cup Vegan Butter (page 249)

¼ cup coconut oil

6 Tbsp almond or oat milk

1 Tbsp pure vanilla extract

Mousse

½ cup dark chocolate chips

4 ripe avocados

½ cup cocoa powder

½ cup maple syrup

2 tsp pure vanilla extract

¼ tsp salt

Fresh raspberries or strawberries, for serving

¼ cup dark chocolate chips, melted in a bain-marie, for drizzling

Prepare the tart shells: Place the almonds and coconut in a food processor, and process until fine. Transfer to a large bowl. Add the flour, cocoa, brown sugar and baking powder and mix well.

In a small saucepan over low heat, melt the vegan butter and oil, stirring with a wooden spoon to combine. Stir in the almond milk and vanilla.

Pour the liquid mixture into the dry ingredients, stirring as you pour. Mix well, using a wooden spoon, until everything is well incorporated. Set aside and allow to cool to room temperature.

Preheat the oven to 350°F.

For individual tarts: In 3-inch fluted tart pans with removable bottoms (or muffin pans), scoop a scant ¼ cup of the dough and press into the pans, taking care to also press it into the fluted sides, with your fingertips. *Alternatively, for one large tart:* Press the dough into the large tart pan with a removable bottom.

Chill the pastry in the fridge for 15 minutes. Bake individual tarts for 10 minutes, or one large tart for 15 to 20 minutes, or until the pastry feels firm to the touch. Remove from the oven and set aside to cool.

Prepare the mousse: Place the chocolate chips in a medium heatproof bowl. Place a saucepan filled with 2 inches of water over medium heat and bring the water to a boil. Cover the bowl of chocolate chips and place it over the boiling water in the saucepan, making sure the bottom of the bowl does not touch the water. Melt the chocolate chips in this bain-marie, adjusting the heat so the water remains at a low simmer. Once the chocolate chips have melted, set them aside to cool.

Process the avocados, cocoa, maple syrup, vanilla and salt in a food processor until smooth. Add the melted chocolate, and process again until smooth.

To serve: Remove the tart shells from the pans. Spoon the mousse into the cooled shells. Top with the raspberries or strawberries and a drizzle of the melted chocolate chips.

FRESH RHUBARB TARTS

Many rhubarb varieties have stalks that are actually more green or wishy-washy pink than they are red. This can be disappointing if you are counting on presenting a dessert that announces itself as beautiful, passionate, vigorous and prone to impulsive actions (i.e. red). The simple addition of a splash of beet juice turns dull greenish-brown rhubarb into a beautiful full-on assertive red. Bonus: it will also add a sweet, earthy flavor.

MAKES SIX TO EIGHT 3-INCH TARTS OR ONE 10-INCH TART

Sweet Tart Dough

¾ cup butter, very cold, cut in small cubes

½ cup sugar

2 egg yolks

2 cups cake and pastry flour

1 tsp salt

Vanilla Pastry Cream

½ cup whipping cream

½ cup milk

½ vanilla bean, seeded (see sidebar), both the seeds and pod

3 egg yolks

3 Tbsp sugar

1½ Tbsp cornstarch

2 Tbsp butter

Stewed Rhubarb

4–5 stalks thin red rhubarb

¼–½ cup sugar, or to taste (see Cook's Note)

1 Tbsp beet juice (optional)

¼ cup sweet cicely, tender stems and leaves (optional, see Cook's Note)

Prepare the dough: In a medium bowl, combine the butter and sugar. Using a stand mixer with a paddle attachment or your hands, mix on low speed for a couple of minutes. Gradually add the eggs, flour and salt until just barely mixed. Form the dough into a cylinder shape 2 inches in diameter, wrap in plastic wrap and chill in the fridge for at least 30 minutes.

Prepare the pastry cream: In a medium saucepan over medium heat, combine the whipping cream, milk and vanilla seeds and pod. Heat until steaming but not boiling.

In a separate bowl, whisk together the egg yolks, sugar and cornstarch.

When the milk mixture is hot, pour about half of it into the egg mixture while whisking vigorously. (This is called tempering; it reduces the chance of the yolks curdling.) Pour the egg mixture into the saucepan with the milk. Turn the heat to low and cook for 2 to 4 minutes, whisking constantly until the mixture thickens.

Strain into a clean bowl. Add the butter and whisk until smooth. Cover with a piece of plastic wrap so that it touches the surface of the pastry cream: this will prevent a skin from forming. Chill in the fridge for at least 2 hours.

Stew the rhubarb: Cut the rhubarb into 3-inch-long pieces. If your rhubarb is particularly thick, you can slice the stalk lengthwise so that it will cook evenly.

In a medium heatproof bowl (try to find one that will fit into the saucepan without touching the bottom), toss the rhubarb with the sugar and beet juice, if desired.

continued on next page

Meanwhile, place a saucepan filled with 2 inches of water over medium heat and bring the water to a boil.

Cover the bowl of rhubarb and place it with the sweet cicely, if desired, over the boiling water in the saucepan (this is called a bain-marie), making sure the bottom of the bowl does not touch the water. Adjust the heat so the water remains at a low simmer.

Gently cook the rhubarb until *just* tender. You do not want to overcook it or the rhubarb will fall apart. After 8 minutes, check if it is tender. If it's not quite there yet, cook for another 3 minutes and check again. Keep an eye on this, as you do not want to miss hitting the sweet spot of tenderness! Remove the bowl from the heat. Let the rhubarb cool to room temperature, then refrigerate until needed.

Preheat the oven to 375°F.

For individual tarts: Cut a ½-inch-thick slice from the dough cylinder. Place between two pieces of plastic wrap and, using a rolling pin, roll to a ¼-inch thickness. Transfer to a 3-inch tart pan and use your fingers to press the dough to line the pan. Trim any overhanging dough from the edges. Repeat with the remaining dough.

Alternatively, for one large tart: Pat the dough cylinder with your hands to flatten into one large disk, following the same wrapping and rolling technique as above, rolling to 12 inches wide. Transfer to a 10-inch tart pan and press and trim as above.

Chill the pastry in the fridge for 15 minutes.

Bake the individual tarts for 7 to 10 minutes, or one large tart for 15 minutes, until a pale golden brown.

To serve: Fill the tart shell(s) with the pastry cream and top with stewed rhubarb.

COOK'S NOTE: Sweet cicely was once a widely cultivated culinary herb but is now only occasionally grown in the herb garden. As a culinary herb, it is a valuable sweetener, especially for diabetics and many others who are trying to reduce their sugar intake. The fern-like leaves smell of aniseed when crushed. When you add it to stewed rhubarb, it will cut through the acidity of the rhubarb; you can then decrease by half the amount of sugar you would normally add.

How to Split and Seed a Vanilla Bean

To remove the seeds from a vanilla bean, use a paring knife to slice the pod in half lengthwise. Use the back edge of the knife (the duller side) to scrape the seeds off the pod. If you're not using the pod for this recipe, don't discard!—stick in your sugar jar and let its essence infuse the sugar. Or add it to a bottle of vodka and make your own pure vanilla extract. (You will need whole vanilla pods, seeds and all, to make an extract with any strength, but it won't hurt to start a collection of scraped vanilla pods to supplement the whole pods—when it comes to vanilla, every little bit is gold!) Homemade vanilla makes a fabulous gift, especially nowadays when you practically have to remortgage your house to buy the smallest bottle of pure vanilla extract.

COOK'S NOTE: To chiffonade mint leaves, simply stack 10 or so leaves and roll them up tightly like a cigar. Use a sharp knife to slice lengthwise across the roll. Fluff with your fingertips to separate the slices.

GRILLED PEACH AND RASPBERRY MELBA

This dessert conjures up memories of endless July days of 100°F Texan heat, when the air is dripping with humidity and there's *got* to be a breeze and it's just so darn hot that ice cream is the only thing that makes more sense than air-conditioning. Peaches were the high point of my childhood summers. We didn't often have raspberries in our house—they are not well adapted to Texas conditions—but when we did, and when this treat was set before me after a Sunday family dinner, I was in peach and raspberry and ice cream heaven. My mom would always fancy up this simple recipe by finding the coolest glassware to present it in. It seemed to my eight-year-old self the height of elegance. I love to modernize retro classics, so my spin on original peach melba involves grilling or broiling the peaches instead of poaching them.

SERVES 4

Melba Sauce

2 cups frozen or fresh raspberries

½ cup sugar

¼ cup orange juice

½ tsp salt

The Melba

4 lusciously ripe peaches, halved and pitted

Oil, for brushing (optional)

1 pint vanilla ice cream (page 213)

1 pint fresh raspberries, for garnish (optional)

¼ cup fresh mint leaves, chiffonade (see Cook's Note), for garnish (optional)

Prepare the melba sauce: In a small heavy-bottomed saucepan over medium heat, combine the raspberries, sugar, orange juice and salt. Cook down until the sugar has melted and raspberries are softened, about 5 to 10 minutes, then stir with a wooden spoon.

Remove from the heat and let cool to room temperature. Using an immersion blender or in a traditional blender, blend the sauce until smooth. This sauce can be made in advance and stored in the fridge for up to 1 week.

Grill the peaches: Brush the cut sides of the fruit with oil. Place the peaches on the grill (you can use a gas or charcoal grill or an indoor grill pan) cut side down over direct heat until the flesh develops grill marks and starts to soften, about 3 to 5 minutes. Brush the skins with oil, then flip the peaches and grill for another 2 to 3 minutes. The skin will loosen, and you can ease it off.

Alternatively, you can broil the peaches: Preheat the broiler or oven to 500°F. Keep the ice cream and melba sauce on hand. Place the peaches skin side down in a broiler pan. Set the pan under the broiler or in the oven for 3 to 4 minutes. Once the tops of the peaches start to caramelize, they are ready.

To serve: Once the peaches are hot and bubbly, assemble your dessert any way you'd like it. I'm a sauce-on-the-bottom-hot-peaches-then-ice-cream-on-top kind of girl.

Garnish with raspberries and fresh mint chiffonade, if you desire.

ICE CREAM SANDWICHES

A strange thing happens at SoBo in the summer around eight o'clock in the evening. The place fills with groups of giggling, glassy-eyed groovy folk ready to succumb to the major munchie attack via our homemade ice cream sandwiches. Watching them try to choose between mint chocolate chip, caramel swirl, fudge brownie, roasted strawberry, cherry chocolate chunk—our flavors are endless—is most entertaining. Pure joy! Tip: Prepare the ice cream a day ahead and let it get nice and hard. And the best ice cream sandwiches marry the perfect firmness of ice cream with the toothsome (read: chewy, *not* rock solid) texture. Crisp cookies crumble, making the sandwich difficult to handle, which could mean a buzzkill for your buzz. Or make the evening even more entertaining.

MAKES 8 SANDWICHES

Plain Ole Vanilla Ice Cream

4 egg yolks

1 cup sugar

1 tsp salt

1 vanilla bean, seeded (see sidebar page 209), both the seeds and pod

1½ cups milk

1½ cups heavy cream

Chewy Chocolate Cookies

1 cup butter, room temperature

½ cup sugar

1 egg

1½ cups flour

½ cup cocoa powder

Prepare the ice cream: In a bowl, whisk together the egg yolks, sugar, salt and vanilla seeds.

In a medium saucepan over medium heat, bring the milk, cream and vanilla pod to a simmer. Do not let the mixture come to a boil. Remove the milk mixture from the heat and, very slowly, ladle ¼ cup at a time into the egg mixture, constantly whisking until well incorporated. (This is called tempering; it reduces the chance of the yolks curdling.)

Return the pot to the stovetop and simmer the mixture, stirring constantly with a wooden spoon. Watch and tend your base so that the eggs do not curdle. The mixture is ready when it registers as 165°F on an instant-read thermometer. (No thermometer? Cook, stirring, until the mixture has sufficiently thickened and coats the back of a wooden spoon.)

Using a fine-mesh strainer, strain the mixture into a bowl to remove any curdled egg. Place the bowl in an ice bath, without allowing any water to infiltrate the mixture. Let chill on the ice bath for 1 hour, then cover the bowl and refrigerate 2 to 3 hours, or overnight.

For processing, follow the manufacturer's instructions for your ice cream maker. If you do not have an ice cream maker, pour the mixture into a shallow freezer-proof container, cover and place in the freezer. Take it out every 30 minutes and mix well with a hand blender. (If you have to stir by hand, well then, stir like crazy.) Repeat 4 to 6 times for a creamy result.

continued on next page

Prepare the cookies: In a stand mixer fitted with the paddle attachment, cream the butter and sugar for 2 minutes. Add the egg and continue beating until incorporated.

With the stand mixer on low speed, gradually add the flour and cocoa. Mix until just combined.

Shape the dough into a 10-inch disk and chill in the fridge, covered in plastic wrap, for at least 30 minutes.

Preheat the oven to 325°F. Line a baking sheet with parchment paper.

Roll out the dough on a lightly floured work surface to a ¼-inch thickness.

Use a 2-inch cookie cutter to cut out the cookies. Arrange the cookies on the prepared baking sheet 2 inches apart from one another to allow for spreading and transfer to the fridge to chill for 30 minutes.

Bake for 10 minutes or until the cookies are firm to the touch, though they should still look a tad undercooked. Let the cookies cool on a wire rack for 1 hour before assembling the ice cream sandwiches.

Assemble the sandwiches: Place a scoop of ice cream on the flat side of a cookie, then top with another cookie, flat side down. Press down to flatten.

ICE CREAM VARIATIONS

You can easily add flavoring to the ice cream base, if desired. (Although, then it won't be Plain Ole Vanilla Ice Cream anymore, which was the whole point to begin with.) But there are no rules here, only effects. No, wait a minute. There *is* one rule. Have fun!

VARIATION CHOCOLATE CHUNK

½ cup dark chocolate chips or chunks

Omit the vanilla bean. Once the ice cream base is almost frozen, fold in the chocolate chips and continue to freeze until solid.

VARIATION ROASTED STRAWBERRIES

1 cup whole strawberries (always use fresh when in season, but frozen will also do)

3 Tbsp sugar

Preheat the oven to 300°F. In a small bowl, toss together the strawberries and sugar. Let sit for 1 hour to macerate (so the sugar melts into the strawberries).

Line a baking sheet with parchment paper. Spread the strawberries on the sheet, and roast for 1 hour, stirring every 15 minutes to prevent burning. They should be soft all the way to the center.

Remove from the oven and let cool to room temperature for 1 hour. When the ice cream base is about half frozen, fold in the roasted strawberries and continue to freeze until solid.

VARIATION CARAMEL SWIRL

¼ cup whipping cream

1 tsp butter

¼ tsp pure vanilla extract

Pinch salt

¾ cup sugar

In a large heat-resistant bowl, whisk together the whipping cream, butter, vanilla and salt. Set aside.

In a small heavy-bottomed saucepan over low heat, place the sugar in ¼ cup water to dissolve. Bring to a simmer. Avoid stirring. If sugar crystals form on the sides of the saucepan, gently dissolve them with a damp pastry brush. Cook the mixture until it is amber in color.

Remove from the heat. Place a tea towel under the bowl of whipping cream to protect your work surface and pour in the hot sugar water. Be very careful with this step! The mixture will foam up and expand before becoming the thick caramel you're looking for. Let cool to room temperature.

Allow the ice cream base to freeze halfway, so that it resembles pudding. Fold in the caramel and continue to freeze until solid.

ROOT BEER FLOAT

Yet another perfect use for Plain Ole Vanilla Ice Cream (page 213), and the tastiest chemistry experiment for kids. That satisfying foam comes from a carbonation process called nucleation —but understanding thermodynamics isn't going to affect the pleasure you get from that first sip of a frothy ice cream float in an ice-cold mug. Ya know?

MAKES 1 FLOAT

2 hearty scoops Plain Ole Vanilla Ice Cream (page 213)

1 bottle root beer or other soda (I like Phillips Soda Works)

Put the ice cream in a frozen mug (I use a glass beer mug). Pour the root beer on top. Ever. So. Slowly. So you can control the foam more carefully and it doesn't erupt over the sides of your glass. Don't love root beer? Try orange soda. Think Creamsicle.

TOASTING SEEDS, NUTS AND MORE

Toasting seeds, nuts and other goodies for your baked goods is a great way to deepen the flavor and add a crisp texture. All you need to do is preheat your oven to 325°F, spread your raw ingredient on a baking sheet and pop it into the oven. Times will vary for each ingredient, but you essentially want to remove the ingredient from the oven the moment they start to color.

Almonds: 7 minutes

Coconut flakes or sunflower seeds: 3 to 4 minutes

Hazelnuts: 5 to 10 minutes

Pumpkin seeds or walnuts: 4 to 5 minutes

With hazelnuts, you'll want to immediately wrap them in a clean tea towel, setting aside to steam for 1 minute. Rub them in the towel to remove loose skins (don't worry about skins that don't come off). Set aside, still wrapped, to let cool to room temperature completely.

TOASTED HAZELNUT BROWNIES

These brownies are super dense and fudge-like. Oftentimes, when I make a batch, they're so dense and rich that I cut them into bite-sized pieces. Hazelnuts are one of the amazing ingredients grown here on Vancouver Island, so I am especially fond of showcasing them, to support local growers. If you want to be extra decadent, serve these with caramel ice cream.

MAKES 8 REGULAR-SIZED BROWNIES (OR 32 BITE-SIZED BROWNIES)

Brownies

2 cups semisweet chocolate chips, divided

¾ cup butter

3 eggs

1½ cups sugar

1½ tsp pure vanilla extract

¾ cup flour

¾ tsp baking powder

¾ cup toasted hazelnuts (see sidebar)

Ganache

1 cup chocolate chips (semisweet, bittersweet or 70% dark)

1 cup whipping cream

Prepare the brownies: Preheat the oven to 325°F.

Fill a medium saucepan halfway with water and bring to a simmer. Put 1¼ cups chocolate chips and butter in a medium heat-resistant bowl. Place the bowl over the pan with simmering water to melt the chocolate chips and butter.

In a large bowl, whisk together the eggs, sugar and vanilla. Add the melted chocolate mixture and whisk together.

In a medium bowl, whisk together the flour, baking powder, the remaining ¾ cups chocolate chips and the hazelnuts. Pour the dry ingredients into the wet ingredients and stir with a wooden spoon until just incorporated. Do not overmix.

Line a 9- × 13-inch baking pan with parchment paper. Pour the brownie mixture into the pan and bake for 30 minutes, rotating the pan halfway through. Remove from the oven and let cool to room temperature for 1 hour.

Prepare the ganache: Place the chocolate chips in a medium heatproof bowl.

Heat the cream in a small heavy-bottomed saucepan until it comes to a gentle simmer. Be careful not to overheat the cream: if it boils, it will be too hot to make the ganache.

Immediately pour the warm cream over the chocolate chips. Let sit for 2 minutes, then stir until smooth.

To serve: Pour the ganache over the cooled brownie slab. Let it sit for about 1 hour before serving (if you can wait that long).

CHERRY PIE

I once read that there was another line after the saying "Another day, another dollar" and that was "I'm tired and I want pie." I didn't write down the source and now do you think I can find where I read it? Not a hope. Part of me wonders if I made that part up. It could be my mantra. I don't eat a lot of dessert, but when I do, it's got to be out-of-this-freakin'-world, otherwise I am content with a modest square of dark chocolate. But every summer, when the livin' is easy, and the ripest fruit is highest on the tree, I will indulge: a slice of cherry pie, then, a few weeks later, a slice of peach pie. If I had to offer just one tip for the crust dough, it would be this: *Do not overwork it!* Channel our pastry chef, Jennifer Scott, when you make this tender, flaky crust.

MAKES 1 PIE

Jen's Pie Crust

MAKES 1 DOUBLE CRUST

(for a single pie crust, halve the recipe)

2½ cups flour

1 Tbsp sugar

1 cup salted butter, very cold, cubed (see Cook's Note)

¾ cup ice water

Filling

6–8 cups (about 1½ lb) fresh cherries, pitted and quartered (see Cook's Note)

¾–1 cup sugar (see Cook's Note)

Juice of 1 orange

¼ cup cherry or orange liqueur (I like kirsch or Grand Marnier)

1 tsp salt

4 Tbsp cornstarch

Prepare the pastry: In a large bowl, whisk together the flour and sugar. Add the butter. Using your hands, two forks or a pastry blender, cut the butter into the flour mixture until it is the size of peas. They won't all be uniform in size, but that's okay: you want to avoid warming up the butter too much.

Add the ice water all at once and gently knead the dough until it just comes together (I repeat: Do not overwork the dough!).

With floured hands, divide the dough in half. Form into two disks, wrap each disk tightly in plastic wrap and chill in the fridge for at least 1 hour.

When you're ready to roll the dough, take the disks out of the fridge and let them rest on the countertop for at least 15 minutes, to take the chill off them. If you roll out cold dough, it will crack and leak.

Lightly flour a clean work surface and roll out one of the disks to a 13-inch-diameter circle. Transfer to a 9-inch pie plate and trim the edges to fit the plate. *For a double crust recipe:* Roll out the second piece of pastry to a 13-inch diameter circle and place in the fridge to chill while you prepare the filling.

Preheat the oven to 400°F.

Prepare the filling: In a large bowl, using a wooden spoon, gently mix together the cherries, sugar (see Cook's Note), orange juice, liqueur and salt. Add the cornstarch and gently toss until the cornstarch is evenly distributed.

continued on next page

Assemble the pie: Pour the filling into the prepared pie crust. Pile it up a bit in the center.

Place the second pie crust over the filling and press around the edges to seal the filling. Use kitchen scissors to trim the excess crust to a 1-inch overhang, then fold the overhang under itself to form an edge. Using your fingertips, crimp the dough along the rim of the pie plate. With a paring knife, cut a few slits in the center of the top crust to allow steam to escape.

Place the pie on a baking sheet to capture any spillage. Bake on the lower rack of the oven for 20 minutes.

COOK'S NOTE: Vegetable shortening or lard make for a traditionally tender-flaky crust, but I am a butter lover, so it is always butter for me. Much trickier to get a tender result, but once you have mastered the art of flakiness, you will be a butter convert! The best cherries for pie are the freshest, ripest you can find. I love a tart cherry, but their season is so short and they are not commonly found in supermarkets. Bing cherries or Rainier are widely available. If using these sweeter varieties, cut the sugar back to ¾ cup.

JENNIFER SCOTT

Even before there was SoBo, there was Jennifer Scott. I met Jen 20 years ago, when I first arrived in Tofino. She was interviewing to be the pastry chef for a new restaurant we were opening, and brought along some photos of wedding cakes she'd made. We sat down for coffee and almost immediately started talking kids: I was a new mom and Jen had three young children, including twin boys. I don't recall if I ever looked at those cake pictures, but I did hire her immediately and we've been colleagues—but most importantly, friends—ever since.

Jen has been the baker and pastry chef at SoBo since we opened our downtown Tofino location. Her baked goods and desserts hit every note for me —they're homey and comforting and made with the finest ingredients. They don't hide behind anything but good flavor, the polar opposite of the molecular gastronomy that was so trendy at the time.

Jen trained to be a cook in college—she had plans to work up north as a camp cook, which really speaks to her adventurous spirit—but soon realized that her forte was baking. She built these skills by taking as many courses as time and money would allow. Jen is such a natural in the kitchen and so organized, and her skills are solid, so I try to bring her along whenever I have to work out of town. I know she can handle whatever tasks I throw at her, even if that means prepping a meal or churning out ice cream for a hundred guests.

On a typical SoBo day, Jen arrives around 7 a.m., after riding her bike to town—year-round, in all weather—and working out at the gym. She gets right down to it on those quiet mornings, prepping the baking for the day, ensuring that the workstations are spotless and that we're organized. (That girl loves her labeler!) This speaks so much to Jen's commitment and work ethic. In our friendship and in our working relationship, she is always there for me and the rest of the restaurant staff. Jen has our backs.

PEACH PIE

My dad's favorite type of pie was cherry, so I channel him while I enjoy my annual slice of cherry. My mom likes *anything* with "pie" in the name, but she lives on a pecan plantation, so I think her choice—feet to the fire—would be pecan chocolate bourbon. The peach is just for me, my guiltless pleasure.

MAKES 1 PIE

12–18 peaches
Juice of 1 orange
¾ cup sugar
2 Tbsp grated ginger
1 tsp ground cinnamon
½ tsp salt
1 Tbsp cornstarch
Jen's Pie Crust (page 219)

Preheat the oven to 400°F.

Submerge the peaches in boiling water for 1 minute, then plunge them into an ice bath for 2 minutes. Using your hands, rub the skins to remove them.

Cut the peaches into ¼-inch-thick slices, and add to a large bowl along with the orange juice, sugar, ginger, cinnamon and salt. Gently mix with a wooden spoon, then add the cornstarch and gently toss until the cornstarch is evenly distributed.

Pour the peach mixture into the prepared pie pastry. Pile it up a wee bit in the center.

Place the second pie crust over the filling and press around the edges to seal the filling. Use kitchen scissors to trim the excess crust to a 1-inch overhang, then fold the overhang under itself to form an edge.

Using your fingertips, crimp the dough along the rim of the pie plate. With a paring knife, cut a few slits in the center of the top crust to allow steam to escape.

Place the pie on a baking sheet to capture any spillage. Bake on the lower rack of the oven for 20 minutes.

Lower the temperature to 350°F and move the pie to the center rack. Bake for 30 minutes and check that the crust is a light golden color; if it's already turning a dark brown, cover with a piece of loose-fitting aluminum foil. Bake for 20 to 30 minutes more: you'll know the pie is just right when the filling is bubbling and the crust is (ideally) golden.

Let the pie cool for a few hours before slicing and serving. If you cut a pie before the filling has had time to set, you will likely have a fruit soup on your hands.

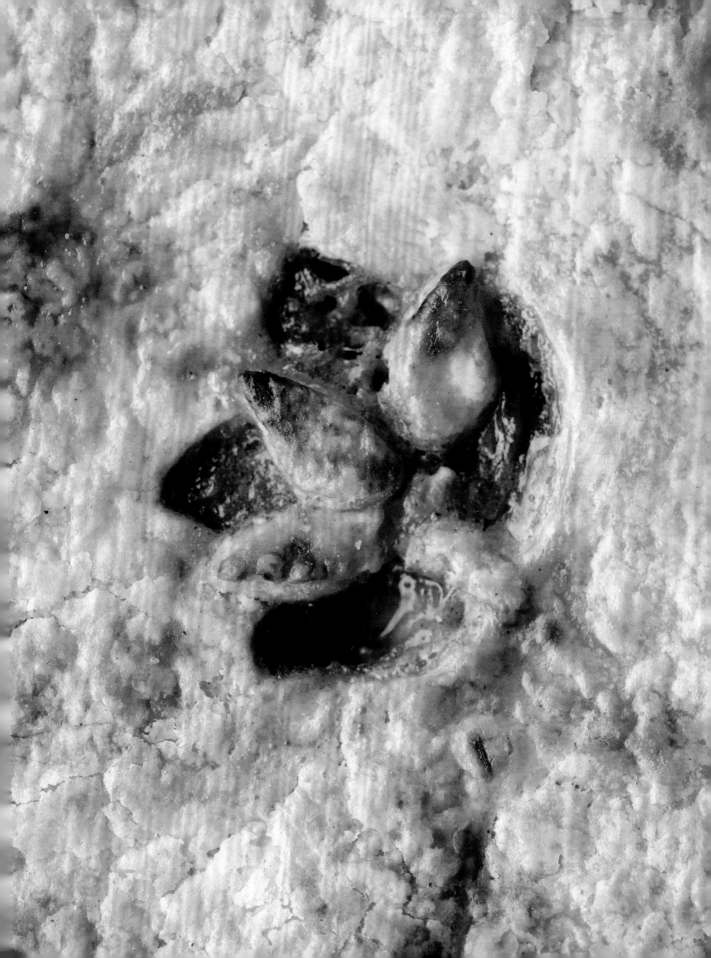

Drinks

SoBo Caesar

Remember that craze of Caesars and Bloody Marys, when the entire appetizer menu was threaded on skewers and hung off the side of the drinks as garnish? Well, sometimes more is not always better, so one day I wondered, how do I get my Caesar to stand out from the crowd? I stared down at a bucket of fresh seaweed—the answer was right in front of me. Just the right crunch, and pretty groovy.

MAKES 1 COCKTAIL

1 Tbsp celery salt

1 lime wedge

2 oz jalapeño vodka (or any small-batch vodka)

6 oz tomato juice (see Cook's Note)

1 oz clam nectar (see Cook's Note)

1 tsp freshly grated horseradish

1 tsp Worcestershire sauce

1 tsp pickling juice from the Pickled Bull Kelp (page 262), or olive brine

½ tsp hot sauce (I like Frank's RedHot or Louisiana)

A few rings of Pickled Bull Kelp (page 262), for garnish

Spread the celery salt on a saucer. Run a lime wedge around the rim of a highball glass, then dip the rim in the celery salt.

Fill the glass with ice. Put the remaining ingredients except the garnish in a cocktail shaker or lidded jar and give it all a good shake or stir.

Pour the drink over the ice and garnish with the kelp. Enjoy.

COOK'S NOTE: In a pinch, you can substitute the tomato juice and clam nectar with 7 oz of store-bought Clamato juice.

SoBo Sunset

When the Tofino Distillery introduced an absinthe to its repertoire, I got super excited. I had never tried any! I had heard of it but thought it was illegal in North America and found only in France. I brought a bottle to SoBo and my teammates Sophie and Mel whipped up this cocktail, just as the sun happened to be setting. So here it is: the SoBo Sunset.

MAKES 1 COCKTAIL

1 lime wedge, for the rim
1 Tbsp brown sugar, for the rim
2 oz dark rum
½ oz triple sec
1 tsp absinthe (I like Tofino Distillery)
2 oz Simple Syrup (page 255)
1 oz freshly squeezed lime juice
1 oz freshly squeezed orange juice
Orange or lime wheel, for garnish

Rim a martini or coupe glass with the brown sugar (see sidebar), then fill with ice.

Put the remaining ingredients except the garnish in a cocktail shaker or lidded jar and give it all a good shake or stir. Pour the drink over the ice and garnish with the citrus wedge.

Mezcal Paloma

Let me start with this little fun fact: mezcal is hands down my favorite alcoholic offering. If I could take one bottle with me to a deserted island, it would be a mezcal. When I am not sipping it straight, this cocktail is my jam. The kick of the salty, spicy, floral and tart complements the mezcal in a natural kind of way.

MAKES 1 COCKTAIL

1 Tbsp salt
1 tsp chili powder
2 oz mezcal
½ oz elderflower liqueur (I like St-Germain or Giffard)
3 oz freshly squeezed ruby red grapefruit juice

Combine the salt and chili powder and use it to rim the glass (see sidebar).

Fill a highball glass with ice. Put the mezcal, elderflower liqueur and grapefruit juice in a cocktail shaker or lidded jar. Give it all a good shake or stir, then pour over the ice.

Alternatively, you can enjoy this cocktail straight up, like a Martini: Put ice in a cocktail shaker, add the ingredients and shake. Strain into a martini glass.

SoBo Sunset

Creating a Rim

To pull a cocktail together, in both taste and style, cut a slice in a lime wedge and run around the rim of your glassware. Pour your powder mixture onto a saucer and place the glass upside down on the saucer so that the powdered mixture sticks.

LAVENDER LEMONADE SPRITZER

Summertime and lemonade just go hand and hand. When Ella was a wee lass, she and her friend Chloe had a lemonade stand on the local bike path. Thirsty cyclists and walkers were stoked to grab some. Chloe's mom is also a lover of gardens and flowers, so she would send a bouquet of fresh herbs and flowers to dress the stand. One day, the girls put lavender flowers in the big beautiful jug of lemonade. (Maybe this should be called Ella and Chloe's Lavender Lemonade Spritzer.) Vancouver Island grows spectacular lavender, as does Salt Spring Island and the Okanagan. This recipe can easily omit the booze, so that anyone can slurp this refreshing drink.

MAKES 1 COCKTAIL

2 oz vodka

2 oz freshly squeezed lemon juice

2 oz Simple Syrup, Lavender Variation (page 255)

2 oz club soda

Sprig lavender, for garnish

Fill a tall glass with ice. In a cocktail shaker or lidded glass jar, combine all the ingredients except the garnish and shake like crazy.

Pour over the ice and garnish with the lavender.

TIJUANA GO SURFING

Our Tofitians love surfing and are known to drive down to the Baja for winter surfing when they're sick of their wetsuits and want to feel the ocean against their skin again. The first stop for many is Tijuana, and after crossing the border, a drink might be in order. Tangy, sweet, spicy—this is a Pacific Northwest twist on a Tequila Sunrise.

MAKES 1 COCKTAIL

1 oz jalapeño vodka (I like Tofino Distillery)

3 oz mango juice

½ oz lime juice

¼ oz Simple Syrup (page 255)

Mango twist, for garnish (optional)

Fill a rocks glass with ice, add all the ingredients except the garnish and stir. Garnish with the mango.

SUSANNE HARE

We value local food at SoBo, and we also value local art.
Susanne Hare provides us with both. It's certainly a
memorable day whenever her daughter arrives with
armloads of fresh kale, mint and rhubarb that Susanne's
grown for us, but it was every day, for many years, that
we were also graced with her art. Susanne's eye-catching
giant metal mobile hung by the window of our main
entrance, one of the first things guests saw when
stepping into the restaurant. Only very recently did we
(reluctantly) part ways with it, as it found a new home.
Still, it lives on in photos throughout this book. Always
and forever an integral part of the SoBo experience.

After studying fine art at McGill University,
Susanne worked as a graphic designer for the World's
Fair, Expo 67, eventually making her way across the
country, landing at Florencia Bay, near Tofino, in the late
'60s. "I remember smelling the sea and thinking I was
home," she says. She's never left the West Coast since.

Now settled on Wickaninnish Island with her family,
Susanne has spent much of her time living off the grid,
involved in environmental activism, homeschooling and
working on her art. Painting is Susanne's first love, but
most of her current works are mobile sculptures—like at
SoBo, the Wickaninnish Inn and Winnipeg's convention
center also feature Susanne's copper, brass or aluminum
hangings—with a focus on driftwood, blown-down wood
from the forest and recycled metal. With the ongoing
fight for the forests, including recent movements at
Fairy Creek, she says she "wanted to show people how
the old-growth forest made these beautiful, time-worn
pieces. I love how time has shaped them. I don't really
think you can improve upon nature."

Susanne and her family welcomed me in the early
days when I was new to town. With no extended family,
it was so wonderful to be enveloped in theirs and to be
included in celebrations, parties and picnics on the
beach. Our tight bond was forged by a love of the
natural world and our choice to raise our families here,
in the heart of it.

BATCHED VESPER

Channel your inner James Bond and enjoy this strong but elegant Martini as an après surf sipper. Although, with all due respect to 007, shaking a Vesper can result in an overly diluted and less smoothly textured drink—and a Martini isn't meant to have ice shards floating on top. The golden rule is stir a spirit-only cocktail.

MAKES 1 COCKTAIL

2 oz gin (I like Tofino Distillery's West Coast Dry Gin)

1 oz vodka (I like Tofino Distillery's Small Batch Vodka)

½ oz Lillet Blanc

1 lemon rind

Pour the gin, vodka and Lillet Blanc in either a lidded glass bottle or jar—a mason jar will do nicely. Stir in 1 Tbsp water. Store in your freezer for when you're feeling risqué!

To serve, gently shake, then pour into a chilled martini glass. Gently twist a generous strip of lemon rind over the glass (this is *expressing*) to spritz the natural oils into the drink, and add the twist as garnish.

STUBBS ISLAND MULE

In 1694, Admiral Edward Russell threw a week-long party and served the world's largest cocktail, involving over 250 gallons of brandy, 125 gallons of Malaga wine and you don't even want to know what else. It was served in a punch bowl large enough to row across. I am envisioning a new gig for my friends, Chris Taylor and Sharon Whalen, who hail from Stubbs Island and their boats: Chris in the *Dick* serving drinks, and Sharon across the cocktail pond in the *Death Trap*, ready to rescue anyone fallen overboard who needs revitalizing with her Sea Wench essential oils.

MAKES 1 COCKTAIL

10 fresh mint leaves

2 oz vodka (I like Tofino Distillery)

6 oz ginger beer (I like Cock 'n Bull or Fever Tree)

¼ oz freshly squeezed lime juice

Dash bitters (see sidebar page 235)

1 lime wedge, for garnish (optional)

Sprig mint, for garnish (optional)

Put the mint leaves in a cocktail shaker or lidded jar. Using the handle of a wooden spoon, crush them up a bit. This will release some of the essence of the mint.

Add the remaining ingredients except the garnishes and give it all a good shake or stir.

Fill one of those fancy copper or stainless-steel mugs with ice (or maybe, like me, you prefer a good old-fashioned glass tumbler). Pour the drink over the ice. Garnish with the lime wedge and mint, if you like the pretty sprig of mint on top—although most people tend to remove the garnish from their drink and look for a place to dispose of it.

Batched Vesper

Cedar Negroni

This version of the essential aperitif takes on subtle notes of our coastal rainforest with the help of the Old Growth Cedar Gin from Tofino Distillery. If this gin isn't on your local liquor store shelves, you could get a dried cedar shaving from a woodcarver and toss it into some standard gin, along with the orange peel. Or maybe it's a good incentive to jump on a plane, train or automobile (or ferry) and come on over to Tofino to pick up a few bottles.

MAKES 1 COCKTAIL

1 oz Tofino Old Growth Cedar Gin
1 oz sweet vermouth
1 oz Campari
Orange rind, for garnish

Pour the spirits into a rocks glass over ice. Stir for 30 seconds or until well chilled. Garnish with the orange rind.

Port of Tofino

With only a splash of club soda, this recipe is straight-up booze, so best-quality spirits are essential. When it comes to the whisky or bourbon, my personal favorite is Ancient Grains from Devine Distillery in Saanich. The master distiller behind this magic potion is Ken Winchester, and, honestly, it's fabulous! Smoky and spicy, with hints of dark fruit and oak. For the port, La Frenz in the Okanagan's Naramata Bench makes an outstanding option, available in very small bottles so your supply stays fresh. (Many people don't realize that port has a shelf life.) All this to say: support your local liquor!

MAKES 1 COCKTAIL

2 orange slices
Dash bitters (see sidebar)
1 oz club soda
1 cup ice cubes
2 oz whisky or bourbon
2 oz port wine

Put the orange slices, bitters and club soda in a rocks glass, and use a wooden muddler to mash the ingredients together.

Add the ice, whisky and port. Sit in front of a crackling fire and sip.

AROMATIC BITTERS

Aromatic bitters come in a range of flavors, like cardamom, nutmeg or cinnamon, and are a key ingredient in classic cocktails—think about the Manhattan or (closer to home) our Stubbs Island Mule. Angostura is probably the most popular brand, instantly recognizable by its yellow cap and oversized label, but these days, artisan bitter cocktail producers are popping up all over. A favorite of mine is Bittered Sling, in Vancouver. Lauren Mote is the bartender and mad scientist behind the line, with products like Autumn Bog Cranberry, Zingiber Crabapple, Moondog Latin and Plum & Rootbeer. I'd buy these simply for the beautiful labels. And they aren't oversized!

Cedar Negroni

Tofino 75

The classic French 75 cocktail was named for the incredible blast it delivers to its drinkers, in the spirit of a French 75 mm field gun. We've concocted a floral, more peaceable twist.

MAKES 1 COCKTAIL

1 oz Tofino Distillery Rose Hibiscus Gin

½ oz freshly squeezed lemon juice

¼ oz Simple Syrup (page 255)

2 oz champagne or your favorite sparkling wine

Lemon twist and rose petal, for garnish

Put ice in a cocktail shaker. Pour the gin, lemon juice and simple syrup over ice. Shake until well mixed.

Strain into a coupe glass and top with the champagne. Garnish with the lemon twist and rose petal.

Red-Eye Medusa

This drink is named after another Tofino local: the red-eye medusa. This plump little jellyfish is translucent, except for the vibrant red mark dotting the stem of each tentacle—no doubt how it earned its name. You stand a good chance of finding these jellyfish while beachcombing around Tofino. Or, stare long enough at the dab of bitters in this drink, enjoy your sips and call it a day.

MAKES 1 COCKTAIL

1 oz absinthe (I use Tofino Distillery's Psychedelic Jellyfish Absinthe)

1 oz freshly squeezed lemon juice

1 oz Simple Syrup, Cucumber Variation (page 255)

Dash orange blossom water

1 egg white

1 cup cubed ice

1 oz soda water

Dash orange bitters (see sidebar page 235)

In a cocktail shaker without ice (this is called a dry shake), shake the absinthe, lemon juice, simple syrup, orange blossom water and egg white for 30 seconds.

Add 1 cup ice to the shaker and shake again for 30 seconds.

Strain the drink twice through a fine-mesh strainer, the second time into a chilled coupe glass. Slowly add the soda water until the egg white rises right to the rim of the glass.

Dot the cocktail with a dash of the bitters, to replicate the jellyfish's red eyes.

TOFINO DISTILLERY

Tofino is worth a visit for any number of reasons. There is surfing, storm watching and brunch at SoBo. There is kayaking, hiking through old-growth forests and lunch at SoBo. There is whale watching, bear watching and dinner at SoBo. (You can see where I am going with this.) There is also Tofino Distillery, whose spirits we use for our cocktails.

Tofino Distillery was founded in June 2018 by three local volunteer firefighters: John Gilmour, Neil Campbell (both pictured here) and Adam Warry. I love that they use certified organic grains from Fieldstone Organics in Armstrong, British Columbia—it means you won't get even a hint of Roundup in your drink. They use water from the Meares Island watershed reservoir, in the heart of Clayoquot Sound, and certified organic botanicals from hither and yon. As they like to say, you are cordially invited to visit their tasting room. It's just off the highway leading to downtown, so you can indulge in their mini-cocktail tasters before heading over to SoBo for much-needed sustenance.

When I call for vodka, gin and absinthe in my drink recipes, I mean vodka, gin and absinthe from Tofino Distillery. Their specialty spirits—like the Psychedelic Jellyfish Absinthe and Jalapeño Vodka, and the Old Growth Cedar and Rose Hibiscus gins—give each cocktail its unique flavor. Meanwhile, their Small Batch Vodka and West Coast Gin are quality takes on staple spirits. If these aren't available to you, substitute another vodka or gin—small batch, if you can.

Because, I have to say, my Tofino Distillery run has become one of my favorite errands. There's something special about being able to stroll directly down to your suppliers and pick up your product directly from the folks and venue where it's made. No middleman, knowing they distill a few rooms over. It's been a pleasure to watch them grow—and I'm more than happy to share them with you.

Sangria for a Crowd

When I worked in a very nice Mexican restaurant in Fort Worth, Texas, in the '70s, red was the only type of sangria offered. It wasn't until the '80s that I started to see white sangrias. White wine spritzers were all the rage, so white sangria was sure to make a big splash at pool parties. Sangria is often associated with Tex-Mex cuisine and patio fun. Historically light, fruity and refreshing. Often made in a large pitcher, like a punch, for sharing. It is traditionally made of wine, fruit and brandy. (Sometimes the drinks are served with a sugared rim, but I am not a fan of that.) Avoid oaky white wines for this one.

Red Sangria

MAKES 1 PITCHER (8 COCKTAILS)

One 750 mL bottle dry red wine
1 cup brandy or cognac
One 355 mL can club soda
1 orange, sliced into rounds
1 lemon, sliced into rounds
1 lime, sliced into rounds

Fill a large pitcher with ice. Add all the ingredients to the pitcher and stir well.

Pour into tall glasses filled with ice.

White Sangria

MAKES 1 PITCHER (8 COCKTAILS)

2 peaches, sliced
½ cup raspberries
1 green apple, sliced
1 cup sliced strawberries
One 750 ml bottle dry white wine
1 cup brandy or cognac
One 355 mL can club soda

Put the fruit in a large pitcher. Using a wooden muddler or spoon, mash the fruit up a little bit. Fill the pitcher with ice. Add the wine, brandy and club soda. Stir until well mixed.

Pour into tall glasses filled with ice.

Tofino 75,
page 236

Batched Vesper,
page 232

Red Sangria,
page 238

Mezcal Paloma,
page 228

SoBo Sunset,
page 228

Tijuana Go Surfing,
page 230

Stubbs Island Mule,
page 232

Staples

SOURDOUGH BREAD

When I couldn't decide whether to include a recipe for sourdough in this book (everyone seems to already have their tried-and-true method, and with whole books written on the subject, what more could I add?) Susan, my coauthor, made it abundantly clear that I *had* to. After all, when she was once forced to evacuate due to a tsunami warning, what did she take with her? Her laptop and her sourdough starter. Sourdough is a must. There's a lot of hoopla around sourdough, and, sure, you should prepare yourself for your daily check-ins, but most people plod through without knowing the ins and outs, and everything usually turns out fine—even delicious and rewarding. Maybe a friend is willing to donate some starter to your cause. But if you are determined to DIY, here's the scoop.

MAKES 2 LOAVES

Sourdough Starter

1 cup (120 g) all-purpose flour (see Cook's Note)

1 cup (120 g) whole-wheat flour or spelt flour

½ cup (120 g) water (80°F)

The starter will double in size, so choose a 2-quart container.

The Levain

1 Tbsp plus 2 tsp (30 g) Sourdough Starter (see above)

1 cup (240 g) water (80°F)

1½ cups (210 g) spelt flour, all-purpose flour or an equal mix of whole-wheat and all-purpose flours

Sourdough Loaves

The Levain (see above)

2 cups (480 g) water (80°F)

4¼ cups (775 g) all-purpose flour

24 g (4 tsp) salt

Prepare the starter: In a large jar, whisk together the flours. Put the water in a small jar and add ½ cup plus 2 tablespoons (100 grams) of the flour mixture. Using a whisk, mix thoroughly until the consistency becomes that of thick batter. Cover with a clean tea towel and store at room temperature until the mixture begins to bubble, 2 to 3 days.

When your starter begins to show signs of activity (bubbling, a faint odor), begin regular feedings. At the same time each day, discard 80% of what's in the jar and feed what's left with equal parts water and the flour mixture (2 Tbsp of each is fine, going forward). You'll want to seal the jar after each feeding. When the starter's bubbling begins to rise and fall predictably and takes on a slightly sour smell (after about 1 week), it is time to bake.

Prepare the levain: In a large bowl, mix together the portion of starter, water and spelt flour. Cover and let sit for 8 to 12 hours, or overnight, at room temperature.

Prepare the sourdough: Add the levain to a bowl with the water, all-purpose flour and salt.

Using a wooden spoon or your hands, mix until the flour is well incorporated and the dough is pulling away from the sides of the bowl. Knead for 10 minutes. Cover the bowl and let rest for 1 hour.

Wet your hands and, working within the bowl, stretch and fold the four corners of the dough toward its center.

continued on next page

Repeat this kneading process and rest cycle two more times, for a total of about 3½ hours.

Divide the dough in half, then shape each half into a loaf. Loosely cover each with a clean tea towel and let rest at room temperature for 2 hours.

Form the dough: Sourdough is a bit tricky because it can get sticky. Be mindful not to add too much flour when forming the loaves. Turn out the dough onto a very lightly floured work surface—a wooden board is perfect. Flatten the dough using a gentle hand, then fold in half. A bench scraper is a good tool for folding, as it helps you get underneath the dough. I fold the dough over in the opposite direction so that, by the end, I have turned the dough over three to four times, with the seam side on the bottom.

Gently shape the dough into a ball or loaf. At SoBo, we use a wicker basket to form, which really helps the dough hold the shape. Rest at room temperature 2 to 3 hours, or in the fridge overnight.

From the wicker basket, turn the dough onto a parchment-lined baking pan and, using a very sharp knife, cut a few shallow slits into the top to allow for expansion.

To bake the sourdough: Preheat the oven to 425°F. Turn the dough out into a cast-iron Dutch oven with a lid. Bake covered for 20 minutes, then remove from the oven, uncover and bake for 20 more minutes. *Alternatively, you can use a baking sheet:* Line a baking sheet with parchment paper. Turn the dough onto the prepared baking sheet and transfer to the oven. Bake for 20 minutes. Turn the temperature to 400°F and bake for a further 15 minutes. You've done it! You've made sourdough! That wasn't too bad, was it?

COOK'S NOTE: Breadmaking is an art, but it's also an exacting science. While measuring cups generally serve home bakers' needs, a cup's actual measurement depends on what is scooped and how —whereas 1,000 grams of flour only ever weighs 1,000 grams. I recommend getting a digital scale for under $60. Once you start weighing your flour, you'll never want to use any other method.

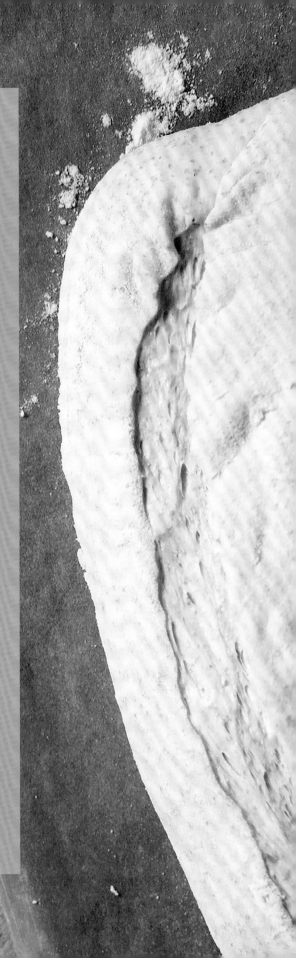

Sourdough Tips

Be prepared to feed and care for your starter for anywhere from 1 to 2 weeks before you even begin to think about baking. If neglected, the surface will get a sinister blue-black or pinkish-purplish mold: the sad, telltale sign that it's kicked the bucket. (Still, all's not lost. Read on!)

Feeding: Try to feed your starter at the same time every day. As long as it's fed fresh flour and water daily, the mixture can stay at room temperature indefinitely.

Water: Tap water is great, just don't use distilled water (it doesn't contain the necessary minerals). If you're using heavily chlorinated water, let it sit at room temperature for 24 hours first, otherwise it might kill your starter.

Container: A glass or plastic jar or container works well. Metal can taint the taste. Place it somewhere you'll be able to keep an eye on it, like the countertop.

Oxygen: Starters need oxygen—a good way to make sure yours gets enough is to whisk briskly. When you cover your jar, don't seal it: leave it ajar to let it breathe, allowing it to expand in a safe environment that won't gather dust.

Reviving: If your starter starts to look off-color from neglect, try leaving it in the fridge for several weeks (it may take a *few* several weeks) to eventually bring it back to a useful and fulfilling life. As long as it's not pink—as soon as it turns pink: throw it away.

On hold: You can pause your starter's growth by putting it in the fridge. Ideally, a starter should be taken out to sit at room temperature and fed the night before it is used in baking.

Hooch: Depending on how long your starter sits in the fridge, you may find a layer of translucent, brown, admittedly nasty-looking liquid on top of your starter. This is called the "hooch," and it might even come in blue, gray or black streaks. It is a normal part of the sourdough's life. (Pink or orange are *not* normal and indicate that the starter should be thrown out.) I simply swirl the hooch into my starter to mix it all up, then feed it once it has come to room temperature. Some people prefer to pour the hooch off and feed the starter with slightly more water at the next feeding.

BISCUITS AND HONEY BUTTER

Every household in the South holds a biscuit recipe near and dear to its heart. We crave what our people make for us. I have many different biscuit recipes stored away, including one for baking powder biscuits in the first SoBo cookbook. This time, I'm sharing the buttermilk variety, and in my next book I will be featuring the cream-style dinner kind.

Oh wait! Did I just say next book? Susan made me do it. We are nearing the end of this book and, well, quite frankly I think she is smitten with me and can't bear to see our relationship end.

(Susan's response: Bless your pea-pickin' lil heart! Will you marry me?)

MAKES 8 BISCUITS

Honey Butter

½ cup butter, room temperature

3 Tbsp honey or maple syrup

Biscuits

2 cups flour, plus 3 Tbsp for kneading

½ Tbsp sugar

1 Tbsp baking powder

½ tsp baking soda

½ tsp salt

½ cup butter, very cold

1 cup buttermilk (see Cook's Note)

Prepare the honey butter: Whip the butter and honey together until well incorporated. I like using my electric beaters to get the fluffy texture. To store, cut the batch into four pieces, then tightly wrap each in plastic wrap or place in a sealed container. Store in the fridge. Let the butter reach room temperature before using, so that it's spreadable.

Prepare the biscuits: Preheat the oven to 400°F. Line a baking sheet with parchment paper.

In a medium bowl, whisk together the flour, sugar, baking powder, baking soda and salt, incorporating all the ingredients evenly.

Using a box grater, grate the butter into the flour. Add the buttermilk. Use a wooden spoon to stir until incorporated.

Turn the dough onto a floured work surface and gently knead 10 to 12 times, dusting with the remaining flour as needed, being careful not to overwork it. With your rolling pin, roll the dough to about 1 inch thick. Cut into even squares, or use a cookie cutter for round biscuits.

Arrange the biscuits a few inches apart on the lined sheet and bake for 12 to 15 minutes, until golden brown.

COOK'S NOTE: If you don't have buttermilk on hand, you can substitute with 1 cup milk mixed with 1 Tbsp lemon juice or vinegar.

VEGAN BUTTER

More and more family and friends are opting for a vegan lifestyle—and there's no need to sacrifice flavor! And, as we all know, butter is flavor.

MAKES 1½ CUPS

1 cup melted refined coconut oil (see Cook's Note)

2 Tbsp canola oil

⅓ cup unsweetened soy or almond milk

1 tsp apple cider vinegar

1 tsp nutritional yeast

Pinch ground turmeric

½ tsp salt

In a blender, pulse the coconut oil and canola oil a few times.

In a medium bowl, stir the soy milk and vinegar together until the mixture curdles into something like buttermilk. Pour into the blender. Add the nutritional yeast, turmeric and salt. Blend until smooth.

Pour the mixture into silicone butter molds or a glass container big enough to hold all the liquid. Place in the fridge to chill for 1 to 2 hours. It will harden to be, well, buttery-like.

COOK'S NOTE: This must be *refined* coconut oil, not extra virgin coconut oil. Refined coconut oil has less coconut flavor, which will let the flavor of the baked goods you're using this butter on shine through.

Egg Pasta Dough

Making fresh pasta is a piece of cake (if you will excuse me for mixing my metaphors). If you don't have a pasta roller, there's nothing wrong with a plain old rolling pin. If you are making a larger batch of this pasta, you might want to use a stand mixer fitted with the dough hook. Or you can take the noble shortcut of buying fresh pasta sheets from the supermarket and slicing the shape yourself, for a handmade feel.

MAKES 4 SERVINGS

2 cups flour
½ tsp salt
2 eggs
1 egg yolk
2 tsp olive oil

On a clean work surface or wooden cutting board, mix the flour and salt together. Make a well in the center. Add the eggs, yolk and oil to the well and use a fork to mix together. With the fork, pull a little bit of the surrounding flour into the well, gently whisking to incorporate. Working your way around the ring of flour, slowly continue to pull more flour into the liquid to whisk, until all the flour is incorporated.

Knead the dough for about 10 minutes or until it feels smooth and elastic-y. I love the process of kneading dough—there's something so satisfying about it. And the whole family, especially the kids, can join in.

Tightly wrap the dough in plastic wrap so that it doesn't dry out. Refrigerate for at least 2 hours, and up to 24 hours (the gluten needs this time to rest).

When you're ready to roll out the dough, either follow the manufacturer's instructions for your pasta roller or use a rolling pin. If using a rolling pin, place dough on a generously floured work surface. Roll the dough out about 1 inch thick, then fold over one-third of the dough from the outer edge to the center, and repeat on the opposite side. Roll out again to 1 inch. Repeat this process a total of three times, adding more flour as needed to keep dough from sticking to the work surface.

Roll the dough out in one long piece. If your work area is small, cut the dough into a few different pieces. Roll the dough until it is quite thin, although ultimately, the thickness is up to you.

Once you have achieved your desired thickness, it's time to cut the dough to your desired shape. When choosing the shape, you'll want to consider what type of sauce you will be using and how heavy it is. A larger, broader pasta such as pappardelle is perfect for braised meats and thicker sauces. Tagliatelle is slimmer, suitable for a Bolognese sauce. Linguini is what you want for delicate seafood, such as clams.

Angel hair is lovely for olive oil–based, simple, two-to-three-ingredient pastas. Pasta rollers can help achieve the smaller pasta, while larger broader noodles are easily cut by hand.

To hand-cut strands, fold the dough over itself about 10 times, or roll it like a cigar, and cut with a sharp knife to your desired width.

Lay the pasta out on a well-floured baking sheet. I like using semolina for this, but all-purpose flour works as well.

When you're ready to cook, follow the method I've given in each recipe. Generally, you only want to stir occasionally, being careful not to break the pasta strands with too vigorous of stirs.

Most fresh pastas cook between 3 to 5 minutes, depending on thickness. Drain the pasta (do not rinse), reserving ¼ cup of the pasta water—the starch in it will help the sauce adhere to the pasta.

VARIATION NETTLE PASTA

For a spectacular variation that makes the most of my beloved nettles (page 160), use this nettle mixture in place of the egg mixture that you pour into the flour well.

1 Tbsp salt

2 cups freshly picked wild nettles (see Cook's Note)

2 eggs

In a large saucepan over high heat, bring 8 cups water and 1 Tbsp salt to a rolling boil. Add the nettles and cook for 3 to 4 minutes. Drain, then let the nettles cool. Transfer the nettles to a blender and purée. Add the eggs and purée together.

COOK'S NOTE: Feel free to substitute spinach for the nettles. Because of the moisture in the nettles (or spinach), be prepared to add more flour, a little at a time, while kneading until your dough reaches the right consistency.

Stocks

Stocks are a great way of honoring a no-waste philosophy. By following a few simple rules, you can have clear, rich, flavorful stock for a fraction of what you would spend on the packaged or tinned kind. Make sure to use good fresh vegetables and cold, fresh water (never hot water). Turn the heat down to a simmer as soon as the stock reaches the boiling point. The lazy bubble is a stock's best friend.

Vegetable Stock

MAKES 4 QUARTS

¼ cup olive oil

8 yellow onions, chopped

8 ribs celery, chopped

3 large carrots, chopped

2 large leeks, greens only, rinsed well and chopped

2 cups chopped vegetables of choice (optional, see Cook's Note)

1 cup dry white wine

6 quarts cold water

2 Tbsp salt

2 bay leaves

3–5 sprigs fresh herbs, like parsley, marjoram, oregano or thyme

Heat the oil in a large heavy-bottomed stockpot over medium-low heat. Sauté the onions, celery, carrots and leeks for about 20 minutes, until tender. If you're using the mixed vegetables, add them now.

Pour in the wine and let it evaporate, 3 to 4 minutes. Add the water, the salt, bay leaves and herbs. Bring to a boil, turn the heat to simmer and cook at a lazy bubble, uncovered, for 45 minutes. Skim off any foam that rises to the top.

Immediately strain the stock through a fine-mesh strainer and cool it down as quickly as possible (see Cook's Note on page 254). Store in a sealed container in the fridge for up to 5 days. If you can't use the stock within a few days, you can freeze it in small containers for up to 6 months and thaw it as needed.

COOK'S NOTE: If I were using this stock in an asparagus soup, I would use the woody stalks of the trimmed asparagus in the stock. If I wanted a corn-flavored stock, I would use the corncobs; mushroom stems for mushroom stock, and so on. Avoid strongly flavored vegetables like cabbage, broccoli and beets.

Fish Stock

MAKES 4 QUARTS

½ cup olive oil

2 carrots, chopped

2 ribs celery, chopped

1 yellow onion, chopped

1 large leek, greens only, rinsed well and chopped

4 lb fish bones and trimmings

2 cups dry white wine

6 quarts cold water

2 Tbsp salt

6 black peppercorns, cracked

4 sprigs fresh thyme

2 bay leaves

Heat the oil in a large stockpot over medium heat. Add the carrots, celery, onions and leeks and sauté for 10 minutes. Add the fish and sauté for 5 minutes. Add the wine and cook, stirring occasionally, for another 5 minutes.

Add the water, the salt, peppercorns, thyme and bay leaves. Bring to a boil, turn the heat to simmer and cook at a lazy bubble, uncovered, for 1½ hours.

Immediately strain the stock through a fine-mesh strainer and cool it down as quickly as possible (see Cook's Note on page 254). Store in a sealed container in the fridge for up to 5 days. If you can't use the stock within a few days, you can freeze it in small containers for up to 6 months and thaw it as needed.

Chicken Stock

MAKES 4 QUARTS

2 Tbsp canola oil

2 onions, chopped

2 ribs celery, chopped

2 carrots, chopped

6 quarts cold water

2½ lb mix of chicken necks, backs and wings (fresh or roasted)

10 sprigs fresh flat-leaf parsley

2 bay leaves

1 tsp salt

¼ tsp black peppercorns

Heat the oil in a large heavy-bottomed stockpot over medium heat. Add the onions, celery and carrots. Sweat for 20 minutes or until all the vegetables are softened.

Add the water, chicken, parsley, bay leaves, salt and peppercorns. Bring to a boil, turn the heat to simmer and cook at a lazy bubble, uncovered, for about 3 hours, skimming the fat off regularly.

Immediately strain the stock through a fine-mesh strainer and cool it down as quickly as possible (see Cook's Note on page 254). Store in a sealed container in the fridge for up to 1 week. If you can't use the stock within a few days, you can freeze it in small containers for up to 6 months and thaw it as needed.

COOK'S NOTE: For a darker, richer chicken stock, add 1 cup tomato paste and 1 cup dry white wine to the sweated vegetables. Stir and cook for another 10 minutes before adding the water, chicken and seasonings.

BEEF STOCK

When roasting bones, do not allow them to burn. Burnt bones means a bitter stock. Beef stock is made from a variety of meaty joints and bones—knuckle and neck bones, shanks and oxtails—simmered for a long time and used as the foundation in sauces, soups and stews. Do not use bone marrow—it makes for poor flavor, greasy texture and no gel. At SoBo, we skim the fat off the top of our stock for a cleaner flavor.

MAKES 4 QUARTS

6 lb beef bones

¼ cup canola oil

½ cup tomato paste

4 carrots, peeled and diced

2 onions, diced

2 ribs celery, diced

4 cloves garlic

1 cup dry red wine

6 quarts cold water

6 black peppercorns

A few sprigs parsley

4 sprigs fresh thyme

4 bay leaves

2 Tbsp salt

Preheat the oven to 400°F.

Place the bones in a single layer in a roasting pan. Drizzle the oil over the bones. Roast for 30 minutes. Remove from the oven and add the tomato paste, carrots, onions, celery and garlic. Stir well so that the tomato paste is evenly distributed. Return the pan to the oven and roast for 30 minutes.

Remove from the oven and transfer the bones, vegetables and any bits left in the pan (excluding any fat!) to a large stockpot. Turn the heat to medium-high and add the wine. Let reduce for 5 minutes, then cover the bones with the water.

Add the peppercorns, parsley, thyme and bay leaves. Bring up to a boil, then turn the heat to simmer and cook at a lazy bubble, uncovered. Frequently skim off the excess fat that rises to the top. Simmer for at least 4 hours but ideally longer—up to 12 hours. If the stock cooks too quickly, you will lose the water ratio and risk burning the stock, so be sure to keep the heat low or it's a goner.

Immediately strain the stock through a fine-mesh strainer and cool it down as quickly as possible (see Cook's Note). Add the salt. Discard the bones, vegetables and bay leaves. Remove from the heat and let cool to room temperature. Store in a sealed container in the fridge for up to 5 days. If you can't use the stock within a few days, you can freeze it in small containers for up to 6 months and thaw it as needed.

COOK'S NOTE: For food safety, chill stocks down quickly, strain them into a container, then submerge the container in a sink filled with ice water for 1 hour or so, stirring the stock every once in a while.

SIMPLE SYRUP

This syrup is called simple syrup because no recipe could be simpler. Boil, stir, cool. If you want to spruce it up, you can also flavor your syrup with herbs such as mint or lavender (variations below), or with wild rose petals. I use the syrup in recipes for beverages in this book, but we often use it to moisten SoBo cakes, too.

MAKES 1½ CUPS

1 cup sugar
1 cup water

In a saucepan, bring the sugar and water to a boil. Stir until the sugar dissolves. Remove the syrup from the heat and let cool. Store in a sealed container in the fridge for up to 2 weeks.

VARIATION CUCUMBER

1 English cucumber, unpeeled, chopped

Prepare the simple syrup as above and let cool. In a blender, blend the cucumber with the cooled simple syrup on high speed for 1 minute.

Strain the mixture through a fine-mesh strainer, pushing on the solids to release their liquid. Store in a sealed container in the fridge for up to 1 week.

VARIATION LAVENDER

2 large sprigs fresh lavender or 1 tsp dried lavender

While preparing the simple syrup, add the lavender to the sugar and water before boiling. Stir until the sugar dissolves. Remove from the heat and let steep for 20 minutes, then strain through a fine-mesh strainer. Let cool to room temperature. Store in a sealed container in the fridge for up to 2 weeks.

VARIATION MINT

1 cup packed fresh mint

While preparing the simple syrup, add the mint to the boiling sugar-water mixture. Remove the syrup from the heat and let the herbs steep for 20 to 30 minutes, then strain through a fine-mesh strainer. Store in a sealed container in the fridge for up to 2 weeks.

CHIPS

Parsnip, potato, yam, sunchoke, beet, taro root, celery root—whatever satisfies your munching cravings will work beautifully as a chip. If you have a mandoline, this is a great time to put it to use, as you can get ultra-thin slices, which are a bit more challenging to make with a knife. Slice your vegetable prior to soaking. The amount you slice is up to you! Once again, whatever satisfies your cravings.

MAKES 4 SIDES

4 large Yukon Gold potatoes, thinly sliced

Salt, for seasoning

Smoked paprika (optional)

In a large bowl, soak the potato slices in ice water for 30 minutes, then dry with paper towel or a clean tea towel until every last bit of surface moisture is gone.

Prepare the fryer: Pour in 2 cups canola or peanut oil and heat to 300°F —test it with a deep-fry thermometer. You can use the bread cube test here (see sidebar page 257), but aim for a light golden crisp. Carefully add the potato slices, and stir with a slotted spoon to prevent them from sticking together. Fry until they are a crispy golden brown, about 3 to 4 minutes.

Carefully remove with a slotted spoon and transfer to paper towel to drain. Season with salt or any other flavor you'd like. Sometimes I use a bit of smoked paprika.

CHIP TIPS

You can (and should!) get creative with your chips. Here are a few of my favorite alternatives to potato, with some helpful hints to get the best results.

Sunchoke: Ensure that the sunchokes have been well scrubbed, as the dirt loves to hang out in the knobby crevices. An unused toothbrush is a helpful tool here!

Beets: Peel the beets before slicing, and watch them carefully: they have a high sugar content so they burn easily.

Yam: Be very careful when slicing yams! They can be tricky, as they are firmer than potatoes and you want to keep all your fingers. Like beets, they are high in sugar and tend to burn more easily than potatoes.

ONION RINGS

You might recognize these addictive crunchy munchies from my first cookbook or their feature in a 1999 *Food & Wine* or in the *Best American Recipes 2000* cookbook. Well, they're a SoBo specialty! Use sweet onions, such as Walla Wallas, or soak yellow onion slices in cold water to dilute the sulfur content, turning them sweet and mild. Dry thoroughly before coating.

MAKES 20–25 RINGS

1½ cups buttermilk

1½ cups flour, divided

2 Tbsp puréed canned chipotle chilies in adobo sauce

2 sweet onions, cut into ¼-inch-thick slices and separated into rings

1½ cups rice flour

1½ cups yellow cornmeal

1 Tbsp ground cumin

1 Tbsp cayenne pepper

4 cups vegetable or peanut oil, for frying

1 Tbsp salt

In a large bowl, whisk the buttermilk with ½ cup of the flour and the chilies until smooth. Add the onion rings. Toss them to moisten, then let them soak for 30 minutes.

In a separate bowl, combine the remaining 1 cup flour, rice flour, cornmeal, cumin and cayenne. Coat the onions in the spiced flour mixture, shaking off any excess.

Heat 2½ cups of the oil in a large cast-iron frying pan to 350°F. Use a thermometer or do the bread cube test (see sidebar). Fry the onion rings in batches, turning them often, until they are golden brown, 3 to 4 minutes. Add the remaining oil to the pan when it is empty (if needed) and heat to 350°F before continuing to fry the next batch of onion rings. Use tongs to transfer the onion rings to a paper towel to soak up any excess oil. Season with salt and serve immediately.

A LESSON IN DEEP-FRYING

If you don't own a deep fryer, use a pot deep enough for the oil to reach one-third of the way up the sides, leaving room for it to bubble without overflowing. Consider the amount of food and oil you will need. (YouTube tutorials are your friends here!)

Know your equipment: Be very careful if you have a gas stove—do NOT turn the heat to high. If the flames underneath whip up the side of your pot, you'll risk the oil igniting. Alternatively, an electric stove can get super hot quickly, so it takes a bit longer to cool the oil down once you've adjusted the temperature.

Tip: Moisture of any kind is an enemy of a deep fryer. Keep any drinks far away and make sure the food hitting the oil is as dry as possible (pat off any excess moisture). If you don't have a fryer basket, use a slotted spoon to remove the food, and be equally mindful when adding *to* the fryer. Never, ever leave the fryer unattended. Fry in small batches and keep the temperature from getting too hot by checking with a deep-fry thermometer.

Bread cube test: Place a bread cube into the oil. If it's the right heat the oil will sizzle and the bread turn golden brown in 60 to 90 seconds. If it darkens too quickly, the oil's too hot. If the oil doesn't sizzle, it's too cold.

ROASTING

ROASTED CORN

In our family we had a saying, "The corn's not perfect until the butter's dripping down to your elbows." The other secret to perfect corn on the cob is, of course, freshness. My mom would put her big stockpot on the stove and, as the water started to boil, send us into the garden to pick the corn. We'd strip each cob of its husk and silk, and run—not walk—back to the kitchen to deliver it to Mom, who would drop it into the boiling water before the corn had the chance to turn to starch (which would make it, in her eyes, inedible). That, and only that, was considered *fresh* corn on the cob.

At SoBo, we like to roast our fresh corn, instead of boiling it. It is so much more flavorful. Think of the difference between a boiled hot dog and a grilled one. Need I say more?

1 EAR OF CORN = ½ CUP
KERNELS

Barbecue: Soak the fresh ear of corn in its husk for 1 hour in cold water. When you are ready to cook it, heat the barbecue to medium-high. Leave the corn in its husk and place it directly on the grill. Cook for about 10 minutes, turning frequently to avoid burning. Pull back the husks, remove the silk and—you know what to do! Add butter and salt and let the melted butter run down to your elbows.

Roasting: Preheat the oven to 450°F. Soak the fresh ear of corn in its husk for 1 hour in cold water, then place on a baking sheet and roast in the oven for 20 minutes. Pull back the husks, remove the silk and . . .

Removing the kernels: There are several ways to remove corn from the cob, but my method of choice is to cut off the bottom end (the one attached to the large stalk; the silk thread comes off more easily this way) to create an even surface to balance on a cutting board. I often put a clean tea towel on the board so the kernels are easier to contain and gather. Then, run a knife down the side of the corn cob to slice off the kernels.

YouTube is a great place to watch different ways to de-cob. At SoBo, we freeze our naked corn cobs for our next batch of vegetable stock.

COOK'S NOTE: If you are determined to boil the corn cobs, here's a tip: don't add salt to the cooking water—it will toughen the corn. Add the salt *after* the corn is cooked. If you *have* to throw something into the boiling water, try sugar instead.

ROASTED GARLIC

When you roast garlic, it transforms from pungent and crisp to sweet, mellow, butter-soft and irresistibly caramelized. It's everything your heart could desire—except perhaps for a piece of fresh sourdough to spread it on (but I've got that for you, too, on page 245). Here are my two methods of roasting garlic. The first uses whole heads, the second uses peeled cloves.

Roasting whole heads: Preheat the oven to 400°F. Using a sharp knife, cut ⅛ inch off the top of the garlic head, exposing some of the cloves inside. Lightly drizzle the garlic with 2 Tbsp olive oil and wrap tightly in aluminum foil. Place the wrapped garlic on a baking dish, in a muffin pan, and roast in the oven for 20 to 25 minutes, until soft enough that you're able to squeeze the cloves out of their skins like toothpaste. (A muffin pan works really well for this, as it keeps the garlic bulbs from rolling around.)

Roasting peeled cloves: Place peeled cloves in a saucepan, cover with olive oil (about ½ tsp per clove) and simmer on low heat until fork-tender and golden brown, about 15 minutes.

Puréed garlic: Pulse the roasted cloves in a blender until smooth. (Great on sourdough!)

To store, transfer the roasted garlic to an airtight container and pour olive oil on top to fill the container. Store in a sealed container in the fridge for up to 2 weeks.

ROASTED CHILIES

Roasting chilies (such as poblanos) is an excellent way to add a lot of depth to your dishes. Here are three methods. For each, you're looking to char the skins until they're black, but you don't want to burn the chilies too deeply.

Barbecue: Preheat the grill to high. Place the chilies directly on the grill. Turn often for even roasting.

Gas stove: Turn on the flame and, using metal tongs, hold the chilies over it. (You'll need to work with one chili at a time.) Turn them often, as you would a hot dog over a firepit.

Oven: Preheat the oven to 500°F. Place the chilies on a baking sheet and roast for 10 to 15 minutes, turning halfway.

When the chilies are blackened, place them in a bowl and cover tightly with plastic wrap. Let sit for 20 minutes. This will steam them, making the skins easier to peel off, simply using your fingers.

CHIMICHURRI SAUCE

This vibrant sauce is a staple in my house. We put it on steak, eggs, vegetables, potatoes, poultry and more. It can be blended smooth or hand-chopped for a more rustic feel. The herbs are interchangeable, like with pesto, but traditionally it's a blend of parsley and oregano—sometimes I add mint or arugula to jazz it up. I often freeze half of what I make so I can have it in a flash when I need it later.

MAKES 1½ CUPS

10 cloves garlic, minced

1 cup packed fresh parsley, finely chopped

½ cup packed fresh oregano, finely chopped

½ cup minced shallot

¼ cup red wine vinegar

¼ cup freshly squeezed lemon juice

½ tsp crushed red chili flakes

¾ cup olive oil

In a medium bowl, place all the ingredients except the olive oil. Mix well, then slowly drizzle in the oil. Store in a sealed container in the fridge for up to 3 days, or in ice cube trays in the freezer for up to 1 month (though fresh is always best!).

LEFT COAST KIMCHI

You might know kimchi as spicy fermented cabbage, but you can use all kinds of vegetables in this recipe: cauliflower, ramps, radishes and (a favorite of mine) seaweed (I like the added brininess and am always looking to use the nutrient-packed ingredient). I see kimchi used not only as a side dish but also as a condiment on tacos, burgers, even grilled cheese. If you have a nice clay pot with a lid, this is a great time to use it, and if not, a mason jar works as well. Traditionally, kimchi is fermented at room temperature, but that might be tricky for first-timers, so, for safety's sake, refrigerate. It just takes a lot longer for the fermentation to occur. That's okay—it's worth the wait.

MAKES 2 QUART JARS (ISH)

One 6-inch bull kelp, cut in rings

¼ small head Napa cabbage, coarsely chopped

¼ head cauliflower, cut in small florets

6–7 ramps, or 1 bunch green onions cut into thirds widthwise

2 radishes

¼ cup salt

¼ cup rice flour (I like brown rice flour)

2 Tbsp sugar

6 green onions, coarsely chopped

6 cloves garlic

2 Tbsp peeled and coarsely chopped ginger

1 Tbsp Korean chili flakes

¼ cup fish sauce

2 Tbsp miso paste

In a large bowl, place the bull kelp, Napa cabbage, cauliflower, ramps and radishes. Add the salt to the vegetables and toss well. Cover with cold water and refrigerate overnight. After 8 to 12 hours, drain the brine into a large saucepan.

Whisk the rice flour and sugar into the brine and bring the mixture to a boil. Whisk frequently for 2 to 3 minutes. Remove from the heat and set aside.

In a food processor, pulse the sugar, green onions, garlic, ginger and chili flakes until a paste starts to form. Add the fish sauce and miso and blend until very smooth. Mix into the flour mixture.

In a large bowl, combine the vegetables and blended spice paste. Massage the paste into the nooks and crannies of the vegetables so they can do their magic.

Pack the vegetables into mason jars or a clay crock, leaving a few inches at the top for the fermentation to do its thing.

Traditionalists can leave the kimchi on a countertop at between 55°F and 60°F, and the fermentation will start in about 3 days. Or do as I suggested and place the kimchi in the fridge right away and wait a few weeks before enjoying.

PICKLING

When it comes to pickling, there are so many kinds of vinegars to try! I generally use apple cider vinegar for classic pickles because it doesn't overpower other flavors. It's a bit softer than red wine or balsamic vinegars, which are wonderful for pickling onions or shallots, since those have stronger flavors that can handle the power of the vinegars. Champagne vinegar is a relatively delicate vinegar, which works well for more subtle ingredients.

PICKLED BULL KELP

This ingredient is what makes the SoBo Caesar a SoBo Caesar (page 226), and it's also tasty with grilled cheese, or just straight, like a dill pickle. The scientific name for bull kelp is *Nereocystis*, which is Greek for "mermaid's bladder," but don't think about that too hard. I make these pickles in the spring while the bull kelp is young and tender. I use only the stipe, or stem.

MAKES FOUR 2-CUP JARS

One 2-foot-long bull kelp stipe

1 onion, sliced

1 jalapeño, sliced

2 cups apple cider vinegar

2 Tbsp sugar

2 tsp salt

1 tsp yellow mustard seeds

5 black peppercorns

1 bay leaf

Wash the bull kelp stipe well and cut into rings (think calamari). Place in a bowl along with 2 cups cold water, the onions and jalapeños. Cover and let soak for 1 hour.

In a small saucepan over high heat, bring 1 cup water, the vinegar, sugar, salt, mustard seeds, peppercorns and bay leaf to a boil. Cook for about 5 minutes, until the sugar dissolves.

Drain the bull kelp and place the rings in four sterilized glass jars. Very carefully, pour the brine over the kelp to cover it completely. Once cool, secure the lids on the jars and store in the fridge. The pickled bull kelp will keep for up to 6 months.

COOK'S NOTE: To sterilize a glass jar, simply pour boiling water into it and let sit for 3 minutes, or run through the dishwasher.

Pickled Kohlrabi

Kohlrabi has made a big resurgence in the culinary world. I love it pickled—total eye candy! The recipe here is for "fridge pickles"—pickles you are going to eat right away. What could be simpler! Kohlrabi is wonderful in vegetable slaws as well.

MAKES 1 QUART

1–2 kohlrabi, peeled and thinly sliced on a mandoline

1½ cups apple cider vinegar

6 black peppercorns

1 bay leaf

1 tsp yellow mustard seeds

1 tsp pickling salt

1 tsp sugar

Place the kohlrabi in ice water for about 1 hour to get the slices extra crisp. (Who wants a limp pickle?) Remove and pack into a sterilized quart-sized jar.

In a small saucepan, bring ½ cup water, the vinegar, peppercorns, bay leaf, mustard seeds, salt and sugar to a boil. Remove from the heat and carefully pour the pickling liquid over the kohlrabi. Let cool to room temperature.

Once the kohlrabi has cooled, put a tight-fitting lid on the jar and refrigerate for at least 2 days before serving. It will keep in the fridge for up to 1 month. Enjoy in salads or as a snack.

Pickled Turmeric Cauliflower

Pickled cauliflower is wonderful in salads or as a snack. Sometimes I add sliced red bell peppers, carrots and onions. If you like it spicy, add a few slices of a chili—try serrano or dried Thai chili.

MAKES 1 QUART

½ head cauliflower, cut in small florets

1½ cups apple cider vinegar

2 tsp ground turmeric

1 tsp ground coriander

1 tsp ground cumin

1 tsp black mustard seeds

1 tsp pickling salt

Pack the cauliflower in a sterilized quart-size glass jar.

Place all the ingredients along with ½ cup water in a small saucepan. Bring to a boil, then immediately remove from the heat. Carefully pour the hot liquid over the cauliflower in the jar.

Let cool to room temperature, cover with a tight-fitting lid and refrigerate for a few days before serving. It will keep in the fridge for up to 1 month.

Pickled Shallots

A tangy, crunchy condiment for tacos, sandwiches and burgers, pickled shallots add a little wow to a dish. I like them with my fish and chips! The sherry vinegar makes the shallot a vibrant pink.

MAKES 1 CUP

½ cup sherry vinegar

¼ tsp sugar

¼ tsp salt

2 shallots, thinly sliced on a mandoline

In a small saucepan over medium-high heat, bring the vinegar, sugar and salt to a boil. Add the shallots, turn the heat to low and cook for 2 minutes. Remove from the heat and let cool to room temperature.

Store in a sealed container in the fridge for up to 1 month.

Pickled Mustard Seeds

How did pickled mustard seeds suddenly become so popular? I am a fan. I would have never dreamed this up, but I love them with poached chilled shrimp, to cut through something fatty like bone marrow, tossed in a salad dressing for extra earthiness and punch, or, really, anything mustard would usually go on.

MAKES ½ CUP

¼ cup yellow mustard seeds

½ cup champagne vinegar, plus extra as needed

1 Tbsp sugar

1 tsp salt

Rinse the mustard seeds in a fine-mesh strainer. Place all the ingredients along with ½ cup water in a small saucepan and cook over medium-low heat for about 1 hour. If the seeds start to dry, add a bit more vinegar. Remove from the heat and let cool to room temperature.

Store in a sealed container in the fridge for up to 1 month. Let the seeds sit for at least 1 day before using.

BOBBY LAX AND THE
TOFINO UCLUELET CULINARY GUILD

The Tofino Ucluelet Culinary Guild was founded in 2010 by six chefs, including me, and a fisherman. The goal was to work collaboratively with local restaurants and resorts to source and deliver more food to the West Coast directly from B.C. fishers, foragers and farmers.

Chefs in Tofino and Ucluelet knew there were a great many independent food producers who deserved their support, but logistics—like the cost of shipping their goods to the end of the road—made it difficult for individual producers to work with any one restaurant. The strategy of group buying and consolidating shipping put more money directly into the producers' hands, while also saving the Culinary Guild members money when purchasing.

The Tofino Ucluelet Culinary Guild's first employee was a SoBo kitchen alumni, Bobby Lax. After working off and on at SoBo from 2006 to 2010, Bobby accepted the role as the guild's community food coordinator, seeking out food producers who prioritized quality and flavor, care of the environment and personal connection. He's nodded to my mentorship as a big reason TUCG is a favorite customer of its many suppliers, treating the folks who grow the produce, fish our waters and gather wild foods with respect. "Often," Bobby says, "they work long hours for little financial reward but are fulfilling their calling as providers, and that deserves our gratitude." From the shellfish farmer to the salad green grower to the blackberry picker at our back door, we should make the time to connect with these people and learn about their stories and their craft.

TUCG now is made up of approximately 25 to 30 restaurants and grocery stores, as well as 500 individual members who have joined the buying group to better access farm-fresh, restaurant-quality ingredients. The community-wide movement continues to grow, helping small-scale food distribution in British Columbia grow along with it.

ACKNOWLEDGEMENTS

My heart is full of love and pride for my family.

Thank you to my father, Harold Barber. I could have never accomplished my culinary dreams without the encouragement from my dad. He could see what my path was long before I knew myself. I miss him so much but somehow, I know it's his strength guiding me through this journey.

Thank you to my mom, Sandy Barber. When most people were aghast by my move from fine dining to food trucks, long before they were really a thing, you knew it would work. Your unwavering support means the world to me. It was your initial investment in SoBo that allowed me to turn my vision into a reality.

To Barkley, you are so naturally gifted as a chef; your focus is beyond anything I've witnessed in a kitchen. I've always known you will succeed at anything you're passionate about. It has been a true honor to have you on our SoBo team.

To Ella, at 45, the last thing I expected was a pregnancy, but I can't fathom a life without you. You are a brilliant writer and I can't wait to see what you do with this life.

Beyond grateful to Jeremy Koreski. Man, you have skills, mad skills, a keen eye—and thank you for choosing such a great life partner in Sarah Davies-Long, whose eye for detail and style makes us both look good. So much love for you both.

To Susan Musgrave. Thank you for walking into my gin joint and sharing your wicked sense of humor. Gosh, we laughed throughout the process. I looked forward to every call. We are really good together, and I hope we will continue to write together.

Thank you, Miss Whitney Millar. You must be the most patient person in the world to have to edit one of my books. I still haven't learned how to dance with my computer without stepping on many toes. Hopefully I didn't break too many of yours.

To Appetite by Random House, for running a damn fine show. Thank you for allowing me to star in it.

To Robert McCullough and Lindsay Paterson, for their ongoing support and encouragement. To the brilliant design team—wow, you polish us up so nicely.

To Jason Puddifoot at Puddifoot in Vancouver. Many thanks for the use of so many groovy dishes from your incredible Vancouver store.

To Wendy Brownie from Inspirati in Calgary. A million thank yous for sharing the most luxurious linens on the face of the planet with little ole SoBo. You are beyond generous and supportive.

A huge thank you to Lynn Crawford for being a great friend and inspiration to us all. Your foreword for this book filled my eyes with tears and my heart with joy.

To all of my SoBo family who, over the last 20 years, have churned out meal after meal for me and have loved our little SoBo so much. It has truly been my pleasure. I love walking through the doors in the morning and sharing this journey with you all.

To all my farmers, foragers, fishers, delivery folks and sales reps. Gosh, y'all work hard.

Thank you to all the artists who have showcased their incredible works at SoBo over the years. It makes our place feel like home. A very, very nice home.

To all my extremely talented chef friends in the biz who have come by to cook guest dinners. These have been a highlight in my memories over the years. I would like to give a huge shoutout to Chef Nicole Gomes, who shows up multiple times a year to make dumplings, pasta and all things delicious. She brings great skills and get-it-done attitude to the kitchen. We are all in awe of and forever grateful for her presence.

A giant thank you to the media who have been so generous in spreading the word about SoBo.

And finally, to my Tofino and Ucluelet community. It is you all who make this such a unique and special place to call home. Sure, the forest and the sea are spectacular, but it's the people who make it home.

INDEX

A

absinthe: Red-Eye Medusa, 236
acorn squash
  Acorn Squash Sauce, 123
  Roasted Acorn Squash and Kale
    Pizza, 127
almond milk: Almond Cream Sauce,
  181–82
almonds
  Fruit and Nut Cookies, 203
  Vegan Chocolate Almond Cookies,
    202
almonds, ground: Chocolate Mousse
  Tarts, 206
apple cider vinegar
  Barbecue Sauce, 171–72
  Pickled Bull Kelp, 262
  Pickled Kohlrabi, 263
  Pickled Turmeric Cauliflower,
    263
  Shrimp and Polenta Grits, 171–72
apples
  Coleslaw, 187–88
  Silky Parsnip, Apple and Celeriac
    Soup, 64
  Waldorf Salad, 94
aromatic bitters, about, 234
arugula
  Green Goddess Salad, 96
  Mushroom, Caramelized Onion
    and Goat Cheese Pizza, 128
  Pumpkin Seed Pesto, 122
  Shrimp, Avocado and Tomato Roti
    Wrap, 75–76
  Smoked Turkey, Bacon, Tomato
    and Arugula on Sourdough,
    85–86
Asiago cheese
  Green Polenta Cubes, 35–36
  Squash Patties, 151–52
  Summer Ratatouille and Polenta,
    142
asparagus
  Asparagus and Potato Pizza, 134
  Buckwheat Crepes, 147–48
  Warm Asparagus, Farro and King
    Oyster Mushroom Salad, 104–5
avocado
  Chocolate Mousse Tarts, 206
  Crab Louis, 37
  Crab Louis Sauce, 37
  Green Goddess Dressing, 96
  Shrimp, Avocado and Tomato Roti
    Wrap, 75–76

  Smoked Turkey, Bacon, Tomato
    and Arugula on Sourdough,
    85–86

B

bacon
  Smoked Turkey, Bacon, Tomato
    and Arugula on Sourdough,
    85–86
  Wedge Salad, 93
Barbecue Sauce, 171–72
bars and squares: Toasted Hazelnut
  Brownies, 217
basil
  Classic Margherita Pizza, 124
  Classic Tomato Gazpacho, 49
  Pumpkin Seed Pesto, 122
  Red Sauce, 122
  Watermelon Gazpacho, 50
Batched Vesper, 232
beef
  Beef Stock, 254
  Braised Beef Cheek Tacos with
    Black Bean Salsa, 189–90
beets
  Green Goddess Salad, 96
  Quinoa Salad, 113
Biscuits and Honey Butter, 248
black beans
  Black Beans, 181–82
  Black Bean Salsa, 189–90
  Braised Beef Cheek Tacos with
    Black Bean Salsa, 189–90
  Seared Halibut, Black Beans, King
    Oyster Mushrooms and Almond
    Cream, 181–82
bocconcini: Classic Margherita Pizza,
  124
bonito flakes: Dashi Broth, 39
Braised Beef Cheek Tacos with Black
  Bean Salsa, 189–90
Braised Chicken and Roasted
  Brussels Sprouts Pappardelle,
  163–64
Braised Lamb, 165–66
brandy: Red Sangria, 238
brassica shoots: Seaweed, Sea
  Asparagus and Brassica Shoots
  Salad, 101–2
bread
  Charcuterie with Grilled Peaches,
    26
  Classic Tomato Gazpacho, 49
  Focaccia, 77–78

  French Baguette, 83–84
  Panzanella with Fresh Mozzarella,
    107–8
  Sourdough Bread, 245–46
  Sourdough Tips, 247
  Tuna Melt, 81
breadcrumbs: Squash Patties,
  151–52
broccoli: Charred Cauliflower and
  Broccoli, 175–76
broccolini
  Seared Wild Salmon, 178
  Seaweed, Sea Asparagus and
    Brassica Shoots Salad, 101–2
Brussels sprouts
  Braised Chicken and Roasted
    Brussels Sprouts Pappardelle,
    163–64
  Roasted Brussels Sprouts and
    Sunchokes, 109–10
Buckwheat Crepes, 147–48
bull kelp
  Left Coast Kimchi, 261
  Pickled Bull Kelp, 262
butter
  about, 19
  Honey Butter, 248

C

cabbage
  Braised Beef Cheek Tacos, 189–90
  Coleslaw, 187–88
  Hot and Sour Chicken Noodle
    Soup, 69–70
  Left Coast Kimchi, 261
Campari: Cedar Negroni, 234
cannellini beans: White Bean and
  Chicken Chili, 58
Caramel, 199–200
Caramel Swirl Ice Cream, 215
carrots
  Beef Stock, 254
  Chicken Stock, 253
  Coleslaw, 187–88
  Curried Wheat Berry and Lentil
    Salad, 99
  Fish Stock, 253
  Green Goddess Salad, 96
  Hot and Sour Chicken Noodle
    Soup, 69–70
  Vegetable Stock, 252
  White Bean and Chicken Chili, 58
cashew butter: Salted Caramel
  Cashew Cookies, 199–200

cashews: Candied Cashews, 199–200
cauliflower
    Cauliflower Purée, 175–76
    Charred Cauliflower and Broccoli, 175–76
    Curried Wheat Berry and Lentil Salad with Poached Eggs and Turmeric Cauliflower, 99
    Fall Harvest Vegetable Soup, 61
    Left Coast Kimchi, 261
    Orecchiette, Braised Lamb and Cauliflower, 165–66
    Pickled Turmeric Cauliflower, 263
    Roasted Cauliflower and Garlic Soup, 62
Cedar Negroni, 234
celeriac
    Celeriac Cream, 169–70
    Silky Parsnip, Apple and Celeriac Soup, 64
celery
    Beef Stock, 254
    Chicken Stock, 253
    Chilled Pea and Mint Soup, 54
    Fish Stock, 253
    Vegetable Stock, 252
champagne: Tofino 75, 236
champagne vinegar
    Pickled Mustard Seeds, 264
Chanterelle Mushroom and Corn Chowder, 57
Charcuterie with Grilled Peaches, 27
Cheddar cheese
    Shrimp and Polenta Grits
    Tuna Melt, 81
Cheddar cheese: Shrimp and Polenta Grits, 171–72
cheese. See also bocconcini; Cheddar cheese; feta cheese; fontina cheese; goat cheese; Halloumi; mozzarella cheese; Parmesan cheese; provolone cheese; ricotta cheese
    Lamb Pizza, 137
cheese, fresh
    about, 26
    Charcuterie with Grilled Peaches, 27
    Lentil Vegiballs with Chimichurri and Fresh Cheese, 145–46
Cherry Pie, 219–20
Chewy Chocolate Cookies, 213–14
chicken
    Braised Chicken and Roasted Brussels Sprouts Pappardelle, 163–64
    Chicken Stock, 253
    Fried Chicken Dinner, Southern Style, 187–88

Hot and Sour Chicken Noodle Soup, 69–70
    White Bean and Chicken Chili, 58
chickpeas
    Falafel Balls, 71–72
    Falafel Pockets, 71–72
chili: White Bean and Chicken Chili, 58
Chilled Pea and Mint Soup, 54
Chimichurri Sauce, 260
Chinook Salmon, 175–76
chocolate chips
    Chocolate Chunk Ice Cream, 215
    Chocolate Mousse Tarts, 206
    Fruit and Nut Cookies, 203
    Ganache, 217
    Salted Caramel Cashew Cookies, 199–200
    Toasted Hazelnut Brownies, 217
    Triple Chocolate Chip Cookies, 204
    Vegan Chocolate Almond Cookies, 202
Chocolate Chunk Ice Cream, 215
Chocolate Mascarpone Cookies, 196
Chocolate Mousse Tarts, 206
cilantro
    Falafel Balls, 71–72
    Falafel Pockets, 71–72
    Halibut, Cucumber and Grapefruit Ceviche, 40
    Herbed Yogurt Sauce, 72
    Salsa Verde, 151–52
clams
    Clam and Corn Vongole, 158
    Mystic Clam Pizza, 131–32
    Nettle, Clam and Shrimp Tagliatelle, 160
    purging, 156
    Seafood Saffron Risotto, 155–56
Classic Margherita Pizza, 124
Classic Tomato Gazpacho, 49
cocoa powder
    Chocolate Chewy Cookies, 213–14
    Chocolate Mascarpone Cookies, 196
    Chocolate Mousse Tarts, 206
coconut, shredded: Chocolate Mousse Tarts, 206
Coconut and Rhubarb Sauce, 147–48
coconut cream: Curried Wheat Berry and Lentil Salad, 99
coconut flakes: Fruit and Nut Cookies, 203
coconut milk
    Coconut and Rhubarb Sauce, 147–48
    Melon and Coconut Soup, 53
coffee: Barbecue Sauce, 171–72

Coleslaw, 187–88
cookies
    Chocolate Chewy Cookies, 213–14
    Chocolate Mascarpone Cookies, 196
    Fruit and Nut Cookies, 203
    Salted Caramel Cashew Cookies, 199–200
    Triple Chocolate Chip Cookies, 204
    Vegan Chocolate Almond Cookies, 202
coriander: about, 19
corn
    Black Bean Salsa, 189–90
    Chanterelle Mushroom and Corn Chowder, 57
    Clam and Corn Vongole, 158
    Corn Purée, 183–84
    Fall Harvest Vegetable Soup, 61
    Pacific Halibut, Chanterelles and Corn Purée, 183–84
    Roasted Corn, 258
cornmeal
    Fried Green Tomatoes, 43
    Green Polenta Cubes, 35–36
    Polenta, 142
    Shrimp and Polenta Grits, 171–72
    Summer Ratatouille and Polenta, 142
crab
    Crab Louis, 37
    Crab Louis Sauce, 37
    Crab Salad, 83–84
crackers
    Seed Crackers, 29
    Wild Salmon Tartare, 29
cream: Heirloom Tomato Quiche, 31
Cream of Mushroom Soup, 67
crepes: Buckwheat Crepes, 147–48
cucumbers
    about, 19
    Classic Tomato Gazpacho, 49
    Cucumber Simple Syrup, 255
    Falafel Pockets, 71–72
    Green Goddess Salad, 96
    Halibut, Cucumber and Grapefruit Ceviche, 40
    Kale, Farro and Grilled Halloumi Salad, 90
    Shrimp, Avocado and Tomato Roti Wrap, 75–76
    Watermelon Gazpacho, 50
Curried Wheat Berry and Lentil Salad with Poached Eggs and Turmeric Cauliflower, 99

D
Dashi Broth, 39
deep frying, about, 257

dressings
  Basic Vinaigrette, 104–5
  Green Goddess Dressing, 96
  Lemon Parsley Vinaigrette, 90
  Parmesan Dressing, 109–10
  Roquefort Dressing, 93
  Seaweed, Sea Asparagus and
    Brassica Shoots Salad, 101–2
  Shrimp, Avocado and Tomato Roti
    Wrap, 75–76
  Tomato Vinaigrette, 107–8
  vinaigrette, about, 103

E
eggplant
  Mediterranean Pizza, 138
  Summer Ratatouille and Polenta,
    142
eggs
  about, 19
  Buckwheat Crepes, 147–48
  Crab Louis, 37
  Curried Wheat Berry and Lentil
    Salad with Poached Eggs and
    Turmeric Cauliflower, 99
  Egg Pasta Dough, 250–51
  Fried Green Tomatoes, 43
  Heirloom Tomato Quiche, 31
  Nettle Pasta, 251
  Plain Ole Vanilla Ice Cream,
    213–14
  Poached Eggs, 99
  Smoked Salmon, Farro and Sorrel
    Fritters, 33
  Spaghetti Squash Patties with
    Poached Eggs and Salsa Verde,
    151–52
  Vanilla Pastry Cream, 207–8
  Warm Asparagus, Farro and King
    Oyster Mushroom Salad with
    Poached Eggs, 104–5
elderflower liqueur: Mezcal Paloma,
  228

F
Falafel Balls, 71–72
Falafel Pockets, 71–72
Fall Harvest Vegetable Soup, 61
farro
  Kale, Farro and Grilled Halloumi
    Salad, 90
  Smoked Salmon, Farro and Sorrel
    Fritters, 33
  Warm Asparagus, Farro and King
    Oyster Mushroom Salad, 104–5
fennel: Buckwheat Crepes, 147–48
feta cheese: Mediterranean Pizza, 138
fiddleheads
  Buckwheat Crepes, 147–48

Halibut Cheeks with Morels,
    Fiddleheads and Celeriac Cream,
    169–70
fish. See halibut; salmon; tuna
fish sauce
  Hot and Sour Chicken Noodle
    Soup, 69–70
  Left Coast Kimchi, 261
Fish Stock, 253
flaxseed: Lentil Vegiballs with
    Chimichurri and Fresh Cheese,
    145–46
flour, about, 19–20
focaccia: Grilled Halloumi and
    Sun-Dried Tomato Tapenade on
    Focaccia, 77–78
fontina cheese: Asparagus and Potato
    Pizza, 134
French Baguette, 83–84
Fresh Rhubarb Tarts, 207–8
Fried Chicken Dinner, Southern
    Style, 187–88
Fried Green Tomatoes with Spiced
    Shrimp and Herbed Mayonnaise,
    43
fritters: Smoked Salmon, Farro and
    Sorrel Fritters, 33
fruit, dried: Fruit and Nut Cookies, 203
Fruit and Nut Cookies, 203

G
Ganache, 217
garlic
  about, 20
  Acorn Squash Sauce, 123
  Braised Beef Cheek Tacos, 189–90
  Braised Chicken and Roasted
    Brussels Sprouts Pappardelle,
    163–64
  Celeriac Cream, 169–70
  Chanterelle Mushroom and Corn
    Chowder, 57
  Chimichurri Sauce, 260
  Clam and Corn Vongole, 158
  Falafel Balls, 71–72
  Falafel Pockets, 71–72
  Garlic Aioli, 35–36
  Grilled Pattypan Squash, Green
    Polenta and Garlic Aioli, 35–36
  Left Coast Kimchi, 261
  Nettle, Clam and Shrimp
    Tagliatelle, 160
  Orecchiette, Braised Lamb and
    Cauliflower, 165–66
  Pacific Halibut, Chanterelles and
    Corn Purée, 183–84
  Parsley Sauce, 178
  Roasted Garlic, 259
  White Garlicky Sauce, 123

gin
  Batched Vesper, 232
  Cedar Negroni, 234
  Tofino 75, 236
ginger
  about, 20
  Hot and Sour Chicken Noodle
    Soup, 69–70
ginger beer: Stubbs Island Mule, 232
goat cheese: Mushroom, Caramelized
    Onion and Goat Cheese Pizza,
    128
grapefruit: Halibut, Cucumber and
    Grapefruit Ceviche, 40
grapefruit juice
  Mezcal Paloma, 228
grapes
  Charcuterie with Grilled Peaches,
    26
  Waldorf Salad, 94
green bell peppers
  Barbecue Sauce, 171–72
  Southern Baked Beans, 187–88
green chilies: White Bean and
    Chicken Chili, 58
Green Goddess Dressing, 96
Green Goddess Salad, 96
greens, mizuna: Grilled Halloumi and
    Sun-Dried Tomato Tapenade on
    Focaccia, 77–78
greens, salad: Crab Salad, 83–84
Grilled Halloumi and Sun-Dried
    Tomato Tapenade on Focaccia,
    77–78
Grilled Pattypan Squash, Green
    Polenta and Garlic Aioli, 35–36
Grilled Peach and Raspberry Melba,
    211

H
halibut
  Halibut, Cucumber and Grapefruit
    Ceviche, 40
  Halibut Cheeks with Morels,
    Fiddleheads and Celeriac Cream,
    169–70
  Pacific Halibut, Chanterelles and
    Corn Purée, 183–84
  Seared Halibut, Black Beans, King
    Oyster Mushrooms and Almond
    Cream, 181–82
  Seared Halibut Cheeks and Tomato
    Dashi, 39
Halloumi
  Grilled Halloumi and Sun-Dried
    Tomato Tapenade on Focaccia,
    77–78
  Kale, Farro and Grilled Halloumi
    Salad, 90

hazelnuts: Toasted Hazelnut
    Brownies, 217
Heirloom Tomato Quiche, 31
Herbed Yogurt Sauce, 72
herbs. *See also* cilantro; mint; parsley
    Green Polenta Cubes, 35–36
honey: Honey Butter, 248
Hot and Sour Chicken Noodle Soup,
    69–70

I
ice cream
    Caramel Swirl, 215
    Chocolate Chunk, 215
    Grilled Peach and Raspberry
        Melba, 211
    Ice Cream Sandwiches, 213–14
    Ice Cream Variations, 215
    Plain Ole Vanilla Ice Cream, 213–14
    Roasted Strawberries, 215
    Root Beer Float, 216

J
Jen's Pie Crust, 219–20

K
kale
    Kale, Farro and Grilled Halloumi
        Salad, 90
    Kale and Heirloom Tomato
        Garnish, 151–52
    Mystic Clam Pizza, 131–32
    Roasted Acorn Squash and Kale
        Pizza, 127
    Wilted Greens, 171–72
kimchi: Left Coast Kimchi, 261
King Oyster Mushrooms, 181–82
kohlrabi: Pickled Kohlrabi, 263
kombu
    about, 38
    Dashi Broth, 39

L
lamb
    Lamb Pizza, 137
    Orecchiette, Braised Lamb and
        Cauliflower, 165–66
lavender
    Lavender Lemonade Spritzer, 230
    Lavender Simple Syrup, 255
leeks
    Chilled Pea and Mint Soup, 54
    Fish Stock, 253
    Mystic Clam Pizza, 131–32
    Vegetable Stock, 252
Left Coast Kimchi, 261
lemon
    Hot and Sour Chicken Noodle
        Soup, 69–70

Melon and Coconut Soup, 53
lemongrass
    Hot and Sour Chicken Noodle
        Soup, 69–70
    Melon and Coconut Soup, 53
lemon juice: Lemon Parsley
    Vinaigrette, 90
lentils
    Curried Wheat Berry and Lentil
        Salad, 99
    Lentil Vegiballs with Chimichurri
        and Fresh Cheese, 145–46
lettuce
    Crab Louis, 37
    Falafel Pockets, 71–72
    Halibut, Cucumber and Grapefruit
        Ceviche, 40
lettuce, iceberg: Wedge Salad, 93
lettuce, mixed
    Green Goddess Salad, 96
    Quinoa Salad, 113
Lillet Blanc: Batched Vesper, 232
lime: Halibut, Cucumber and
    Grapefruit Ceviche, 40
lime juice: Salsa Verde, 151–52

M
mango juice: Tijuana Go Surfing, 230
maple syrup
    about, 20
    Barbecue Sauce, 171–72
    Chocolate Mousse Tarts, 206
    Coconut and Rhubarb Sauce,
        147–48
    Vegan Chocolate Almond Cookies,
        202
mascarpone: Chocolate Mascarpone
    Cookies, 196
mayonnaise
    Crab Louis Sauce, 37
    Fried Green Tomatoes with Spiced
        Shrimp and Herbed Mayonnaise,
        43
    Green Goddess Dressing, 96
    Herbed Mayonnaise, 43
    Roquefort Dressing, 93
    Tuna Melt, 81
Mediterranean Pizza, 138
Melba Sauce, 211
Melon and Coconut Soup, 53
Mezcal Paloma, 228
milk, about, 20
mint
    Chilled Pea and Mint Soup, 54
    Coleslaw, 187–88
    Halibut, Cucumber and Grapefruit
        Ceviche, 40
    Melon and Coconut Soup, 53
    Mint Simple Syrup, 255

Stubbs Island Mule, 232
Tuna Melt, 81
Watermelon Gazpacho, 50
mozzarella cheese
    Heirloom Tomato Quiche, 31
    Lamb Pizza, 137
    Mediterranean Pizza, 138
    Mushroom, Caramelized Onion
        and Goat Cheese Pizza, 128
    Mystic Clam Pizza, 131–32
    Panzanella with Fresh Mozzarella,
        107–8
    Roasted Acorn Squash and Kale
        Pizza, 127
mushrooms
    about, 20
    Chanterelle Mushroom and Corn
        Chowder, 57
    cleaning, 184
    Cream of Mushroom Soup, 67
    Halibut Cheeks with Morels,
        Fiddleheads and Celeriac Cream,
        169–70
    Hot and Sour Chicken Noodle
        Soup, 69–70
    Lentil Vegiballs with Chimichurri
        and Fresh Cheese, 145–46
    Mushroom, Caramelized Onion
        and Goat Cheese Pizza, 128
    Pacific Halibut, Chanterelles and
        Corn Purée, 183–84
    Seared Halibut, Black Beans, King
        Oyster Mushrooms and Almond
        Cream, 181–82
    Summer Ratatouille and Polenta,
        142
    Warm Asparagus, Farro and King
        Oyster Mushroom Salad, 104–5
mustard: Barbecue Sauce, 171–72
mustard seeds
    Pickled Mustard Seeds, 264
Mystic Clam Pizza, 131–32

N
navy beans: Southern Baked Beans,
    187–88
nettles
    Nettle, Clam and Shrimp
        Tagliatelle, 160
    Nettle Pasta, 251
noodles, vermicelli rice: Hot and
    Sour Chicken Noodle Soup,
    69–70
nuts, toasting, 216

O
oils
    canola, about, 19
    olive, about, 20

olives
  about, 20
  Grilled Halloumi and Sun-Dried
    Tomato Tapenade on Focaccia,
    77–78
  Lamb Pizza, 137
  Mediterranean Pizza, 138
  Orecchiette, Braised Lamb and
    Cauliflower, 165–66
onions
  about, 21
  Barbecue Sauce, 171–72
  Beef Stock, 254
  Chicken Stock, 253
  Classic Tomato Gazpacho, 49
  Coconut and Rhubarb Sauce, 147–48
  Fish Stock, 253
  Lamb Pizza, 137
  Lentil Vegiballs with Chimichurri
    and Fresh Cheese, 145–46
  Mushroom, Caramelized Onion
    and Goat Cheese Pizza, 128
  Onion Rings, 257
  Sumac Onions, 72
  Vegetable Stock, 252
  White Bean and Chicken Chili, 58
onions, green
  Halibut, Cucumber and Grapefruit
    Ceviche, 40
  Hot and Sour Chicken Noodle
    Soup, 69–70
  Left Coast Kimchi, 261
  Seared Scallops and Quinoa Salad,
    113
onions, red
  Salsa Verde, 151–52
  Tuna Melt, 81
oranges
  Cherry Pie, 219–20
  Peach Pie, 222
  Quinoa Salad, 113
Orecchiette, Braised Lamb and
  Cauliflower, 165–66
oregano: Chimichurri Sauce, 260

P
Pacific Halibut, Chanterelles and
  Corn Purée, 183–84
Panzanella with Fresh Mozzarella,
  107–8
Parmesan cheese
  Classic Margherita Pizza, 124
  Parmesan Dressing, 109–10
  Roasted Brussels Sprouts and
    Sunchokes with Parmesan
    Dressing, 109–10
parsley
  about, 21
  Chilled Pea and Mint Soup, 54

Chimichurri Sauce, 260
Falafel Balls, 71–72
Falafel Pockets, 71–72
Herbed Yogurt Sauce, 72
Lemon Parsley Vinaigrette, 90
Parsley Sauce, 178
Roasted Cauliflower and Garlic
  Soup, 62
Salsa Verde, 151–52
Smoked Salmon, Farro and Sorrel
  Fritters, 33
Tuna Melt, 81
parsnips
  Parsnip Fries, 75–76
  Parsnip Puffs, 175–76
  Shrimp, Avocado and Tomato Roti
    Wrap, 75–76
  Silky Parsnip, Apple and Celeriac
    Soup, 64
pasta
  Braised Chicken and Roasted
    Brussels Sprouts Pappardelle,
    163–64
  Clam and Corn Vongole, 158
  Egg Pasta Dough, 250–51
  Nettle, Clam and Shrimp
    Tagliatelle, 160
  Nettle Pasta, 251
  Orecchiette, Braised Lamb and
    Cauliflower, 165–66
peaches
  Charcuterie with Grilled Peaches,
    27
  Grilled Peach and Raspberry
    Melba, 211
  Peach Pie, 222
  White Sangria, 238
peas: Chilled Pea and Mint Soup, 54
people of SoBo
  Barber, Sandy, 95
  Campbell, Neil, 237
  Davies-Long, Sarah, 198
  Fisette, Laurence, 152
  Gilmour, John, 237
  Hare, Susanne, 231
  Koreski, Jeremy, 198
  Law, Dan, 32
  Lawson, Cosy, 174
  Lax, Bobby, 265
  Peters, Katrina, 68
  Ponak family, 80
  Schwab, Brenda, 133
  Scott, Jennifer, 221
  Southcott family, 80
  Taylor, Chris, 41
  Tofino Distillery, 237
  Tofino Ucluelet Culinary Guild, 265
  Warry, Adam, 237
  Whalen, Sharon, 41

Pickled Bull Kelp, 262
Pickled Kohlrabi, 263
Pickled Mustard Seeds, 264
Pickled Shallots, 264
Pickled Turmeric Cauliflower, 263
pie crust
  Jen's Pie Crust, 219–20
  Par-Baked Pie Crust, 30pies
    Cherry Pie, 219–20
    Peach Pie, 222
pita: Falafel Pockets, 71–72
pizzas
  Asparagus and Potato Pizza, 134
  Classic Margherita Pizza, 124
  Lamb Pizza, 137
  Mediterranean Pizza, 138
  Mushroom, Caramelized Onion
    and Goat Cheese Pizza, 128
  Mystic Clam Pizza, 131–32
  Pizza Dough, Tofino Style, 119–20
  Pizza Sauces, 122–23
  Roasted Acorn Squash and Kale
    Pizza, 127
Plain Ole Vanilla Ice Cream, 213–14
Poached Eggs, 99
polenta
  Green Polenta Cubes, 35–36
  Grilled Pattypan Squash, Green
    Polenta and Garlic Aioli, 35–36
  Polenta, 142
  Shrimp and Polenta Grits, 171–72
port wine: Port of Tofino, 234
potatoes
  Asparagus and Potato Pizza, 134
  Chanterelle Mushroom and Corn
    Chowder, 57
  Chips, 256
  Seared Wild Salmon, 178
provolone cheese: Lamb Pizza, 137
pumpkin seeds
  Fruit and Nut Cookies, 203
  Pumpkin Seed Pesto, 122

Q
quiche: Heirloom Tomato Quiche, 31
quinoa
  Lentil Vegiballs with Chimichurri
    and Fresh Cheese, 145–46
  Quinoa Salad, 113
  Seaweed, Sea Asparagus and
    Brassica Shoots Salad, 101–2

R
ramps: Left Coast Kimchi, 261
rapini: Curried Wheat Berry and
  Lentil Salad, 99
raspberries
  Grilled Peach and Raspberry
    Melba, 211

Melba Sauce, 211
White Sangria, 238
Ratatouille, 142
red bell peppers
    Classic Tomato Gazpacho, 49
    Green Goddess Salad, 96
    Mediterranean Pizza, 138
    Quinoa Salad, 113
    Summer Ratatouille and Polenta, 142
    Tuna Melt, 81
Red-Eye Medusa, 236
Red Sangria, 238
Red Sauce, 122
rhubarb
    Buckwheat Crepes, 147–48
    Coconut and Rhubarb Sauce, 147–48
    Fresh Rhubarb Tarts, 207–8
    Stewed Rhubarb, 207–8
rice
    Lentil Vegiballs with Chimichurri and Fresh Cheese, 145–46
    Seafood Saffron Risotto, 155–56
ricotta cheese
    Acorn Squash Sauce, 123
    Mystic Clam Pizza, 131–32
    White Garlicky Sauce, 123
Roasted Acorn Squash and Kale Pizza, 127
Roasted Brussels Sprouts and Sunchokes with Parmesan Dressing, 109–10
Roasted Cauliflower and Garlic Soup, 62
Roasted Chilies, 260
Roasted Corn, 258
Roasted Garlic, 259
Roasted Strawberries Ice Cream, 215
rolled oats
    Fruit and Nut Cookies, 203
    Lentil Vegiballs with Chimichurri and Fresh Cheese, 145–46
Root Beer Float, 216
Roquefort Dressing, 93
roti: Shrimp, Avocado and Tomato Roti Wrap, 75–76
rum: SoBo Sunset, 228

S
salads
    Coleslaw, 187–88
    Crab Salad, 83–84
    Curried Wheat Berry and Lentil Salad with Poached Eggs and Turmeric Cauliflower, 99
    Green Goddess Salad, 96
    Kale, Farro and Grilled Halloumi Salad, 90

Panzanella with Fresh Mozzarella, 107–8
Roasted Brussels Sprouts and Sunchokes with Parmesan Dressing, 109–10
Seared Scallops and Quinoa Salad, 113
Seaweed, Sea Asparagus and Brassica Shoots Salad, 101–2
Waldorf Salad, 94
Warm Asparagus, Farro and King Oyster Mushroom Salad with Poached Eggs, 104–5
Wedge Salad, 93
salami: Charcuterie with Grilled Peaches, 27
salmon
    Chinook Salmon, 175–76
    Seared Wild Salmon, 178
    Smoked Salmon, Farro and Sorrel Fritters, 33
    Wild Salmon Tartare, 29
Salsa Verde, 151–52
salt, about, 21
Salted Caramel Cashew Cookies, 199–200
sandwiches
    Crab Salad, 83–84
    Falafel Pockets, 71–72
    Grilled Halloumi and Sun-Dried Tomato Tapenade on Focaccia, 77–78
    Ice Cream Sandwiches, 213–14
    Shrimp, Avocado and Tomato Roti Wrap, 75–76
    Smoked Turkey, Bacon, Tomato and Arugula on Sourdough, 85–86
    Tuna Melt, 81
Sangria for a Crowd, 238
sauces
    Acorn Squash Sauce, 123
    Almond Cream Sauce, 181–82
    Barbecue Sauce, 171–72
    Black Bean Salsa, 189–90
    Chimichurri Sauce, 260
    Coconut and Rhubarb Sauce, 147–48
    Crab Louis Sauce, 37
    Herbed Yogurt Sauce, 72
    Melba Sauce, 211
    Parsley Sauce, 178
    Pizza Sauces, 122–23
    Pumpkin Seed Pesto, 122
    Red Sauce, 122
    Salsa Verde, 151–52
    White Garlicky Sauce, 123
scallops
    Seafood Saffron Risotto, 155–56

Seared Scallops and Quinoa Salad, 113
sea asparagus
    Seafood Saffron Risotto, 155–56
    Seaweed, Sea Asparagus and Brassica Shoots Salad, 101–2
Seafood Saffron Risotto, 155–56
Seared Halibut, Black Beans, King Oyster Mushrooms and Almond Cream, 181–82
Seared Halibut Cheeks and Tomato Dashi, 39
Seared Scallops and Quinoa Salad, 113
Seared Wild Salmon, 178
Seaweed, Sea Asparagus and Brassica Shoots Salad, 101–2
Seed Crackers, 29
seeds, toasting, 216
shallots
    Chimichurri Sauce, 260
    Pickled Shallots, 264
sherry vinegar: Pickled Shallots, 264
shrimp
    Fried Green Tomatoes with Spiced Shrimp and Herbed Mayonnaise, 43
    Nettle, Clam and Shrimp Tagliatelle, 160
    Seafood Saffron Risotto, 155–56
    Shrimp and Polenta Grits, 171–72
Shrimp, Avocado and Tomato Roti Wrap, 75–76
Silky Parsnip, Apple and Celeriac Soup, 64
Simple Syrup, 255
    Cucumber Variation, 255
    Lavender Variation, 255
    Mint Variation, 255
Smoked Salmon, Farro and Sorrel Fritters, 33
Smoked Turkey, Bacon, Tomato and Arugula on Sourdough, 85–86
smoking, stovetop, 86
SoBo Caesar, 226
SoBo Sunset, 228
sorrel: Smoked Salmon, Farro and Sorrel Fritters, 33
soups. See also chili
    Chanterelle Mushroom and Corn Chowder, 57
    Chilled Pea and Mint Soup, 54
    Classic Tomato Gazpacho, 49
    Cream of Mushroom Soup, 67
    Fall Harvest Vegetable Soup, 61
    Hot and Sour Chicken Noodle Soup, 69–70
    Melon and Coconut Soup, 53
    Roasted Cauliflower and Garlic Soup, 62

Silky Parsnip, Apple and Celeriac
    Soup, 64
for summer, 49
Watermelon Gazpacho, 50
Sourdough Bread, 245–46
Sourdough Tips, 247
Southern Baked Beans, 187–88
spaghetti: Clam and Corn Vongole,
    158
Spaghetti Squash Patties with
    Poached Eggs and Salsa Verde,
    151–52
spinach
    Green Goddess Salad, 96
    Pumpkin Seed Pesto, 122
    Smoked Salmon, Farro and Sorrel
        Fritters, 33
    White Garlicky Sauce, 123
squash
    Grilled Pattypan Squash, Green
        Polenta and Garlic Aioli, 35–36
squash, yellow: Summer Ratatouille
    and Polenta, 142
Squash Patties, 151–52
strawberries
    Roasted Strawberries Ice Cream, 215
    White Sangria, 238
Stubbs Island Mule, 232
Sumac Onions, 72
Summer Ratatouille and Polenta, 142
sunchokes: Roasted Brussels Sprouts
    and Sunchokes, 109–10
Sun-Dried Tomato Tapenade, 77–78
sunflower seeds: Fruit and Nut
    Cookies, 203
sweet cicely
    about, 208
    Fresh Rhubarb Tarts, 207–8
sweet vermouth: Cedar Negroni, 234

T
tarts
    Chocolate Mousse Tarts, 206
    Fresh Rhubarb Tarts, 207–8
Thai basil: Melon and Coconut Soup,
    53
Tijuana Go Surfing, 230
Toasted Hazelnut Brownies, 217
Tofino 75, 236
tomatoes
    about, 21
    Barbecue Sauce, 171–72
    Braised Beef Cheek Tacos with
        Black Bean Salsa, 189–90

Classic Tomato Gazpacho, 49
Fall Harvest Vegetable Soup, 61
Fried Green Tomatoes with Spiced
    Shrimp and Herbed Mayonnaise,
    43
Heirloom Tomato Quiche, 31
Kale and Heirloom Tomato
    Garnish, 151–52
Mediterranean Pizza, 138
Panzanella with Fresh Mozzarella,
    107–8
Red Sauce, 122
Seared Halibut Cheeks and Tomato
    Dashi, 39
Smoked Turkey, Bacon, Tomato
    and Arugula on Sourdough,
    85–86
Summer Ratatouille and Polenta,
    142
Tomato Vinaigrette, 107–8
Tomato Water, 39
Watermelon Gazpacho, 50
tomatoes, cherry
    Panzanella with Fresh Mozzarella,
        107–8
    Seared Halibut Cheeks and Tomato
        Dashi, 39
    Shrimp, Avocado and Tomato Roti
        Wrap, 75–76
tomatoes, sun-dried
    Grilled Halloumi and Sun-Dried
        Tomato Tapenade on Focaccia,
        77–78
    Mediterranean Pizza, 138
tomato juice: SoBo Caesar, 226
tomato paste: Beef Stock, 254
tortillas: Braised Beef Cheek Tacos
    with Black Bean Salsa, 189–90
Triple Chocolate Chip Cookies, 204
Tuna Melt, 81
turkey
    Smoked Turkey, Bacon, Tomato
        and Arugula on Sourdough, 85–86

V
vanilla bean, splitting and seeding,
    209
Vanilla Pastry Cream, 207–8
Vegan Chocolate Almond Cookies,
    202
Vegetable Stock, 252
vinaigrettes. See dressings
vodka
    Batched Vesper, 232

Lavender Lemonade Spritzer, 230
SoBo Caesar, 226
Stubbs Island Mule, 232
Tijuana Go Surfing, 230

W
Waldorf Salad, 94
walnuts: Braised Chicken and
    Roasted Brussels Sprouts
    Pappardelle, 163–64
Warm Asparagus, Farro and King
    Oyster Mushroom Salad with
    Poached Eggs, 104–5
Watermelon Gazpacho, 50
Wedge Salad, 93
wheat berries: Curried Wheat Berry
    and Lentil Salad, 99
whisky: Port of Tofino, 234
White Bean and Chicken Chili, 58
White Garlicky Sauce, 123
White Sangria, 238
Wild Salmon Tartare, 29
Wilted Greens, 171–72
wine, red
    Beef Stock, 254
    Braised Beef Cheek Tacos with
        Black Bean Salsa, 189–90
    Braised Chicken and Roasted
        Brussels Sprouts Pappardelle,
        163–64
    Orecchiette, Braised Lamb and
        Cauliflower, 165–66
    Red Sangria, 238
wine, white
    Clam and Corn Vongole, 158
    Cream of Mushroom Soup, 67
    Mystic Clam Pizza, 131–32
    Seafood Saffron Risotto, 155–56
    Silky Parsnip, Apple and Celeriac
        Soup, 64
    Vegetable Stock, 252
    White Sangria, 238

Y
yellow bell pepper: Coleslaw, 187–88
yogurt: Herbed Yogurt Sauce, 72

Z
zucchini
    Fall Harvest Vegetable Soup, 61
    Mediterranean Pizza, 138
    Summer Ratatouille and Polenta,
        142